The Most Pai

The Most Painful Choice

A Dog Owner's Story
of Behavioral Euthanasia

BETH MILLER

DOGS IN OUR WORLD
Series Editor Brian Patrick Duggan

McFarland & Company, Inc., Publishers
Jefferson, North Carolina

All photographs are by the author.

ISBN (print) 978-1-4766-9019-3
ISBN (ebook) 978-1-4766-4878-1

Library of Congress and British Library
Cataloguing data are available

Library of Congress Control Number 2023005498

Front cover: Champ, 2011–2020, a black-and-tan German Shepherd
(photograph by the author)

Printed in the United States of America

*McFarland & Company, Inc., Publishers
Box 611, Jefferson, North Carolina 28640
www.mcfarlandpub.com*

To Champ, 2011–2020,
the most handsome black-and-tan
German Shepherd Dog who ever lived.
He gave everything he had to give,
including so much love.
He will always have my heart.

Disclaimer: The descriptions of the treatment methods and training I conducted with Champ are by no means training or treatment advice for anyone else. These were specific to Champ's needs at the time. If you have behavioral issues with your dog, please seek a qualified and certified trainer or board-certified veterinary behaviorist who can help.

I intentionally did not list the medications Champ was taking for anxiety because those were prescribed to him by his veterinarian and were prescribed for his needs. Please consult your veterinarian and a board-certified veterinary behaviorist for specific medication advice.

Throughout this book I use dogs as the main pet, however, many other pets have been subject to behavioral euthanasia, including cats, other small animals, and horses. My experience was with a dog.

Table of Contents

Acknowledgments

I want to thank Paula Roberts-Banks and Caroline Caligiuri, both talented writers, for reading the manuscript and for their constant support both before and during this project; my writer's group, graduate school classmates and professors for their encouragement; Serendipity German Shepherd Dog Rescue, Redemption German Shepherd Dog Rescue, and Miracle GSD Network for their work rescuing Champ and other German Shepherd Dogs in need of a fresh start; Colleen Koch, DVM, and the staff at the University of Missouri Veterinary Health Center in Wentzville, Missouri; Caitlin DeWilde, DVM, and the staff at Brentwood Animal Hospital for their excellent care and love for Champ; Linda S. for her training, guidance, and advice; Toni Morrison for the inspiration; and most of all, my husband, Dan, for agreeing to adopt Champ and for helping to make him the best he could be.

Preface

The Most Painful Choice: A Dog Owner's Story of Behavioral Euthanasia recounts six years of my life during which my husband and I had a rescued German Shepherd Dog, Champ. (Per the American Kennel Club, Dog is part of the breed name and capitalized; it will be shown that way throughout this book). Since we don't have children, our pets have always been a huge part of our life. Champ was our only pet for most of the time that we had him, and due to his needs, he got 100 percent of our attention in our attempt to rehabilitate him from whatever trauma or abuse he may have experienced in his first three years of life.

I love to do research and to learn. After Champ's death, I searched for a book or in-depth resources on behavioral euthanasia and came up with just a few websites. I found numerous books and memoirs about the loss of a beloved pet, but those were due to illness or aging, not because the dog had unsolvable behavior and mental issues. Inspired by Toni Morrison's quote "If there's a book that you want to read, but it hasn't been written yet, then you must write it," I decided to write our story for those who have also had to make the painful choice of behavioral euthanasia, as well as to inform and educate those in the dog world who have never heard of it. There are thousands of pet owners who have had to make this choice, yet there is little to no support for us, mostly due to lack of knowledge and understanding, but also due to the very real expectation of judgment.

As a science writer, I wanted to see what the scientific literature said about behavioral euthanasia. Not surprisingly, there was very little about it. However, I scoured the literature for research on dog behavior, including its origins, biological and genetic basis, and emotions in dogs to see if they have similar emotional systems to humans. I read hundreds of papers and journal articles and as many books about dog behavior as I could, all by the top researchers in the field of animal behavior and veterinary research over the past fifty years. In addition to the hard science, I also looked at the social aspects of pet behavior by

1

Preface

exploring the effects on owners of these pets as well as grief after losing them.

This book is about dogs with severe behavior issues, not dogs who misbehave. It is not about dogs who chew on shoes, tear up the newspaper, or dig holes in the backyard. It is about dogs whose brains are abnormal in ways that are still unknown, causing them to deal with life in very unhealthy and unsafe ways. It is about dogs whose suffering and mental anguish is so strong that their owners must make the unthinkable choice of ending their life prematurely. I simply ask that all readers keep an open mind and reserve judgment on these owners until the end of the book.

While my husband was also involved in Champ's care, this story is told from my point of view only.

Introduction

"It is amazing how much love and laughter they bring into our lives and even how much closer we become with each other because of them."—John Grogan[1]

We had just left our house for an evening walk and crossed the street to get on the walking path. I had the remote for the electronic collar in my right hand and Champ's leash in my left hand, wrapped securely around my wrist. We made it two steps on the path, and Champ saw another dog about fifty feet from us. He went airborne lunging toward the dog and barking like crazy, pulling me down into the grass. As I lay there, I kept pressing the button on the remote that would deliver a small nick to his neck. But instead of stopping the behavior as intended, it only spurred him on. I was on the ground yelling, "No!," my husband was yelling, the other dog was barking; it was pure chaos. It felt like it went on forever, but I'm sure it was only five or ten seconds. After the other dog had moved on and things calmed down, I remember being too shaken to get up, and I had to sit on the ground for a few minutes to catch my breath and stop shaking.

This was our life several months after adopting three-year-old Champ from a local German Shepherd Dog rescue group in spring 2014. With our previous dogs, walking was a relaxing and social activity we did after work every day. With Champ, we had to prepare ourselves for episodes such as this one because of his extreme reactivity to other dogs, driven by fear, insecurity and likely a lack of socialization at the most critical time in his life.

For six years, I moved heaven and earth to try to help Champ become a "normal" dog. I hadn't planned for a dog like Champ, but that's what we got. We spent a fortune on training, some of which helped, some of which didn't; medications; agility classes; veterinary behavior specialists; puzzles and games; homemade food; even an animal communicator. I stopped at nothing to give him a chance at a better life. I

3

Introduction

always believed that he had potential to overcome his demons from his prior life and enjoy the life he had if I just worked hard enough to help him. And I loved him so much that I would do anything to help him.

Honestly, he was a good dog and tried so hard to please us. But some scars are too deep to heal, and at the suggestion of his two veterinarians and a trainer, I chose behavioral euthanasia for Champ in March 2020. Behavioral euthanasia (BE) was an unfamiliar term to me up to that point—I was familiar with euthanasia at the end of life for a pet, but not familiar with choosing it for behavior issues. Like me, many owners of pets with behavioral issues will do anything to help their pets and only choose BE when there is no other choice to make. It's a horrible choice for the owners, who often feel wracked with guilt and feel like they have failed to help the pet. But it also can be the most loving choice, as it is the only way to provide their beloved pet the peace it was unable to find in its troubled life.

This is my story of life with Champ, an incredibly handsome and loving rescued German Shepherd Dog with many behavioral issues that we were unable to relieve in the six years that he was with us. I don't believe that I did anything extraordinary for him, but those we worked with tell me that I went above and beyond. I did everything I did because I loved him and believed that he deserved the best life we could give him. I want to share our story so that others understand what it's like to have a dog with severe anxiety, global fear, and stress from previous traumas, as well as what it's like to make the painful choice to euthanize. I also review the scientific literature, as well as the literature from leading veterinary behaviorists, to look for reasons why pets like Champ are the way they are.

1

Bringing Champ Home

"When I needed a hand, I found your paw."—Unknown

In early 2014, I was still reeling from the loss of my beloved seventeen and a half-year-old cat, Skipper, in mid–December 2013, and our Golden Retriever, Luke, in September 2013. I had spent the previous two years as primary caregiver for Skipper, who had diabetes, kidney disease, and hyperthyroidism. He required at least twice-daily blood glucose monitoring and insulin shots, subcutaneous fluids three times a week, and a couple of medications. My whole life was centered around his care schedule, so when he died, I suddenly had a lot of time on my hands, and I didn't know what to do with it.

It was a repeat of 2010, when my beautiful black-and-cream German Shepherd Dog, Lindy, passed away at the end of July at the age of thirteen. I had gotten her from a breeder as a thirteen-week-old puppy in 1997, and she was a great dog. As is typical for a German Shepherd, she was very energetic and very smart. She got along great with my two cats, Skipper and Mulligan, who were both under eighteen months old when Lindy came in their lives. We went to puppy classes to socialize her with other people and other dogs, then followed through with general obedience training. She got her American Kennel Club Canine Good Citizen certification on the first try. We even did an agility class together, which she hated, but I wanted her to do it to help build her confidence since she could have a touch of separation anxiety. She could do all the obstacles in the agility course, though reluctantly, not very quickly, and with a lot of cheerleading and pieces of cheese.

Lindy was not only a great pet, but she was very intuitive and an emotional support for me during a difficult time in my life. I got her when I was in a relationship, and it was clear from the first day that I was her "person." She followed me everywhere. Once when I was taking the trash out to the backyard, she followed along so closely that our legs got tangled up, and I fell flat on my face. I had gotten a serious concussion

5

several months before, and I felt the same sensation after I fell in the yard. A visit to the doctor showed a mild concussion and a nose that looked like a boxer's who had been punched during a fight.

After that relationship ended, Lindy, the cats, and I moved to a new city where I didn't know anyone. I rented a house with a huge fenced-in backyard so she could run as much as she wanted. We took a lot of long walks around the neighborhood and played a lot of frisbee. It was a difficult time for me, both emotionally and financially, but she helped me get through it. When I got laid off from the job I had moved there to take, we moved again, this time to St. Louis, my home city.

I rented a small house with a nice fenced-in backyard near a lot of parks so that we could continue our walks. About five months later, it was on one of those walks that we met a neighbor, Dan, walking his two dogs: Clara, an English Setter, and Luke, a Golden Retriever. We would run into each other frequently since we both walked after work, so eventually we started walking together. The dogs got along well, and we would let them play and wrestle in a school field. Four years later, Dan and I got married. We called our combined menagerie of three dogs and two cats our "blended family" or our "Brady Bunch family." Thankfully, all five of them got along, and there were never any issues. The dogs wrestled every morning in the backyard after breakfast, and the cats ruled the roost, often choosing to sleep in the middle of the dogs' beds just because they could.

As she got older, Lindy started to develop a little more separation anxiety and started to get a little reactive on walks. I tried several things to fix it, such as a Gentle Leader, which helped some, but since she was a long, lean seventy-five pounds, I sometimes had difficulty restraining her. I was referred to Debra Horwitz, DVM, who was at that time the only veterinary behavior specialist in the area. She taught me some counter-conditioning techniques to try with Lindy on walks. One of them, the "look" command, solved the problem in just one walk. The key is to say "look" the very instant that your dog sees another dog, then give it a high value treat so that they make the connection that the other dog means they get a reward. By the third dog we encountered, she was already looking at me on her own without me having to say "look." But it was a temporary solution because she started walking more slowly and getting reactive again. Another visit to Dr. Horwitz proved that Lindy had arthritis and was using her reactivity to warn people and other dogs to stay away from her because she was in physical pain. So, she and I went on shorter, slower walks by ourselves until she wasn't able to go on walks anymore. I took her for acupuncture, which worked really well for about a year. We tried a few anti-inflammatory medications to help with the pain. For the last two years of her life, I had to hand feed her all her meals.

Lindy developed a cough that didn't go away, and imaging showed she had a tumor in her lung. Since she was approaching thirteen years old, I was not going to pursue aggressive treatment, so we kept her comfortable for her remaining months. Making the decision to let her go was so hard. I wanted her to make the decision for me by passing away in her sleep, but she didn't. One morning, I looked in her eyes, and they told me she was done. We helped her cross the Rainbow Bridge in late July 2010, five days after my birthday. She was thirteen years old.

I don't remember anything that happened after that day for about six weeks. I went to work, but I was in a terrible fog and just went through the motions. I didn't break out of the fog until mid–September. It was a slow healing process, and I didn't think I'd ever get over the loss. I burst into tears whenever I saw another German Shepherd. Gradually, though, I healed. I even recognized when she sent me signs that she was ok. On the first three Mother's Days after her death, I saw a German Shepherd Dog being walked while I was running or cycling. I knew she had sent it just for me.

Dan's English Setter, Clara, died a year later of hemangiosarcoma, then Luke, the Golden Retriever, died in the fall of 2013 after collapsing on our front porch one Saturday morning. Our house was empty of dogs, and our whole routine was disrupted. But I was so involved with Skipper's care that I hardly noticed.

I'd been taking Skipper to a veterinary internal medicine specialist for his diabetes for a couple of years, and I was managing the best I could. One day in early December 2013, the day that my twenty-page research paper for my first graduate school class was due, Skipper was not acting like his usual self. He curled up in the corner of a couch that he never went near, and I knew something was wrong. I called the specialist, but she was not available, so I called our regular vet and said it was time. My patched-up heart was being ripped open again. After more than seventeen years with him, I couldn't imagine life without him. I'd gotten him when he was about five months old when a neighbor of a coworker found him as a stray and couldn't keep him. He was full of spunk from the very first day. He slept on my pillow every night and was never far from me. He was so intuitive to what I was feeling that when Dan came to wake me the first morning that I was home from the hospital after a major surgery, Skipper got between Dan and me and hissed at Dan. He knew something was wrong with me and did not want Dan to bother me.

After Skipper passed away, I went into a funk again. I didn't put up a Christmas tree for the first time in my life, and I was in no shape to celebrate Christmas. I went through the motions, but I was in deep grief.

Skipper's loss left us with just sweet Mulligan, my little black cat. She relished being the only pet in the house. She was sixteen by this time and was starting to have some health issues, as well. One January Sunday, we got a rare blizzard and were snowed in. About midday, Mulligan started seizing for what seemed like forever, but in reality, it was just a few seconds. After she stopped seizing, I comforted her as much as I could. There were no veterinary offices open that day or for a few days afterward because of the snow, so I had to wait to talk with her vet until mid-week. There wasn't much they could do, but they told me to watch her.

Over the next two years, Mulligan had more frequent seizures, then she would walk in a counterclockwise circle after it was over. My vet said it was likely she had a brain tumor that was causing the seizures and the circling. I believe she eventually lost her sight, as well.

I had been following a social media account for a while of Rico, a retired Customs & Border Protection German Shepherd Dog that had been adopted by a local family after his retirement due to a spinal injury. I got up the courage to ask to meet him, and they allowed me to meet him in November 2013, just a few weeks before Skipper died. We got to be friends with the family, and when they went on vacation in March of 2014, Rico stayed with us for two weeks. I loved it. He was partially paralyzed, so he needed some extra care, but it was so great to have a dog in the house again.

Rico wore a red vest with a handle on the top to help pull him up when he needed assistance and to lift him in and out of cars. One day while he was staying with us, I had to go to the eye doctor where they dilated my eyes, so I couldn't wear my contact lenses home. It was a sunny day, so they gave me some temporary dark glasses to put under my regular glasses so I could drive home. I took Rico for a walk after I got home, not thinking about the fact that I had the dark cover over my eyes and that he was wearing an assistance vest. I couldn't understand why people were looking at us with such funny looks when they passed by. I think they thought I was visually impaired, and Rico was my service dog!

After Rico went home, I realized I was ready for another dog and started looking at adoptable dogs through the local breed rescue group, Serendipity German Shepherd Dog Rescue (SGSDR). I was watching its

Champ in spring 2014 on a park outing while in the care of Serendipity German Shepherd Dog Rescue. When I saw this photograph on Facebook of their dogs available for adoption, I knew this was my dog.

website and social media posts for the right dog. One day in late April 2014, they posted a photo of a three-year-old male named Champ with the typical GSD head tilt lying on a yellow blanket, and I knew that he was my dog. I talked to Dan about it, and we agreed to meet him. At the time Champ was in boarding because his foster home didn't work out, so we met the rescue volunteer at the boarding facility. Champ never really came up to us to check us out—he mostly just ran around and played with a ball. We were told he was ok with cats, which was important to

Dan and I as we tried to hold onto Champ the evening we adopted him in 2014.

1. Bringing Champ Home

me because Mulligan was sixteen, and I didn't want to compromise her safety. He was very thin—only about sixty-five pounds—and was missing a lot of hair on his hind end. I was already in love with him, so we signed a foster-to-adopt contract, and on May 1, 2014, Champ came home with us.

In the car on the way home, I sat in the backseat with him. He ran back and forth across the seat and across my lap, screamed, whined, and cried. I was trampled. When we got home, I thought I'd take him for a short walk to work off some energy. That's when I learned he had no leash skills. He dragged me down the street, and when we saw another person or another dog, he went ballistic barking, and I could barely hang on. When we got back home, he ran around the house, checking everything out. I had bought two toys for him: a blue squeaky ball and a hard nylon bone. He took the ball and ran around the house squeaking it as loud as he could. When it got close to bedtime, I put the ball away so we didn't have to listen to it squeak all night. He grabbed the bone and ran into my small home office. When I walked to the doorway of that room, he started growling, and it wasn't a play growl—he was resource guarding. Dan told me not to approach Champ, so we walked away. I don't remember how long he was back there, but I do remember he eventually came out, and I exchanged the bone for a treat. He slept through the first night pretty well. I took the next day off to be at home with him and to finish a paper for my graduate school class. I was working at the dining room table most of the day. Champ got the blue squeaky ball and literally ran circles around the table squeaking the ball all day. He rarely stopped except for when I took him outside in the backyard.

He was protective of his food, too. When we fed him, he would growl if we happened to walk by or talk to him while he was eating. I tried counter conditioning, gradually getting closer an inch at a time over a period of weeks, and he eventually stopped. We had put away the nylon bone after the first night and didn't give him any more bone-type toys.

Since our neighbors knew us for always walking three dogs and knew that we'd lost them all, they were excited that we got a new dog. We wanted to introduce Champ to them. But every time we got within a few feet of a person, he would lunge toward them, barking and growling and trying to attack. Our friends and family wanted to come over to meet him, but they couldn't even get into the house because he was so aggressive. We have a bay window in our dining room from which we can see a lot of neighbors walking their dogs on the sidewalk or walking path across the street. Champ posted himself there and would nearly go through the window every time he saw a person or a dog, so we had to line our dining room chairs up in front of the windows to keep him away.

Despite being told Champ was good with cats, he was not good with my cat. A few days after we brought him home, I came home from work and class at about 9 p.m., and when Mulligan came to greet me, he picked her up with his mouth. Terrified, I screamed, and he dropped her, unharmed, thankfully. From then on, I put up baby gates to give Mulligan access to part of the house and Champ access to the other part. But Champ could easily leap over the baby gates, so I had to stack two of them in the doorways.

In the first week or two that we had Champ, I took him to an introductory meeting with the veterinarian who had cared for Lindy, Skipper, and Mulligan because I really liked their holistic approach of using both natural and Western medicine treatments depending on the situation. I talked about Champ's reactivity and resource guarding with the veterinarian who knew me well, and she said it was beyond her experience and referred me to another veterinarian in the area. When I went to that practice's website to get more information, I had to complete an online form before making an appointment for a behavior evaluation. A day later, the veterinarian called me and said he had reviewed my form, and he believed that Champ and his issues were out of his scope of practice. He referred me to a behavior veterinarian through the University of Missouri, Colleen S. Koch, DVM. I kept that information on a note tacked to my bulletin board for months, but I never called because I didn't think we needed it, but I didn't yet understand what we were dealing with.

When we had our three other dogs, our daily routine began with Dan walking them in the morning then feeding them. Then we would all go together on a longer walk in the evening right after work. We were looking forward to getting back to that routine with Champ. We didn't realize how much work we would have to do to take two walks a day with him. He was terrible on a leash—he pulled, he barked at everything, he was extremely reactive, and the ordeal exhausted all of us. I had torn rotator cuffs in both my shoulders at the time from swimming, and his pulling made the pain even worse.

After the first week, I knew we were in over our heads. I was referred to a local dog training organization that offered behavior evaluations. We went for an evaluation two weeks after bringing Champ home. He was so anxious and hyper that he was yipping and pulling against the leash the whole time. I remember they asked me to connect his leash to a bolt fastened into the painted cement-block wall for a test in which they were going to bring out a life-size stuffed dog to see his reaction. I asked them how much tension the bolt could withstand, and they just looked at me strangely. I connected the leash to the bolt, and I was to keep him turned away from them until they brought the stuffed dog out, then let him turn around to see the stuffed dog. I remember holding my breath while watching them bring out the stuffed dog and trying to hold Champ still. When I could let go of him, he turned around, saw the stuffed dog, started barking ferociously and pulled toward it as hard as he could. His front legs actually went up about three feet in the air. I wanted to cry. What had we gotten ourselves into? What kind of dog reacts this way to a stuffed animal?

The evaluators said that Champ displayed "disruptive, fearful, threatening, or aggressive behavior" and recommended a class (appropriately) called "Dogs with Issues" for reactive dogs. Their method for the class was to have each dog in a partitioned space and gradually get them closer to the other dogs. As part of the owner preparation for the class, we were required to attend a four-hour class for owners on dog body language. We learned a lot, but what we didn't learn was what to do with Champ once we recognized he was giving these signals.

After we finished the required owner's class, we learned that the organization wouldn't be able to offer the Dogs with Issues class until fall, which was four months away, and we knew we couldn't wait. Walking was nearly impossible, and being in the house all the time wasn't helping, either. We couldn't leave him free in the house when we weren't there because it was too stressful for him. Neighbors said they could hear him barking all day. While he knew his crate was a safe place and would sleep in it by choice, he also broke out of it numerous times when we were at work and demolished the hard plastic crate liner. We ended up using about a dozen wire ties to reinforce the crate, and he wasn't able to break out of it again.

One of the books I bought at this time was *Don't Leave Me!* by Nicole Wilde about how to help a dog's separation anxiety, the term used to describe when the dog becomes emotionally distraught when separated from a specific person or when left alone. Champ had both issues—he would get upset when I was out of his eyesight or when we left him alone. I had some experience with this as Lindy and Luke developed some separation anxiety as they got older, though theirs was manageable and considerably milder than what Champ had. When Luke was the only dog left, he started tearing up some papers and books when we weren't home, so we started to crate him when we left. That seemed to take care of things for him. But Champ was on a whole different level with the ability to break out of a locked crate. Some other behaviors he had that indicated a separation issue were his hyper attachment to and hypervigilance with me. He always knew where I was because he was practically attached to me. He followed me everywhere, and I was never out of his eyesight. While the book was very helpful and informative, I believed we needed more help with Champ.

We ultimately decided not to wait for the Dogs with Issues class and to seek training elsewhere. I was disappointed that this class didn't work out for us, and I have no idea whether it would have worked and changed the rest of Champ's life, or if it would have failed.

A neighbor recommended a trainer from the local facility where she trained her dog. I gave him a call and described some of Champ's issues, which at that time included not eating well and guarding his food. He told me to withhold Champ's food for a few days, and that would solve the problem. I was shocked and horrified. What kind of "professional" trainer recommends starving an already underweight dog to treat behavior problems? To how many other people had he given this advice? Needless to say, we didn't work with him.

We contacted another trainer that the evaluators recommended and worked with her for a few sessions. She specialized in clicker training, where the owner uses a clicker to mark good behavior and gives a reward (a treat). We bought clickers and dove into this form of positive reinforcement. I read several books on the theories behind clicker training on a road trip. Ultimately, Champ understood the meaning of the clicker, but his anxiety was too high for him to take the treat. You know there is something wrong when a dog refuses a treat.

Then, to take pressure off my shoulders when I was walking him, the trainer brought a leash that went around my waist and connected it to Champ. He dragged me along behind him, and I had to run to keep from falling. I felt like I was being dragged behind a pack of sled dogs. As that trainer was walking out of our door the last time she left our house, she said, "You know, Champ's never going to be a dog you can take to the dog park." We were stung. Taking Champ to a dog park was not our goal and not why we asked for her help. The goal was to have a calmer, less reactive, and less fearful dog that we could take on walks in the neighborhood. We never called her again. We needed help, not judgment.

14

1. Bringing Champ Home

We went back to square one. I reached out to the rescue volunteers and told them we needed help. It was then that I learned Champ's back story from the man who had gone to get Champ from his first home. Champ had belonged to a young couple and was the woman's "baby." The woman died, and the widower went to live his mother in her trailer. The mother didn't want Champ inside the trailer, so he was left outside on a five-foot chain. A woman who lives in the area and is involved with rescue found out about Champ and worked with the widower to surrender Champ. He was surrendered in February, so he had been outside all winter in the elements in a very cold part of the country. When the rescue volunteer went to get Champ, the widower was passed out inside the trailer and never awoke to say goodbye. Champ weighed only about 60 pounds, making him very thin. We found out that they had used hydrogen peroxide on his skin to "help" his constant scratching, likely from the allergies we learned about later. That's why he had no hair on his hind end when we met him months later.

The wonderful volunteers with Miracle GSD Network, a national network that pulls German Shepherds from extremely difficult

Champ being rescued by a volunteer with a local German Shepherd Dog rescue in 2014.

situations, raises funds for their care, and places them with regional German Shepherd rescue groups across the U.S., brought Champ into the network and made him Miracle GSD #306. His initial veterinary care was taken care of in Indiana by the wonderful volunteers with Redemption German Shepherd Rescue before he was transported to St. Louis to Serendipity. Once in Serendipity's care, his medical needs were addressed, and he was neutered. After his neuter surgery, he developed a hematoma, an injury to a blood vessel that causes blood to pool near the surgical region, and for the rest of his life, he was extremely sensitive to anyone touching him in the groin area.

This story still upsets me, and I was angry at the prior owners for a long time. Over the first year, I realized I had to forgive them, because my anger wasn't helping Champ recover from that horrible experience. How confusing it must have been for him to go from a spoiled dog to being left outside in the winter on a short chain in a trailer park, then given up without even a farewell. I had to give them credit for surrendering Champ to rescue, which would give him a chance at a better life instead of taking him to a shelter, having him put to sleep because he was an inconvenience, or worse, letting him loose somewhere to fend for himself. It took me a long time to get there, but I felt like I had to forgive them to be able to help Champ.

The SGSDR volunteers recommended a local trainer with experience with reactive and aggressive dogs. He had been in the military and had German Shepherds himself. When we went to meet him for an evaluation in early July, Dan and I were sitting in chairs at the desk in the training room, where there were a few other people with dogs in private lessons. Champ was so anxious that he kept trying to claw his way up on my lap. He was about 70 pounds at this point and way too big to be on my lap. He panted heavily, yipped, and would not sit down. Then he noticed the owner's two dogs lying quietly behind the desk. When he saw them, he started barking and lunging, showing his teeth, jumping toward them with his front paws up on the desk, and I could barely hold on. The trainer's eyes got huge, and he said, "Oh, boy." But he said he could help us and suggested we bring Champ for a two-week board-and-train program, then when he was ready, we could take him to weekly group training with other dogs.

We arranged to leave Champ with them while we went out of town for a week and the week after. I called to check on him every other day. About a week into his stay there, they posted a photo on social media of Champ lying nicely only a few feet from one of the trainers' dogs. I

1. Bringing Champ Home

Champ close to a trainer's dog during board and train in 2014. We couldn't believe he was that close to another dog!

couldn't believe it. I remember crying when I saw the picture because I was so happy that he was able to be that close to another dog. I was so hopeful that he could change! When we picked him up, we had a session to go over everything he had learned. They had put a prong collar on him, and one of the trainers yanked it so hard when she corrected him that he yipped, and I gasped. I was shocked. Was this what it was going to take to help him? But I told myself that it had to be that way to help him because these trainers knew what they were doing.

After the two weeks of intense work, Dan and I took him back to that facility for group training classes once a week for the next three years. Eventually, he was able to be about three feet from a few dogs in group without being reactive. But if a dog came into his three-foot bubble of safety, he would go after them. Since we went to the same group each week, we got to know the other dog owners, and they understood that Champ needed space. I had to explain to new people in the class that Champ didn't greet other dogs and asked them to please respect his space. Not everyone understood, and more than one owner was quite afraid of him and would keep their dog far away from us.

Champ (in front), close to another Serendipity German Shepherd Rescue dog while in group training in 2017. She was the only dog who could get this close to him without him trying to attack.

Other than the reactivity, he did really well in those groups. He was very smart and a quick learner. He could do anything that the trainers asked him to do: sit in a wheelchair; sit his big body on a tiny stepstool; walk through a ladder on the floor; and stay inside the door while I went outside and out of sight. When the trainers had contests for the dogs, such as a tic-tac-toe game with the dogs as the markers, Champ frequently won. He was a model student—on the outside.

But just being there exacerbated his anxiety. When we would walk in a circle at the beginning of class with our dogs on our left side in

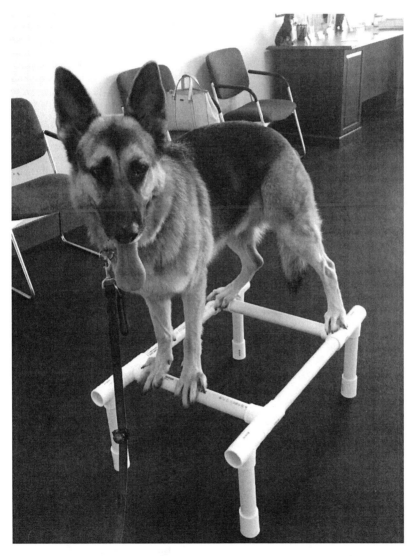

At weekly group training, Champ excelled in all the activities they asked him to do, including standing on a frame made of PVC pipe in 2015.

a heel, Champ would nip my pants legs at the ankles. If I was wearing shorts, he would bite my feet or my thighs. He panted and drooled excessively through class, and a large portion of his tongue would be hanging out of his mouth, all classic signs of anxiety. When we had to put our dogs in a sit, then walk ten to fifteen feet away to practice recall, I held my breath every time that he would come straight to me and not detour to go after another dog or run away from the group.

One of the trainers suggested that we get him a pack to wear to give him a job. We found a pack, and I put a can of pumpkin on each side to add weight. He would wear it when we walked and to group training. I didn't really notice much of a difference in him when he had it on, but he didn't mind wearing it, so we kept using it until it fell apart.

Another milestone for Champ in this program was the ability to "place," or sit and stay, on top of a fire hydrant. We practiced the place command often in class, whether on a place board, a Bosu trainer, mini trampoline, large box, or a tiny footstool. He always did well. We worked very hard with him to place on a neighborhood fire hydrant, and one

The "holy grail" of group training was for the dog to be able to balance on a fire hydrant. Champ became a member of the trainer's Fire Hydrant Club in 2015.

20

1. *Bringing Champ Home*

evening, he did! We made a huge deal out of it, and I managed to snap a couple of photos before he jumped off. We printed one of the photos and took it to the trainer, and they put it up on a bulletin board with photos of other dogs that had joined the "Fire Hydrant Club."

While he wasn't terribly reactive in the group training sessions unless a dog encroached on his space, he was still reactive at home. One of the trainers said she would come to our house and go for a walk with us to see how he reacted to other dogs in the neighborhood. She could only come during the weekday, however, so I had to take a half-day of vacation to accommodate this. When she and I walked Champ that day, everyone else in our neighborhood was at work, so no dogs were out, and he wasn't reactive. But when the neighbor across the street brought his dog over at my request, it took both me and the trainer to hold Champ back. It wasn't productive, she offered no solutions or suggestions, it wasn't cheap, and I had used a half-day of vacation.

Another time, one of the other trainers came over to help us start using an electronic collar. I was not in favor of using it, but they suggested it, and we didn't know what else to do. The session was somewhat helpful, though I noticed Champ negatively reacting to the e-collar right away, and I didn't like it.

At home, Champ's bubble of safety was more like 100 yards—the length of a football field. One Sunday when I was at church, Dan tied Champ on a longline outside in our driveway while Dan washed his car. He used to have Luke out with him with no leash when he washed the car. Luke was so gentle and obedient that he just enjoyed being outside with Dan and would stay in the yard. But Dan forgot that Champ was not Luke. A neighbor walked by with his dog, and Champ went after it, snapped the longline in two and attacked the dog, causing injuries in two places that required multiple stitches.

After church that day, I went to a local outdoor flea market. I had just gotten there and parked when Dan called. I could tell by his voice that something was wrong. He told me what had happened, and I asked if he was ok. I left the flea market right away and drove home. I was angry at him for trusting Champ on a longline out in the open. I also understood that he wanted another dog like Luke and wanted Champ to be that dog, but Champ wasn't and couldn't be that dog.

When I got home, we walked over to the neighbors' house to apologize and to tell them we would pay their costs resulting from Champ's attack. Thankfully, the dog recovered and only had physical scars, not emotional ones. The neighbors were upset, naturally, but they didn't report the bite to the police department. It helped that we shared a common veterinarian.

That was a large dose of reality of what we were dealing with—a large, muscular German Shepherd with dog and fear aggression who was gaining weight with regular meals. It was easy to see why dogs built like Champ are used in the military and in law enforcement because they are so strong. After that event, a friend advised us to get an umbrella insurance policy to cover ourselves in case Champ attacked again. It was a miracle that our neighbors didn't sue us or have Champ taken away from us.

Things got somewhat better. We still walked him twice a day, and it remained difficult, but I tried different things to help. I tried teaching him the same "look" command that I had taught Lindy when she was reactive. Champ's reaction from the instant he saw the dog and the time he got ramped up was much faster than I could even say, "look" or use the clicker, so I was not successful. I tried carrying a tennis ball, which he loved, and giving it to him when he saw another dog. It worked somewhat, but not enough for him not to bark and drop the tennis ball, sending me scrambling after it.

He also was extremely reactive around moving bicycles and would bark and lunge toward them in the same way he reacted toward other dogs. One evening we were walking, and a neighbor stopped us to talk after he had seen Champ's reactive behavior toward another dog. He told us he was a dog trainer and would be willing to help us. He said he was starting a program for dogs and their owners to exercise together, and he thought that we would be good candidates and that it would help Champ. We made plans for him to walk with us one evening.

The neighbor wanted to hold Champ's leash while we walked so that he could be "in control" of Champ's behavior. A person on a bicycle rode up from behind us unexpectedly, and Champ lunged toward it, nearly pulling the neighbor over and getting very close to the cyclist. We all moved to get control of Champ, then had to stop and catch our breath. We finished the walk, but that was the last time we ever saw or heard from that neighbor.

Often, kids would see us walking and ask if they could pet him. I wanted to explain it in a way they would understand, so I said that Champ used to live with some people who weren't very nice to him, so when he met new people, he wasn't sure if they would be nice to him or not, so he was afraid. I told them that if he wanted to be petted, he would come to them. This explanation worked remarkably well with

22

kids: they seemed to immediately empathize that someone hadn't been nice to him and would respect his boundaries. Champ could sense this, and more often than not, he would allow the empathetic children to pet him. But if he sensed any sort of fear or uncertainty in the kids, he would hide behind me. In those cases, I explained to the kids that he was feeling scared, but it wasn't their fault, and maybe we could try again another day.

Interestingly, though, Champ loved babies and toddlers. He would go right up to a baby in a stroller with his tail wagging. Champ never once growled, snapped, or showed any kind of fear or aggression around babies or toddlers. I always thought he liked toddlers because they were at his eye level. He would pull toward a toddler and give a big wet kiss across the face before anyone knew what was happening or before I could stop it. More than one parent was at first horrified, but many were understanding, particularly if their child giggled after the lick.

One morning in the first several months, I was leaving for work, and Champ was trying to leave with me. As I opened the front door, a neighbor's outdoor cat ran across our yard. Champ saw it before I did, pushed the storm door open and ran after the cat, eventually chasing it up a tree halfway down the block. I ran screaming behind him in my heels, praying he didn't catch and kill the cat or that either or both wouldn't get hit by a car. He thought it was great fun. I caught up with him and was able to grab his collar and drag him home, and the cat stayed safely in the tree until we were well out of sight. It took fifteen minutes for my heart to stop pounding.

During Champ's two-week intense training stay, the trainers taught Champ to walk on a treadmill and recommended that we continue this at home a couple of times a day. They said the exercise would help burn off some energy and anxiety. Dan and I found a used treadmill at the Goodwill store and set it up in the basement. We set the pace at three miles an hour. He loved it—he would actually smile when he was on it. After his outside morning walk, he would get on the treadmill to walk for another thirty minutes. Every evening, his internal clock told him that it was time for the treadmill, and he would go down to the basement on his own and stand on it, then wait for one of us to come down and turn it on—even when we had already taken a long walk outside. One of us always watched him while he was on it.

Occasionally, when the weather was bad, I would have to borrow his treadmill for my runs. He wanted to join in and would try to get on it with me, not understanding that it was set much faster than three miles

23

an hour, and that treadmills weren't made for more than one user at a time. He went right off the back while I was frantically pulling the emergency stop cord. Thankfully neither of us was hurt, and he only did it twice before he learned not to try it again.

I also started taking Champ on short runs with me thinking that it would help to burn off some of his energy and anxiety. At first, I took him a mile to see how he would do and gradually increased his mileage up to five miles. Our legs got tangled up a couple of times—just like they had with Lindy—and I fell several times. My knees are covered with scar tissue from all the falls. He did pretty well except when we saw another dog. Then his reactivity took over, and I had a very hard time holding him back and staying upright while continuing to run. I carried a bag with small pieces of hot dog in it to give him when we would see another dog. It was a balance challenge trying to reach in and get pieces of hot dog, feed them to Champ and try to continue running without falling. I was not always successful. I would take him for a five-mile run on Saturday mornings before we went to group training, thinking that he would be worn out and would be less anxious in class. But it had the opposite effect—he was even more energetic and anxious in class. He was experiencing the same "runner's high" that I do and was becoming more and more fit. The trainer then told me to stop running with him because it was conditioning him like an athlete and not helping his anxiety. After that, I felt guilty on my Saturday morning runs for not taking him with me.

Some other clients at the same training facility had an informal group that would take their dogs on pack hikes on weekends at area parks. Dan took Champ a couple of times, and he did ok. He knew many of the other dogs from group training, and the other owners understood his issues, so no one was concerned if he needed to be taken out of the pack for a minute to regroup or walk some distance behind the pack. When he came home, he would crash from the stress of the situation—the car ride and being in a group of people and dogs in a strange place were a lot for his brain to process. A couple hours after he got home from one of those pack walks, I saw him lying flat on his side in the cool grass in our backyard, completely spent. It was so unusual for him to be so still.

At the time, we shared a fence with neighbors who had a Yorkshire Terrier that would burst out of their back door barking and run straight for the shared fence. That was gasoline on a fire for Champ. Our wood fence had vertical boards about two inches apart, enough for Champ and the Yorkie to bite at each other. The neighbors wouldn't come out and get their dog, even when I was yelling as loud as I could at both dogs

24

In the first year that we had Champ, 2014, I took him on short runs on weekends.

to stop, so I had to try to grab Champ and wrestle him in the house. But he would run back and forth along the fence and was impossible to catch. I would get trampled trying to grab him. On the rare occasion that I did catch him, I had to try to drag him into the house while he was still going after the Yorkie. It happened almost daily, and it was horrible. We had the same issue with the neighbor on the other side of the shared fence, though this was with a Labrador Retriever with no socialization.

One rainy morning I had taken Champ out before I left work, and the Labrador came out and charged the fence, and World War III ensued. I managed to grab Champ's collar and start to pull him back toward the house while he was still wiggling around, and I slipped and fell flat on my back in the mud, losing my grip on his collar, which released him back to the fence. My work clothes were covered in mud, and I had to go in and change before I could leave for work.

For the first several years, we continued to walk Champ daily. I tried to change the route for some variety but also to avoid known triggers: dogs that would bark from their backyard through the fence or dogs inside an invisible fence. One evening shortly before Christmas, I was walking Champ alone, and two unleashed dogs came charging out of their backyard and went right for him. I was screaming as loud as I could and kicking the dogs to try to keep them away from Champ, who was in full fear-aggression mode: barking, thrashing, showing teeth and lunging toward the two loose dogs. No one came out of the houses to see why a woman was screaming in the street, and no cars drove by. Eventually the dogs ran back to their yard, and I walked quickly in the opposite direction to get away from them as fast as I could. I was shaking so much that once we got a couple of blocks away, I had to sit down. I chose the curb in front of a house adorned with Christmas lights and yard ornaments with lights choreographed to music. We stayed there for about five minutes until I stopped shaking and felt like I could continue walking.

One day I walked to the dry cleaners, which is a few blocks away from our house, and took Champ with me. The owners welcome dogs inside the small lobby and keep treats on hand, so I thought it would be ok. However, I forgot that they have a very large floor-to-ceiling mirror on the wall in the lobby. When Champ saw his reflection in the mirror, he barked loudly and ferociously and tried to attack his reflection. Unfortunately, an older man who works at the dry cleaners was sitting next to the mirror sorting laundry and was terrified. I apologized profusely, but they weren't very happy with me. I wasn't able to take Champ back to the cleaners with me again. Thankfully he did not break the mirror.

Another time, though, I took him with me to the neighborhood shoe repair shop, and he sat quietly while I bought what I needed. The

1. Bringing Champ Home

store owner complimented him for how well behaved he was. It was times like these that I thought we were making progress.

At the suggestion of the trainers, we tried walking with trusted neighbors when they walked their dogs. We'd see the neighbor walking their dog, and we would start walking a hundred feet or so behind them and eventually fall in line right behind or right next to them. Sometimes this worked, but most of the time Champ was too anxious. He wouldn't try to attack the other dog, but wouldn't walk in a straight line, always trying to jump up on me while whining and drooling. His behavior made the other dogs anxious and made the walk unpleasant for everyone.

Champ's problems were not only outside, but inside as well. From the beginning, he had a compulsion to nibble on bedding with his front teeth. Whenever he saw it, he could not help himself—he had to nibble on it. I kept a sheet over our living room chair and couch to try to keep some of the ever-present German Shepherd Dog hair from them, and he nibbled on those sheets every morning when I was putting my shoes on for work or when he saw that I was preparing to leave. But he also did it when no one was paying attention to him because he knew that he would get my attention that way.

He also would drink a lot of water when he was anxious. He'd drink so much he'd empty the large bowl we had, then would start again when I refilled it. I know he couldn't have been dehydrated because he only did it when he was anxious.

Champ rarely stopped moving. In the house, he was usually right at my heels. I tripped over him more times than I can count. I could never watch TV because as soon as I sat down, he would get in my face and start whining. I couldn't sit out on the front porch because he couldn't handle me being out there without him, but we couldn't take him out there for fear that he would see someone walking their dog or a neighborhood cat and run after it and we wouldn't be able to catch him, or that he would bite another dog or a person or be hit by a car in pursuit of another dog.

We did have some really good times with him. After about six months with us, he finally wagged his tail for the first time, and it was about eighteen months before he would sit down next to one of us on the floor. He was never much of a snuggler, but he did love to be petted and brushed. He tolerated baths at a local dog-washing place but expressed his displeasure with the whole situation by yipping through the whole experience. We had to make sure there was enough space between him

27

and any other dogs there at the time, and the staff there was always very helpful with that.

We often took him to playgrounds in the neighborhood when children weren't present to let him walk around on the equipment to help build his confidence. I would usually go up with him onto the platforms,

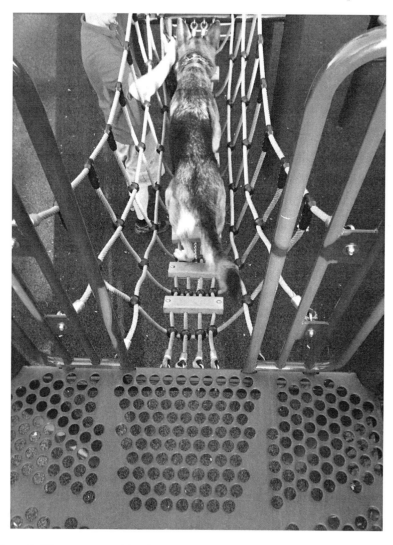

We took Champ to neighborhood playgrounds when children weren't present to build his confidence on the obstacles. Getting him to go across this swinging bridge was a big accomplishment in 2016.

then he would run down the slides. One playground near us has a swinging bridge, and we taught him how to walk across it. That was a big accomplishment for us all.

Champ loved to be in the backyard. He had balls of all sizes, and he almost always had one in his mouth. If not a ball, then he had one of several Kong toys on ropes. Those were easy to throw, and he loved to carry

Champ loved to soak in his pool on hot summer days.

them around. We also had a kiddie pool for him most summers, and he loved to go out and soak. Unfortunately, he would get hot spots on his skin if he spent too much time in the water, so we had to limit it to short periods.

One Friday evening right after work, I walked Champ to a nearby pet supply store about a mile from our house. Since driving with him was so difficult, I thought the walk while wearing his pack would tire him enough to take the edge off. I chose that day and time thinking not many other people would be there with their dogs, and I was right. We were able to walk around the store without much interaction with other people and dogs, and he got a lot of attention from the employees for being so good. After the walk home, he crashed hard for the rest of the evening. The stress of being in a new environment with so many smells had tired him out, not to mention the long walk.

Despite never having a formal obedience class, at least with us, Champ knew the basic commands, including sit, down, place (another word for stay), on your mat, and shake. I also taught him "hug and kiss." When I would come home from work and let him out of his crate, he would often lie on the floor and roll onto his side. I'd get down on the floor next to him so it looked like we were hugging, and I'd say, "Give me a hug." Then I'd say, "Give me a kiss," and he would lick my face. It was the one trick we would do if someone came over and was wary of him. I'd say, "Give mama a hug and kiss!" and he'd get on the floor and roll on to his side. When others were watching, though, he would only stay on the floor long enough for the trick, then he'd get up right away. He rarely put himself in a submissive posture when other people were around.

His rescue group, Serendipity, holds an alumni picnic for adopted dogs and their families every fall at a park about forty-five minutes away. For the first couple of years that we had Champ, we didn't go because we thought it would be too much for him, but one year, I thought he was doing well enough to go. Still terrible in the car, he was already tired by the time we got there—as were we, quite honestly—but the stress of being in a new place with lots of people and dogs had him at his highest level of anxiety. Most of the people who volunteer with the rescue knew him, but he didn't know them. They all wanted to come up and pet him, and he was not comfortable with that. He got a bandana with his name on it when we checked in, and I tried to keep him away from the other dogs as much as I could. There was a nice playground there, so I took him up on the playground equipment so he could focus his energy on that rather than all the other dogs there. We were able to stay a couple of hours before he was absolutely done, complete with tongue hanging all the way out to the side, panting and drooling. He was still anxious in the car, but less so than on the way out there. When we got home, he slept the rest of the evening, only waking to eat dinner and go outside a few

Champ wearing his pack on a visit to the pet supply store in 2014.

31

The Most Painful Choice

hours. We went again the next year, but after that, it was just too much for him, and for us as well, since we were working so hard to keep him away from other dogs that we didn't really get to talk with any of the volunteers or other owners.

I also took him to a local fire station several times at Christmas to see a Santa Claus specifically for pets. I took him the first year we had him, even though Dan didn't think it was a good idea, and for the next three years. Each time we went, there was only one other dog there at the same time, and he was surprisingly good. He let Santa pet him and sat nicely in front of Santa for the photos. Santa explained that he also had a rescued dog, so he understood. The final time that I took him, I put a Santa hat on him, which he tolerated long enough to get one decent photo, which is what I wanted.

By the end of 2016, I thought things were going pretty well. He was excelling in our group training and agility classes, walking ok, though not great, was comfortable with our routine, and was learning a lot. Since we didn't have any papers on his breeding, I got the Purebred Affiliate Listing from American Kennel Club that indicated he was a purebred German Shepherd Dog. I knew we wouldn't be able to get any

Dan, me, and Champ at the Serendipity German Shepherd Dog Rescue alumni picnic in 2016.

Champ with Santa Claus in 2016.

other AKC certifications, such as the Canine Good Citizen certification, I knew we could get at least this one.

One of the other Miracle GSD Network adopters, who had adopted Miracle GSD #307, had a blog and asked me to write a post about Champ and his progress. Looking back, that was when he was probably at his peak, and things were as good as they were going to get. We had seen so much progress in him at the time, so it was a very optimistic and positive post. But there were still issues, and as is typical for the situation, I did not share those. I hadn't seen anyone else in the Miracle GSD Facebook group sharing similar issues, and I didn't want to be the only one admitting we had problems.

2

Treating Champ

"Do not say you didn't try. Remember: You did the best you could in the situation you were in with the materials you had."—Blythe Baird[1]

Eventually, I sought out help from our vet, Caitlin DeWilde, DVM, who prescribed fluoxetine for him. It helped to tamp down some of the anxiety, but it was by no means a miracle drug. It stopped working after about a year, and she said she had no more experience with these kinds of issues, so she referred us to a behavioral vet, Colleen Koch, DVM— the very one whose name I had previously been given and had tacked on my bulletin board.

We had to wait three months to get in to see Dr. Koch, a board-certified veterinary behaviorist at the University of Missouri Veterinary Health Center in Wentzville, about forty-five minutes away, and the only veterinary behaviorist in Missouri and within a six-hour radius. She was only in the office on certain days of the week, so we each took a half day of vacation for Champ's appointments.

While we were looking forward to the appointment, we weren't looking forward to getting Champ there given his behavior in the car, and this was a long drive. I drive a manual transmission car, so when I drove, he would push against the back of my right arm, sometimes knocking it so hard it pushed my gear shift into neutral. I tried various types of restraints to keep him in the back seat, but he would strain against them so hard that they would detach, and he would quickly end up in my face, drooling profusely. Several times, I had to pull over to try to restrain him again, and after a few minutes back on the road, he'd be loose again. On top of that, he would yip and scream so loudly that I had to wear earplugs whenever he was in the car. Sometimes it was so bad that I would cry the whole way.

When we arrived for our first appointment, we were already completely worn out by the time we arrived at the clinic, which also was an

34

oncology center. We walked Champ around in the green space around the building before we went in. After several visits, he knew where we were and would pull toward the door. He would bark and yip so loudly with anxiety that the staff inside could hear him and know we had arrived before we even checked in. One time when we arrived, there was another client with her dog in the lobby, so we needed to wait to go in until they had left. I told Dan to keep Champ outside, and I would go in to let them know we were there. But as I walked away from Champ, he went into full meltdown mode, essentially screaming because I was walking away from him. Dan was struggling to hold on to him while I went inside. I saw the two staff members at the desk, and they both gave me a look of sympathy. I was embarrassed for the way Champ was acting, and I was stressed from the harrowing car ride and from Champ's anxiety level. They had us wait outside, then walk around to take Champ into the building through a side entrance to avoid seeing any other dogs. From then on, we always had to use the side entrance instead of the main entrance.

Prior to our first visit, Dr. DeWilde contacted Dr. Koch and asked if there was anything she could recommend for us while we waited for our appointment. Dr. Koch asked that we send some videos of Champ's behavior issues. One evening when we were walking him, we saw someone walking a dog in our direction, so I had Dan record the interaction on my phone while walking behind us. Champ was extremely reactive, even though the dog was on the other side of the street. Champ pulled, barked, spun around, and was extremely aggressive. At that time, we were using the electric collar. I tried saying "no" several times while delivering a nick on the electric collar as we'd been trained. Champ turned around and snapped at my hand with a yip each time. It was redirected aggression, but it was affecting me. Thankfully I was wearing gloves, so I wasn't bitten. Dr. DeWilde sent that video to Dr. Koch in an email, then forwarded Dr. Koch's response to me. Her first words were "Oh my."

Dr. Koch recommended we change from the electric collar to a Freedom Harness, which allows a leash to connect to a strap across the front of the chest and between the shoulders; start using a rubber basket muzzle whenever he was out of the house or our backyard; and to walk Champ at off-peak times in places other people weren't walking dogs. That's not easy to do in our small suburb, but we started walking him through an industrial court. The problem was that getting to the industrial court required walking on a path frequented by dog walkers at all times of the day or driving there. Neither option was good, so we got creative on ways to get to the industrial park. It wasn't a perfect solution—there were dozens of stray cats in one section that we had to avoid, and there is a small, fenced-in dog park in another section that we couldn't go near because it was too overwhelming for Champ.

When we finally went for our first visit to Dr. Koch, she had a knee-level fence dividing the room in half. On the side Champ and I were ushered into, there was a chair for me and several food puzzles on the floor for Champ. Dr. Koch was at a desk in the center of the room, and there were four veterinary students, sitting in a row with their laptops, who were observing. Dan was in a chair on the other side of the fence. Champ was very anxious and tried to climb up in my lap. I was trying to look like I could handle him, but it was obvious he was anxious, and I was glad that Dr. Koch could observe his behavior. He was too anxious at first to play with the food puzzles—he drank the whole bowl of water right away, so they got to see how his anxiety made him thirsty—but eventually, he found the food puzzles.

After an hour or more of us talking and Dr. Koch and the students observing Champ's behavior, she gave us her diagnosis: "generalized anxiety; global fear; fear-related aggression; possession aggression; suspect separation anxiety or confinement distress."

We got a four-page, single-spaced treatment plan with tools for managing the behaviors, learning his body language, avoiding all punishment, and trying new medications. Because of his behavior in the car, she gave Champ a dose of an anti-anxiety medication shortly before we left. It took effect by the time we got in the car, and it was the only time in his life that we had a quiet ride with him in the car. We left there with so much hope. I felt like we finally found the answers we had been looking for all along.

Dr. Koch emphasized that this was going to take a lot of work and that aggression is never cured. We were to manage him and teach him new ways to cope with the things that stressed him so that he would be less likely to choose aggression. We were not to use any punishment—no saying no, no "ah-ah," no prong or electronic collars. We were to reward him when he was being good so that he would make an association to the behavior we wanted him to do. However, Champ was not food motivated, so I used some of his favorite toys as rewards while I worked to get him more interested in food. I filled Mason jars with his dog food and placed them around the house so I'd have it available when I needed it. I'd give him a piece at a time and ultimately reduced the food I gave him at meals so that he wasn't overfed.

2. Treating Champ

Dr. Koch also encouraged us to get him some toys that would work his brain, so I got several food puzzles, starting with level one. That took him about five seconds to figure out, so I moved to level three. The best one was a tray with four bone-shaped pieces in the center surrounded by eight boxes that opened with flaps. The dog was supposed to lift the bone pieces out of the tray to get the treats underneath, then open the flaps of the boxes with his nose to get the treat inside. The boxes also slid to the center space once the bones were removed, so there was another treat under each of the boxes. It took me about four minutes to fill the toy with treats in all the spaces and snap the flaps tightly. The first time I gave it to Champ, I timed him. It took him two minutes and fifty seconds—less time than it took me to fill it up! The second time, it took two minutes and thirty seconds. I needed to find level ten food puzzles!

I was supposed to give him these puzzles to encourage independent play, but Champ never did anything independently. He had to be with one of us at all times. I could not go anywhere alone, and he was always underfoot. Imagine a toddler wrapped around mom's leg. Now imagine the same scenario with a 100-pound German Shepherd. While I liked that I was the person he felt safest with, it was often a burden because I couldn't get anything done. I felt like I had to always provide one-on-one interaction and supervision. Sometimes his clinging would get to me so much that I'd have to leave for a while and take a walk in the neighborhood just to get some space.

Champ couldn't—and wouldn't—stay out in the backyard alone. He could not stand to be away from either of us. We tried it a few times, but he would stand at the back door and whine until someone dared to walk past our yard, then he would run down to the fence and bark at them until they passed by, then run back to the door.

We were also supposed to teach him that a mat was a safe space with the command "go to mat." I found a yoga mat we were no longer using and would get him to lie on it, then say, "go to mat" and give him a treat so that he would know that was what I wanted him to do. We had a mat in several rooms in the house so that he would have a spot to go no matter where I was. He did ok with it as long as the mat wasn't much farther than six feet from me. If any farther, he wouldn't stay on it. We were supposed to get him more comfortable being farther away from me but were never successful.

Champ did get stressed whenever I left, even though I always kept my departure low-key. Dr. Koch suggested giving him a food-filled Kong-type toy when I left to give him something to divert his focus. We had several of those type of toys, so I tried various things in them that I thought he might like—peanut butter, canned dog food, or a large treat. I ended up getting about a dozen of this type of toy from a subscription box and would fill them with dry treats and braunschweiger, then put them in the freezer. Every morning before I left for work, I'd open the freezer to take out my ice pack for my lunch bag and grab a frozen toy for him. He figured it out quickly, and every time I opened the freezer, he would stick his big head in and try to choose one for himself.

At the first visit, Dr. Koch changed his medication. She increased the fluoxetine and added medications meant to reduce anxiety. She also recommended a probiotic. Eventually, we added a second probiotic that was supposed to have calming effects.

We worked on all those things over the next three months before our next visit, when I said we needed some help at home with some of the training. She gave us a few names of trainers she knew well, and I contacted one of them. Linda called me one Saturday, and we talked for about an hour about Champ's issues and Dr. Koch's recommendations. Linda told me she completely understood how stressful the situation was because she had had a dog with severe anxiety. We agreed to have her come and meet Champ and talk with us about how to move forward.

Linda sent me several questionnaires and assessments to fill out before our first visit. I was to monitor Champ's body language for signs of stress, such as yawning, panting heavily, licking his lips or nose, tucking his tail, stopping to sniff, whining, raising his hackles, freezing, raising one paw, or even a general look of worry on his face. Champ's most frequent signs of stress were whining, raising his hackles, freezing, lip licking, excessive sniffing, and raising his paw. Once I figured those out, I had to determine what was causing him the stress. In the house, he would whine whenever I was out of his eyesight or if I went outside without him. Most of the other behaviors happened when we were outside.

Linda also had me complete a behavioral assessment called the Canine Behavioral Assessment & Research Questionnaire (C-BARQ) that compared Champ's behavior with other German Shepherds. The assessment was scored with colors: green was good, yellow was less desirable than average, and orange and red were causes for concern. Champ received scores in the orange or red for all but four areas: trainability (green); stranger-directed fear, separation-related problems, and excitability (yellow). He scored red, the highest scores possible, for dog-directed aggression, dog-directed fear, and energy; and orange, or slightly below the highest score, for attachment/attention-seeking.

2. *Treating Champ*

While I knew this from living with him, it was hard to see it on paper knowing how serious his issues were and how much work we had ahead of us.

When Linda first came to our house, I did my best to keep Champ quiet, but he could be very intimidating to strangers. I kept him on a leash so that I could keep him as close to me as possible. Linda admitted that she was fearful of him, but she eventually won him over by throwing tiny bits of cheese down at him while we were talking. He learned to associate Linda with good treats and cheese, and he always liked her.

One of the exercises that Dr. Koch and Linda taught us was "touch." I first taught it to Champ using a spatula. Whenever he touched the spatula with his nose, I gave him a piece of food. Then we moved to him touching my index finger and middle finger with his nose and getting a treat. This was to be used to refocus him in stressful situations, such as someone coming in the house (which was rare because of his stranger aggression) or going to the vet. I'd ask the vet tech to hold out his or her two fingers and ask Champ to touch, then give him a treat, then ask the vet to do the same. It seemed to help, so we used it often.

A similar exercise we worked on was shaping. I'd set a cast-iron doorstop down in the middle of the floor and not say anything. If he touched it, he'd get a treat. He picked up on that quickly, so we changed the object to his mat. Whenever he went to his mat, even just to touch it or to lie down on it, he got a treat. This was supposed to encourage him to use his brain to figure out why I was giving him a treat and encourage him to go to the mat more often. That worked fairly well, but again, the mat had to be close to where I was for him to stay on it.

Dr. Koch also had us set up tethers so that I could have some space without Champ under my feet all the time and to help when people came into the house. We got two bolts from the hardware store and drilled them into the baseboards in the hall and in the TV room. We attached a six-foot length of climbing rope with a leash clip on one end to attach to his collar. When Champ was attached to the one in the hall, he could still lie outside of the kitchen door and see me when I was in there. The one in the TV room allowed him to come out a bit into the hall, but he couldn't see me if I was in the kitchen or another room. We didn't use that one as much because he would whine and cry when I was out of eyesight, and that got really stressful for all of us.

I also told her that I could not sit down without Champ getting in my face and begging for attention. I watch one TV show a week, and every time I would sit down to watch it, Champ would stop what he was doing and come over to where I was sitting, put his face in my face, and whine and pant. Dr. Koch suggested that I toss him pieces of kibble during the show, which took away from my concentration and attempted relaxation. She also suggested giving him a food-stuffed toy, which I did, but he would finish it in minutes and be back in my face with his braunschweiger breath. It was as though he refused to allow me to relax.

Linda referred me to an online course and group called Dogs in Need of Space (DINOS). Jessica Dolce, a dog walker, animal advocate and compassion fatigue educator, started the movement and course about dogs in need of space after writing a blog post titled "My Dog Is Friendly! A Public Service Announcement." In it, she explained how dogs are often approached by well-meaning dog owners on every street. Said dog owners will often call out, "My dog is friendly!" as their dog is pulling them across the street to visit. But many dogs, including reactive, insecure, and fearful dogs like Champ, as well as dogs with chronic illnesses or in chronic pain and those who are old and cranky, don't want to be greeted or approached by other dogs, even if the other dog is "friendly." Service or working dogs are not supposed to be approached by other dogs or humans.

I took Dolce's online course and learned a lot about dog reactivity as well as caregiver fatigue. I knew about caregiver fatigue in people who care for humans, but I didn't realize that humans could get it from caring for animals, as well. Along the journey with Champ, I never would have said I had caregiver fatigue because I was doing what I needed to do for him and didn't think twice about it. But after this course, I realized I had been suffering from it with Skipper over the last two years of his life when his health needs were extensive, though I didn't realize it at the time. When in the throes of caregiving, you don't take time to think about yourself.

Another thing I learned from the course was that it was more than OK to tell people to please keep their distance and not give them the chance to allow their dog to run toward us to greet. I learned that my protection of Champ's boundaries would make some people unhappy or make them think I was rude, but it was what I had to do to keep Champ safe. They suggested a yellow sleeve that went over the leash that read "I need space!" or tying a yellow bandana on the leash as a signal for people to stay away, but I didn't see either of those things working for us. I didn't think the people determined to greet us would even notice, and I didn't think a yellow bandana had a universal meaning that people would know.

2. Treating Champ

The course discussed threshold, which is basically how much a person or a pet can take until he or she breaks. I had to learn Champ's thresholds, such as the distance between him and another dog that he could tolerate without reacting, as well as my own. I also learned about management techniques for my stress along with Champ's stress, though I did a better job of managing Champ's than my own. I knew that he picked up on my stress, so it was almost a vicious cycle: his stress fed my stress about caring for and protecting him, then my stress fed his stress. It was damaging to both of us, as well as to Dan.

At our second visit with Dr. Koch, she asked me to start keeping track of his anxiety and aggressive behaviors. I started a Google spreadsheet so that I could easily share it with her, Linda, and Dr. DeWilde. I updated the spreadsheet daily—even on the day he died.

At the end of every day, I'd give Champ's anxiety and behavior a ranking from one to ten, with one being no anxiety and ten being absolutely unmanageable. I also had columns for his behaviors that indicated stress, such as lip licking, water drinking and chewing on fabric, reactive barking, whining, freezing, paw raising and others. Whenever he exhibited those behaviors, I'd make a tick mark. Sometimes there were ten tick marks in one box. I also wrote a brief summary of his behavior that day—good and bad. I shared the document with Dr. Koch every Monday with a summary of how the week went and my observations and questions.

This was when we brought in behavior management along with modification. We knew that we would not be able to modify every anxious or aggressive behavior Champ had, so we had to manage them. Using a muzzle whenever we were outside of our yard was one management tool, as was the Freedom Harness. Giving him the frozen stuffed food toy every time I left the house was a way to manage his separation anxiety. Keeping NPR playing on the radio whenever we were gone was another management tool that allowed him to hear even-toned human voices when he was alone (I often said Champ was the most well-educated German Shepherd around from listening to NPR all day). Using the "touch" command was a way to redirect his anxiety when people came in the house or when we were at the vet.

Champ also was very reactive to my voice, which is not a big, booming voice—I am a soft-spoken person. But whenever I would talk on the phone, he would run to the front windows and bark. If I was working on something and repeated something to myself out loud so I would remember it, or if I said something to Dan that was anything above a whisper, Champ would bark. To avoid that, if Dan was in another room and

Champ wearing the basket muzzle and Freedom Harness on a neighborhood walk in 2018.

I needed to tell him something, I either had to get up and go tell him in person, which meant Champ would get up and go with me, or I had to text Dan. But even that made Champ bark. Dan had to change his text tone that sounded like crickets because Champ would bark every time he heard it. One spring afternoon, I was getting ready to watch the St. Louis Cardinals' home opener on TV. I said, "Champ, this is my favorite day of the year" in my normal speaking voice. He jumped up and ran to the front windows barking as if there were someone banging on the front door.

Dogs bark for a lot of reasons, but all barks have a message. I tried to decode Champ's barks. I knew certain barks were alerts that he had heard a noise or seen someone outside and some were reactive barks toward other dogs or people. What I could never decode were what I called nuisance barks—the barking when there was nothing to precipitate it, at least that I could see or hear. Was he in pain? Did he hear something I couldn't that was causing stress? Was he looking for attention? Dr. Koch suggested maybe he heard some trains in the area that I couldn't hear, or possibly he was having small seizures. I never could figure it out, but it exhausted me.

2. Treating Champ

I talked to Linda about this, and she suggested that I read to him in a louder voice than usual to desensitize him to my voice. While reading to him, I was to toss tiny pieces of treats his way. She suggested the Dr. Seuss books because they were rhythmic, so I got out my childhood copies and read a couple to Champ every day. When I got tired of those, I checked out some others from the library.

Champ loved our reading time, most likely because of the treats, which were sometimes blueberries, but it was a time just for us. He was

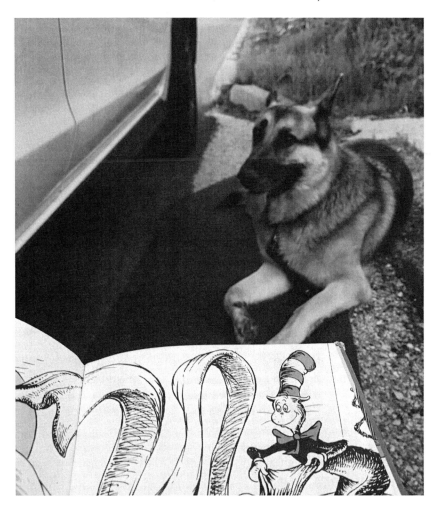

Me reading a Dr. Seuss book to Champ in the driveway next to my car in 2018.

also very attentive and mostly calm during that time. Since Champ was so anxious in the car, Linda also suggested that I read to him outside next to my car so that he would become desensitized to it, as well. One summer, every evening after dinner, Champ and I would take our Dr. Seuss books outside and sit on a yoga mat next to my car while I read. When it got too dark to do that, we moved our reading inside, and I branched out on books. Initially, I was reading books for preschoolers, but they were so short, and I wanted to keep him calm for as long as I could, so I chose some chapter books for younger readers—the *Stick Dog* series; the *Bobbsey Twins* series; several books about a girl named Lucky and her horse, Spirit; the Ramona Quimby series by Beverly Cleary; the *Junie B. Jones* series by Barbara Park; and Roald Dahl's classics such as *Charlie and the Chocolate Factory, Matilda,* and *James and the Giant Peach.* I liked to do different voices for the different characters. We also read all the *Diary of a Wimpy Kid* series, which made me laugh out loud as I read, and Champ really liked when I laughed. The last book we read together was *The Wind in the Willows* by Kenneth Grahame, a delightful story about anthropomorphized woodland creatures that easily lent itself to many opportunities for different voices.

Sometimes when Champ was barking a lot or exceptionally hypervigilant to noises, I would put on soft music. A friend of ours recorded an album of soothing folk-style music, and I played it for him often. By the end of the second song, he would relax on his bed and start to doze. I told my friend how much we played her album and how much it helped Champ, and thankfully, she took that as a compliment.

One of the other things we worked with Champ on was to gradually make him more comfortable being away from me. I began by saying, "Be right back," then going just out of eyesight for five to ten seconds and coming back so that he would be more comfortable with me being away for longer and longer periods of time while knowing I always came back when I said that. I even said it when I went down to the basement for a minute. I also said it whenever I left the house so he would learn to associate that with me returning. It seemed to work, though it's hard to say, but I always returned when I said I would, and saying it became so ingrained in me that I still say it today.

Because we had so much difficulty walking in our own neighborhood which has so many other dogs, I started taking him to large parks at off times on the weekends to walk around without risk of running into many people with dogs. We would stay off the beaten path, instead walking the perimeter of the park or in the less-populated areas.

I would try to find obstacles for him to climb on, such as large boulders, benches, or retaining walls, to give him something else to focus on. A lot of times, though, he would still be really anxious. Linda suggested I spray deer urine spray on some trees ahead of us when we were walking so that the scent would attract his attention, not the fear that we might run into other dogs. He never showed much interest in the deer urine, and it became clear that the outings were causing him more anxiety than relieving it, so I had to stop those, too.

We tried to teach Champ a whistle recall exercise with the goal of interrupting his reactivity to a trigger, specifically, fighting with the neighbors' dogs at the fence. However, he always went to threshold so quickly that he wasn't interested in the treat offered to him when I blew the whistle. I'm sure he heard the whistle, but he never showed any reaction to it, and I could never find a treat enticing enough to take him away from the fence.

One of the biggest issues with having Champ was finding safe and appropriate care for him when we traveled. When we adopted Champ in May 2014, we were preparing for a long-planned trip at the end of May to one of my races. I hated to leave him so soon, but we talked with the rescue group about it before we adopted him, and they agreed it would be better for him to go home with us in early May rather than wait until we returned from our trip in early June and keep him in boarding for another month. With his issues, I was concerned about having a pet sitter come into the house, so I looked into boarding him. Initially I called a nearby daycare and boarding facility, but the woman told me that he would have to pass a test in the facility before being allowed to stay, and I knew that he wouldn't pass due to his reactivity. She recommended a local kennel, and I talked to them about his recent adoption and reactivity, and they said they would be glad to have him. I signed him up for a hike to the park every day with a kennel worker and individual playtime rather than group playtime. I thought that since he had been in a kennel for a couple of weeks a month prior to that time he would be comfortable there, but I was also afraid that he would feel like we were returning him.

I called the kennel every day to check on him, and they said he was anxious but doing ok. We were all happy to see each other when we returned so we could try to help him feel more secure at home.

Every visit to the kennel was traumatic for him and required several days for him to get back to "normal" once we were home. When we would go to pick him up, once he saw us in the parking lot, he would take off running toward us, dragging the kennel worker, usually a high school student, behind him. It would take the kennel worker, Dan, and me to get him into his leash and collar because he was jumping up on us, whining, crying, and trying desperately to get in the car. I got scratched and nipped more than once from his exuberance.

In 2018 we took a long-planned trip to British Columbia for eight days. We decided to have our fence replaced while we were gone to try to solve the fence-fighting problem with the neighbors' dogs. Dan and I had both been bitten several times trying to pull Champ away from the fence, and the constant threat of a fence fight every time we went outside was too much and kept us from spending as much time outside as we would like.

The shared part of our fence would go from its existing four feet to six feet high with no space between the boards. This way, we could prevent any contact that happened during fence fighting and keep Champ from climbing over to get to the other dogs. He never succeeded in doing that but came dangerously close a few times. The rest of the fence would be four-foot-tall boards with two inches of space between each. These shorter, spaced-apart boards would still allow him to see what was going on in the neighborhood. The new fence wouldn't completely solve the fence-fighting problem because the dogs could still hear and smell each other and run along the fence line barking, but they could no longer see or bite at each other through the fence openings, so this eliminated that risk.

We had to start the travel day at 3 a.m. to get to the airport for our 5 a.m. flight—the first of three that day—so I took Champ to the kennel the day before. I had my phone off during the first flight, and when I turned it on during the first layover, there was a message from the kennel that Champ wasn't eating, wouldn't take his medicine, and had diarrhea. I called them back and said I wasn't concerned about him not eating but I was concerned about the medicine. They said they had some canned food on hand and could try to get him to take his medicine in the canned food instead of the peanut butter we usually used.

Trying to explain the medication schedule to the workers at the kennel was difficult, and I know they tried their best. Their feeding schedule was different from ours at home, so we had to work together to design a medication schedule that would allow Champ to get all his medications in the time that someone was on duty. I had to sort out the medications before I dropped him off then go through all of the doses with the manager to make sure they completely understood. They had a fee per medication dosage, and thankfully, they always gave me a break on that cost because that would have been an unbelievably high amount.

Our second flight was longer, and I didn't have any messages when we landed. Our third and final flight was to be forty-five minutes on a fourteen-seat plane. We had just gotten seated, and my phone rang. It was the kennel again. I told them to do their best with him, and if I needed to, I would call someone to take some medicine out to him for his diarrhea and some other canned food. I said that he would likely eat out of someone's hand if they were patient. I told them we were getting ready to take off, so I'd call them back when we landed.

I talked to the kennel workers six times that day and several times a day for the rest of the trip. They were doing all they could, but Champ wasn't really responding. I gave them permission to give him whatever it took to get him to take his medicine and not to worry about his food. I felt completely helpless because I was over two thousand miles away. But even if I'd been two hours away, there was still nothing I could do. If I had sent someone over there whom he knew, he would think he was getting out, and that wouldn't be fair.

I knew the kennel workers were stressed trying to take care of him. I knew, because I dealt with this every day, and this was my one week away to recharge. But it was hard for me to relax because I was so worried about him and felt completely helpless.

We had appointments with Dr. Koch every three months to see how his medications were working and to determine if any changes needed to be made to either his medications or his behavior modification. At our final visit, she said she would continue to prescribe Champ's medications for as long as he needed them, but there was not much more we could do to manage his behavior because there were likely underlying physical problems that we had been unable to diagnose or manage. I left there in a state of shock. It felt like a punch in the stomach, and I wondered how to go forward.

3

Anxiety and Post-Traumatic Stress Disorder in Dogs

"Loving you changed my life. Losing you did the same."—Unknown

I truly believe Champ had a canine version of post-traumatic stress disorder from which he never recovered despite our efforts. Moving from a home where he was supposedly loved to being chained outside—unwanted and underfed—to going into a foster home that didn't work out, going into a noisy boarding kennel for two weeks, then to us was likely too much for his brain to process. I believe that that combination of traumas to his emotional state led to his constant state of anxiety. His "fight or flight" stress response was always on, leaving him hypervigilant.

Animal behaviorist Temple Grandin, PhD, writes that anxiety is related to fear, though a milder form of fear, and that dominance aggression is related to fear aggression. "A fear-aggressive dog just wants to get away, but a dominance-aggressive dog is anxious about his control over resources (food, toys, sleeping spot) or behaviors (running off leash, getting up on the bed)," Grandin writes. The dominance-aggressive dog that is growling at the person touching his food bowl doesn't run away because that won't solve his problem. Grandin says that if a dog is anxious or has anxiety aggression, it is the opposite of relaxed and happy, and instead of focusing on dominance, owners should focus on treating the aggressive dog's fear and anxiety and training it for emotional restraint and good manners.[1]

Anxiety has a purpose in life—it is an adaptive reaction when an animal or human is confronted with potential danger or threat.[2] It prepares a person or animal to escape from danger or perceived danger. However, researchers are not sure if animals experience anxiety in the same way as humans do. The physical signs of anxiety in animals are

48

freezing, panting, restlessness, aggression, hypervigilance, and sleep disturbances. A team of researchers in the Netherlands suggested a need to define pathological anxiety in animals, which they describe as

> a persistent, uncontrollable, excessive, inappropriate, and generalized dysfunctional and aversive emotion, triggering physiological and behavioural responses lacking adaptive value. Pathological anxiety-related behaviour is a response to the exaggerated anticipation or perception of threats, which is incommensurate with the actual situation.[3]

These researchers point to genetics, environmental stressors, and epigenetics, or how a person's or animal's behaviors and environment can cause changes that affect the way their genes function.[4] Environmental changes such as divorce, birth of children, frequent moves, or being rehomed can lead to a pet's pathological anxiety. Unfortunately, treatments for pathological anxiety are limited.

Separation anxiety is a behavioral and emotional disorder that has physical, physiological, and behavioral signs and can cause poor health and physiological state of a dog.[5] Dogs who are suffering from separation anxiety may whine, bark, drool or howl excessively, tremble, attempt to escape, scratch at door frames or windows, hide, or urinate or defecate in the home or crate, typically within 30 minutes of the owner leaving the house.[6] It is one of the most common reasons why people seek help from veterinary behavior specialists and trainers and is the first behavioral disorder in dogs to have an on-label pharmaceutical treatment. Clomicalm, the brand name for clomipramine hydrochloride, is a tricyclic antidepressant used to treat depression and obsessive-compulsive disorder and phobias in humans.

The degree of anxiety and symptoms shown by some dogs with separation anxiety mimics the diagnostic criteria for panic attacks and bipolar disorders in humans. People with bipolar disorders may cycle between agitation and lethargy, similar to dogs with this disorder, when separated from their owner, cycling from agitation, such as barking, howling, and being destructive, to lethargy or depression.[7]

It directly affects the well-being of the dog as well as the owner, who may be frustrated by the destroyed items, damage to the home or by complaints from the neighbors about the dog barking while the owner is away. More importantly, it can damage the human-animal bond, which is what dog owners cherish.

Interestingly, dogs with separation anxiety are often exhausted when their people come home and show a very different sleep-wake pattern on days when their owners are at home.[8] Dogs learn the owner's routine, such as making coffee, taking a shower, getting dressed, putting on shoes and coat, and picking up keys, and will be clingy and restless during this process. Some dogs will even grab the owner's clothing or bite their hands in an attempt to prevent them from leaving.[9]

Some risk factors that have been associated with separation anxiety include a history of traumatic separation, unfamiliarity with being left alone, excessive greetings or drawn-out departures by owners, changes in owner's routine, moving to a new home, adding a new caregiver, or loss of a family member. In addition, dogs that follow their owners are more likely to develop separation-related behaviors.[10]

Rescued or shelter dogs are thought to be more likely to have separation anxiety, according to veterinary behaviorists E'Lise Christensen, DVM, and Karen L. Overall, DVM, PhD. Veterinarians are not sure whether this is due to the trauma of being given up, the time spent in a shelter, or whether their separation anxiety was the reason they were surrendered. When owners surrender their dog to a shelter, they typically do not report separation anxiety to the shelters because they are afraid the dog will be euthanized.[11] Up to 30 percent of dogs in shelters are thought to have been surrendered for separation-related behaviors.[12]

It is estimated that 20 percent to 40 percent of cases at U.S. veterinary behavior clinics and 30 percent of dogs adopted from shelters suffer with separation anxiety, though other estimates go up to nearly 50 percent of all canines having some level of separation anxiety.[13]

Various studies have looked for consistency among dogs with separation anxiety, however, no common thread has yet been found. Two studies showed that male dogs were more likely to have separation anxiety, while one found no difference in males or females. Another study suggested males with separation anxiety are more annoying than females because they are larger and louder.[14] One study indicated several breeds that were more likely to have separation-related issues, while another found very different breeds and yet another found that 50 percent of dogs with separation anxiety were mixed breeds.[15,16] One study suggested that early neutering or spaying might increase the likelihood of fear and anxiety.[17] Still others showed that owners who do not react to distress signals from their dogs can increase the risk of separation-related behaviors.[18] For a behavior problem that is so prevalent among dogs and seen so frequently in veterinary clinics and shelters, there are few concrete answers.

One study showed that when dogs are separated from their owners, most dogs stay close to the chair where the owner usually sits. In contrast, dogs with separation anxiety do not show a preference for objects touched or left behind by their owner. These dogs may not be able to associate their owner with his or her home or possessions, so they do not feel safe when the owner is not present.[19] Owners who do not teach their dog how to respond to social cues can also unknowingly foster with separation anxiety, which can develop at any age. Other research found that abandonment, or being left alone without human contact, was more important in dogs with separation anxiety than attachment to the owner. Some of these dogs are happy only when with their owners, showing distress even when with people who aren't their owners.[20]

Nicholas Dodman, DVM, a veterinarian, animal psychologist and professor emeritus at the Tufts University Veterinary Center, said dogs that bark during periods of separation anxiety often have a dysfunctional or abusive background that makes them "bond like Velcro to caring owners. These dogs almost literally love too much."[21]

Some websites for owners of dogs with separation anxiety try to provide helpful suggestions about ways to manage it, including giving the dog a "calming" supplement, providing more exercise, trying a compression vest, providing distracting toys, using a pheromone diffuser, or giving a pain medication.[22] We tried all those things from the beginning, and none of them worked long-term. I read that list now and shake my head, knowing how many other owners of dogs with severe anxiety tried these things with as much hope as I had, only to be disappointed if they didn't work.

Dogs show many physical signs of stress, though owners are not always aware of them or are not paying close attention. A study in Italy found that owners reported the indicators of stress in their dogs were trembling or shaking and whining, which correlate with most people's idea of fear and anxiety. The researchers also noted aggression, excessive barking, hyperactivity, and excessive drooling and stated that it is important for owners of dogs showing these signs be aware that these may be indicators of stress, which can be treated instead of relinquishing, abandoning, or euthanizing their pets as a result.[23]

In humans and other species, exposure to a stressor causes a physiological stress response, such as a release of cortisol, faster heartbeat, and tensed muscles, all which can have effects on health and lifespan of an individual. While these responses are not as well studied in dogs as they have been in humans and other mammals, it is assumed that their responses are similar. While different stressors affect different parts of the stress response system, they all influence well-being. If a dog is constantly exposed to a stressor—for instance, thunderstorms—its stress response may become chronic. This would also apply in the case of separation anxiety. If a dog is left alone daily, its stress response will be activated daily.[24]

In Wilde's book *Don't Leave Me!*, she assigns various reasons for a dog's separation anxiety: genetics, assimilation into the household, abandonment/rehoming, breed, traumatic experience, and aging.[25] It may also include loss of family or companions, loss of freedom, stress, and abuse.[26] We could check most of those boxes with Champ, though he was only three years old when we adopted him.

Much of the research into separation anxiety looks at the role of hyper attachment, an exaggeration of normal attachment, an evolutionary process that young animals are born with toward their caregiver, usually their mother. A healthy attachment with the mother reduces fear and encourages puppies to explore their environment.[27] While hyper attachment is often given as a leading cause of separation anxiety, it can be found in pets without a formal diagnosis as well, those that are simply labeled as needy or insecure. One clinical trial sought to use hyper attachment as a measure to diagnose separation anxiety, however, the researchers were unable to find a relationship between hyper attachment and separation anxiety.[28] After all, some dogs seem to have been born with separation anxiety, while others develop it later in life. When it appears in older pets, it may be the result of underlying medical conditions, such as hypothyroid or metabolic disease, hearing or vision loss, kidney disease, or arthritis, as it did with my first German Shepherd, Lindy.[29]

Some researchers claim that separation anxiety is sometimes caused by frustration, not necessarily fear and anxiety. They claim that inappropriate elimination can be from improper housetraining, a dog not receiving enough physical or mental stimulation, or a dog with little impulse control.[30] Hungarian researchers claim that an owner's permissiveness lowers the threshold of frustration in the dog, resulting in barking when the owner is absent. In addition, they claim that when dogs experience unpredictability in their owners' permissive behavior, they react with frustration when separated.[31]

A study of canine anxiety among nearly 14,000 pet dogs in Finland showed that noise sensitivity was the most common anxiety trait among the group surveyed with nearly one-third of all dogs showing sensitivity to at least one noise. Separation anxiety and aggression were the least common with 5 percent and 14 percent, respectively. Dogs with separation-related behavior were more than four times more likely to also be hyperactive or impulsive and 3.4 times more inattentive than dogs without separation-related behavior. Male dogs were more likely to show separation anxiety, aggression, and hyperactivity/impulsiveness. The researchers also ranked the top fifteen breeds of dogs that show certain anxious behaviors, including fear of thunder, strangers, and surfaces; hyperactivity/impulsivity; inattention; aggression toward strangers; tail chasing; fly snapping or chasing light; and vocalizing or salivating while alone. The German Shepherd Dog was in the top fifteen breeds experiencing these symptoms for every behavior, ranking second for hyperactivity/impulsivity and for fly snapping/light chasing and third for aggression toward strangers.[32]

The few times I would get brave and try to talk about Champ's issues with friends who also had dogs, they would look at me quizzically and say, "My dog just sleeps all the time. Isn't that what dogs do?" Normal dogs do tend to enjoy their rest. Dogs like Champ, though, rarely rest. He acted as though he expected something bad to happen to him, and he had to be prepared for it. He rarely sat down or laid on his bed, and never napped. He was always listening, always watching for something to happen. He would jump at a crackling leaf outside or at the sound of a car door closing on the street. At the beginning, before we knew the extent of his issues, we would say that he didn't have an off switch. That was true, but the reasons behind it were problematic.

Can dogs have post-traumatic stress disorder? How would it be diagnosed? A dog can't tell us verbally about its past or traumas it has experienced. Canine PTSD is very similar to PTSD in humans, says Dorothy Black, DVM, clinical assistant professor in emergency and critical care at the Texas A&M College of Veterinary Medicine and Biomedical Sciences.

"Dogs and people display similar behaviors after traumatic events and have similar biochemical changes," Black explained.[33]

The pioneering neuroscientist Jaak Panksepp, PhD, wrote that one of the most horrible experiences of life is to be stricken by sudden terror.

Another is to be continually consumed by the persistent feelings of anxiety that gnaw away at you, destroying your sense of security in the world. It is likely that the affective impact of both experiences emerges ultimately from the differential arousal of one and the same brain system—a coherently operating fear circuit that produces terror when precipitously aroused and chronic anxiety during milder, more sustained arousal.[34]

The Most Painful Choice

Those "persistent feelings of anxiety that gnaw away at you, destroying your sense of security in the world" is likely how Champ felt. Anxiety was gnawing away at him, both his mental and physical state, for as long as we had him and likely even before. Despite everything that we did to make his life feel more secure, it didn't work.

In PTSD in humans, and likely other mammals, the amygdala, an almond-shaped structure in the brain that plays a role in aggression, overreacts to fearful stimuli and is slow to calm after being activated. It expands in size in prolonged PTSD and becomes hyperreactive.[35]

In fact, military dogs serving in Afghanistan and Iraq where they were exposed to explosions, gunfire and other violence are being diagnosed with PTSD more frequently, according to the *New York Times.* More than 5 percent of the about six hundred and fifty military dogs deployed by American combat forces are developing canine PTSD. As with humans, symptoms vary: hyper-vigilance; avoiding buildings or work areas; changes in temperament; aggression with their handlers; or being clingy and shy.[36]

Dodman wrote about a patient of his, a German Shepherd Dog that had been in Iraq with the U.S. military for six months searching for explosives. When she returned to the U.S., she was fearful, overwhelmingly anxious, became hypervigilant and was always looking for trouble, displaying "the full range" of PTSD symptoms. Dodman compared the dog's symptoms with the qualifications necessary for diagnosis of PTSD in humans and found that she had them all, despite her being unable to explain what had happened to her.[37]

As with humans, not every dog that experiences trauma or goes to war experiences it. What is the difference? Dodman suspects genetic predisposition, environmental events, and resilience.[38]

Perhaps one of the best-known cases of resilience in dogs was in the group of dogs that became known as the Vicktory Dogs after they were rescued in 2007 from former National Football League player Michael Vick's Bad Newz kennels, where they had been used as fighting dogs and subjected to various other forms of abuse. Of the fifty-one dogs rescued, two were euthanized; two died while in shelters; ten dogs went to BAD-RAP, a pit bull rescue organization in California; and twenty-two of the most traumatized went to the sanctuary at Best Friends Animal Society in Utah to recover and heal. Many of them were adopted into families, earned an AKC Canine Good Citizen certificate, got involved in agility and other activities, or became service or therapy dogs.[39] The last surviving Vicktory Dog passed away in December 2021.

3. Anxiety and Post-Traumatic Stress Disorder in Dogs

Patricia B. McConnell, PhD, an applied animal behaviorist and professor in Wisconsin, wrote in her memoir *The Education of Will* that there is no doubt that dogs are capable of being psychologically traumatized and suffering from some PTSD-related symptoms, including hyperarousal, or always being "on."[40] To them, the world is a scary and dangerous place.

McConnell wrote that she believes that many of the dogs she worked with were victims of some kind of trauma, either from an attack by another dog, abusive treatment by a previous owner, or having lived in a puppy mill.

> It's time to view them as we see survivors of war or of sexual and physical violence—not as examples of deficient individuals who should be blamed for their inadequacies or need for "dominance" but as individuals who can be healed through skill and compassion. These dogs need, first and foremost, the patience and understanding that provide them a sense of safety, and the belief that they can have some influence on the world around them.[41]

We tried to give Champ the sense of safety. He had a calm, safe home with a fenced-in yard, the best veterinary care, training, and nutrition we could give him, and so much love. He had 100 percent of my attention when I was at home. I am a very determined person, and when I set my mind on something, I work hard until I get it. I applied that determination to making Champ feel safe and loved, but it wasn't enough to eliminate his fears or anxiety. He was physically healthy, as far as we knew, until the arthritis flared toward the end, but mentally and emotionally, he was not a healthy dog, and I couldn't fix him. It still frustrates me that the efforts of the team we had in place ultimately could not heal him.

But we were not alone in our failure to heal Champ. Many others have been unsuccessful in rehabilitating dogs with PTSD. Dodman told the *New York Times* that the disorder may not be able to be cured. "It is more management," he said. "Dogs never forget."[42]

Do dogs ever forget being abandoned or rehomed? Maybe not, says Overall. "Relinquishment may be a shattering experience for dogs. Anything that we can do to prevent their neuroimmune system from sinking into depression may benefit their transition and—as an unexpected plus—long-term outcomes. It is likely that medicating dogs and cats for distress, arousal, and anxiety when entering sheltered environments can be done with a host of medications that may provide profound benefits."[43]

Few people knew how stressful and taxing managing Champ's

behavior was. Dan saw it most frequently, and Dr. Koch knew from my daily entries of Champ's anxiety on a shared spreadsheet and emails. I didn't say much to anyone else, simply because people didn't understand, even if they said they did. People could not understand that such a big, solid dog was acting out because he was afraid. A few people close to me could see the toll it was taking on me, but they also knew I was not going to give up on Champ.

At one point, Dr. Koch and I had a phone conversation in which she told me she suspected Champ had some medical conditions we hadn't been able to identify or treat that may have been contributing to his anxiety. She suspected he had a gastrointestinal component and something going on in his brain and recommended an MRI of his brain and spine. I decided against the MRI because of the stress it would have created for Champ and because I knew it wouldn't change the outcome of the situation. If he had a tumor, I wouldn't put him through brain or spinal surgery or chemotherapy. She indicated that there may be several "little time bombs coming together" that created his physical and emotional pain.

Me with Champ in 2016. My shirt says, "All dogs were created equal. Then God made a German Shepherd."

56

3. Anxiety and Post-Traumatic Stress Disorder in Dogs

Several groups of researchers have found that chronic health problems cause prolonged stress in animals, which leads them to adapt, either through physiological changes in the brain and nervous system, or through psychological changes, as in behavior and emotions. These adaptations take a lot of energy away from normal functioning. They determined that prolonged health conditions are themselves a stressor that may affect an animal's well-being.[44] This may have been the case with Champ if there were truly underlying conditions that we could not diagnose.

In the fall of 2018, at a vet visit to Dr. DeWilde, she told me that it might be time to start thinking about letting him go. At that point, there was nothing more we could do medically for him, and we were maintaining his mental health and behavior as best as we could. I remember thanking her for telling me that and being honest with me, but I wasn't ready to stop trying.

About that same time, I had a phone call with Dr. Koch, and she told me the same. She said without knowing if there was anything physical affecting his behavior, such as a brain tumor, there really wasn't more that we could do. I told her I wasn't ready to give up on him and would keep looking for ways to help him.

A week or two later, when Linda had come over to work with us, she told me the same thing. Linda was also a nurse, and she had told us early on that Champ's anxiety would shorten his life, simply because of the physical toll it takes on the body—clenched muscles, continuous high levels of cortisol from being in the "fight-or-flight" state, or other physical manifestations of the disorder. I asked her if she had been talking to Dr. DeWilde or Dr. Koch, and she said no. I told her that they both had given me the same recommendation within a couple weeks from the other, but that I was not ready to make that decision.

I told Dan what all three of them had said, then told him I could not consider that option at that time. If I just tried harder, I could find something that might work. And I was not ready to even think about not having Champ in my life. Looking back, I can see how selfish that was of me to refuse to consider euthanasia at that time, but the decision is one never to be made lightly, and I was not ready to make it. Champ deserved more—whatever that looked like—and I was going to find it and give it to him.

4

Nature vs. Nurture

"Don't give up on the hard dogs. They will give you something you never knew you needed."—Modern Canine Training

I think about what little I know about Champ's first three years of life and whether whatever happened in those years made him beyond repair in the six years that we had him. Was it poor nutrition in his mother that caused some developmental issues in his brain? Poor genetics and breeding? Was he abused or malnourished in his first home, and that's what made him anxious and fearful? Did someone do something to him when he was tied out on the five-foot chain in the trailer park?

There's a common quote attributed to John Grogan, author of *Marley and Me: Life and Love with the World's Worst Dog*, that reads: "There's no such thing as a bad dog, just a bad owner."[1] I have several problems with this. First, the subtitle of his book is terrible—he did not have the "world's worst dog." I understand that Grogan's title is tongue-in-cheek, but I don't think he has any idea about what it is like to have a dog with behavior issues.

Second, his quote implies that all dogs are good and are corrupted only by their owners. While that is true in select cases, such as the Vicktory Dogs, it's not universally true. Some dogs, like Champ and the others like him, may have had genetic or physical issues that led to their behavior problems, not "bad owners."

Eventually Grogan admits, "Dogs are great. Bad dogs, if you can really call them that, are perhaps the greatest of them all." He falls in love with Marley and is devastated when he passes. But I don't like that his premise is that Marley is a "bad" dog.

Sue Alexander, a certified dog behavior consultant, certified professional dog trainer and certified behavior consultant canine in Guelph, Ontario, Canada, and Trish McMillan, who has a master's degree in animal behavior, said it's not nature versus nurture, but "it's always both."

58

4. Nature vs. Nurture

"You can do everything right—have the best environment, give the best training and the best socialization—and still end up with a dangerous dog," McMillan said.[2]

Dodman writes that while environmental experiences play a role in developing canine behaviors and temperaments, including reactivity, some animals are born with genetic tendencies to develop behavioral problems, while others have these behavior problems forced on them by owners.[3]

"All behavior is determined by both nature and nurture—the precise contribution of each depending on the stage in the dog's life and the opportunity that has occurred for modification of the behavior by learning," Dodman writes.[4] "That behaviors arise spontaneously when there has been no opportunity for learning to occur is evidence that they are preprogrammed. Exactly how this happens is a bit of a mystery, but the answer lies somewhere in the genes."

Dodman adds that most of the seriously affected dogs that he has seen in his practice have experienced a traumatic event, often while young, that shaped the beginning of their fear.[5]

Nancy Tanner, a dog trainer and writer, indicates that the following building blocks—both genetic and environmental—can create a dangerous dog: heredity, sex/reproductive status, early experience, socialization, training, health, quality of owner, and victim behavior. "One indicator does not a bad dog make. But put all eight of these together and you have a real problem, and most of the time a problem that will result in euthanasia. ... Any dog that has teeth has the potential to cause harm, it is the care and well-being that is provided that indicates how this will most likely play out," she writes.[6]

Stanley Coren, PhD, a psychologist who studies dog behavior, wrote that aggressive personalities are both born and made. "It is possible to create an aggressive dog that is willing to attack other animals or people, even when it has not been threatened or challenged. People can create vicious, even ferocious dogs using variations of the selective breeding techniques and rearing practices that produce sound and agreeable dogs."[7]

Even researchers studying genetics in dogs acknowledge that phenotyping behavior is difficult, in part because behavior is almost always influenced by the environment.[8]

A phenotype is the physical expression of one or more genes. For example, in dogs, the phenotype includes coat color and texture, eye color, and stature. Phenotypes are influenced by the genetics, physical, and maternal environments as well as the interaction of those environments on the dog's brain. This is why dogs from the same litter can have very different behaviors: one puppy may be terrified of storms and fireworks, while another is not.[9]

Having a gene means a behavior could happen but is not a definite prediction.

"All behaviors are the result of the interaction of the genetic background with the physical and cognitive environments found in the individual patient," write Overall and colleagues.[10] "Even when diseases are heritable in a simple manner, their phenotypes and presentations can be altered through interaction with the environment. Nowhere is this truer than for behavior: it occurs when pharmacologic treatment and behavior modification are used for behavioral problems, and when problems are prevented simply because the patient is in a household that may not promote Them."

Alexander and McMillan provide a variety of options to clients with dogs with behavioral issues: work with it; manage it; rehome the dog; surrender it to a shelter or sanctuary; or euthanize.

Working with the dog, they say, has several obstacles. Finding the right help can be difficult, as we experienced with Champ, and it can be cost prohibitive. Management of the dog carries an emotionally high cost for the humans and the dogs, and will almost always eventually fail, they said.

"Environment can't fix everything. Making the behavior stop doesn't necessarily make the problem go away,"[11] Alexander said. While an owner may have been able to stop behaviors such as lunging and barking, he or she might not be able to stop the dog from feeling the inner turmoil and conflict that was driving that behavior.

The Biological Aspects of Behavioral Disorders

There is no such thing as a superdog. Humans' desire for perfection is an understandable weakness. However, a dog cannot be both gentle and reliable with strangers and children and an effective sentry dog—as some beloved characters in movies are shown to be. The television superhero dogs are fictional: Dogs that are tough enough to do police work will not make trustworthy family pets, and vice versa. Even individuals from the most versatile breeds, such as the German Shepherd Dog, cannot simply be trained to be guide dogs for the blind or military dogs. Markedly different lines are bred within a breed for different purposes.[12]

Researchers say dogs are excellent models to study behavior because the different breeds have been specifically created to have certain behaviors and to perform specific tasks, giving dogs differences in emotions, aggression, activity, and predatory behavior. For example, Labrador Retrievers, the most popular breed in America, were designed as working gun dogs and bird retrievers, but they also make good family dogs.[13] They are generally easy to train and eager to please.

In a study of thirteen behavior traits in the fifty-five most registered breeds of the American Kennel Club, researchers found vast differences, as one might expect. For instance, for the watchdog barking trait, the Bloodhound ranked at the least likely to have the trait while the miniature Schnauzer ranked most likely. For the excitability trait, the Bloodhound again ranked at the lowest end for the least excitable, and the Fox Terrier ranked highest. For the housebreaking ease, the Bassett Hound ranked at the lowest end, or most difficult to housebreak, while the Doberman Pinscher ranked at the highest end. The researchers concluded that there is more impact from early training and environment on the traits that differentiated the least well, such as housebreaking ease, than on traits such as excitability that differentiated better. In addition, the behavior of the dog's parent was also important to consider, as well as the characteristics of the particular line of dog within the breed and the breeder's environment.[14]

Another analysis of those thirteen traits found that the most variance among breeds was in aggression, trainability, and emotional reactivity, which includes excitability, general activity, snapping at children, excessive barking, demanding affection, and fearfulness or distress.[15]

One of the first studies of genetics and behavior in dogs was in the book *Dog Behavior: The Genetic Basis* by John Paul Scott and John L. Fuller, published in 1965. The researchers raised multiple litters of dogs of five breeds: Basenji, Beagle, Cocker Spaniel, Shetland Sheepdog, and Wire-Haired Fox Terrier. They studied the dogs for multiple traits and behaviors, including fear and noise reactivity, biting and jerking the leash, timidity, barking, aggression, dominance, tail wagging, and problem-solving skills, among others. In addition, they found that there are few general behavioral traits. Each breed showed a combination of characteristics that were related to the specific behavioral tasks for which they were created. They noted that from the beginning of their work, there was a lot of variation between individual dogs, making it impossible to generalize about any one breed from experience with one dog or one line of dogs, because some behavior can change over generations.[16]

The Influence of Early Life Experience

Highly stressed or anxious dogs are physiologically on edge because of an abnormal function of the hypothalamic-pituitary-adrenal (HPA) axis, writes Ilana Reisner, DVM, PhD, and Stefanie Schwartz, DVM, in *Decoding Your Dog: Explaining Common Dog Behaviors and How to Prevent or Change Unwanted Ones.*[17] The HPA axis regulates production of glucocorticoids, a class of steroid that is linked to physical and emotional stress and helps to regulate stress responses. A well-known glucocorticoid is cortisol, known as the stress hormone. In studies in rats and primates, researchers found that while some glucocorticoid exposure is necessary for development and learning, excessive exposure is harmful to a young animal's brain development.

Stress in the prenatal period affects the development of the brain regions that control the HPA axis, including the hippocampus, the frontal cortex, and the amygdala. The hippocampus modulates HPA axis activity. If its functioning is altered, it may cause fewer glucocorticoids to be secreted in abuse situations or higher cortisol levels if kept away from the mother.[18]

In humans, excessive exposure to glucocorticoids during development has been shown to make adults more prone to anxiety and depression. If the effect is the same in dogs, then puppies born to mothers in a stressful or overwhelming environment, such as in a crowded shelter, a puppy mill, or on the street, may also have physical changes to their brains leading to behavior problems later in life, such as increased aggression[19] or what some trainers and owners of these pets refer to as "being wired differently."

In newborns, glucocorticoid production is suppressed during brain growth, which also is the socialization or stress hyporesponsive period that is so critical to healthy development in dogs. In young rats, glucocorticoids rise when they are separated from their mother, but return to lower levels when the mother is close by. Researchers found that adult rats who were exposed to prenatal stress have shown three major effects on adult behavior: learning impairments, greater sensitivity to drugs, and increased anxiety and depression-related behaviors.[20]

In dogs, the stress hyporesponsive period lasts about four weeks. If puppies are separated too early from their mother, their brains experience a surge in glucocorticoids, which can give them the impression that the world is stressful and frightening. The longer the mother is separated, the more impact there is on the puppies' developing brains.[21]

4. Nature vs. Nurture

Disease and death related to stress from being separated from the mother occurs more often in puppies that are weaned at six weeks than puppies that are weaned at twelve weeks. Puppies permanently separated too early from their mothers, as occurs in commercial breeding situations and puppy mills, may go on to develop behavioral disorders.[22]

A group of developmental researchers in Japan found an increase in cortisol in Labrador Retriever puppy urine after five weeks of age when separated from the mother. This suggests that a stress hyporesponsive period persists until four weeks of age in dogs, similar to what exists in rat models. They found that at five weeks of age, the puppies' distress sounds, such as whining, yelping, or howling, during separation changed and the nursing behavior decreased, which they determined was related to a change in the interaction between the mother and the puppies. The researchers concluded that the behavior and stress levels of the mothers needs to be considered in future research given their influence on the stress response of their puppies.[23]

A study of German Shepherd Dog puppies and their mothers found that the quality and quantity of the mother's care may also affect the behavior development of the puppies. Puppies that received the most interaction from the mother, including physical contact, nursing, licking, sniffing or poking the puppy with the nose, showed more engagement with humans and inanimate objects at eighteen months old.[24]

While all stress is unavoidable, and some stress is necessary for proper brain development and socialization, too much stress can cause damage and later behavioral and emotional problems. Thus, a behavior problem that begins when a dog is three or four years old may be the result of the mother's stress during pregnancy or a stressful experience as a weeks-old puppy.

There are two camps of thinking about how this happens. One camp is the neurotoxicity hypothesis, which claims that continued exposure to glucocorticoids reduces the ability of the neurons to resist injury, thereby increasing the rate at which they are damaged. This leads to years of post-traumatic stress disorder, depression, or chronic stress, which results in a smaller hippocampus, the part of the brain responsible for emotional and behavioral responses. The other camp supports the vulnerability hypothesis, which claims that the smaller hippocampus is a pre-existing factor for these disorders due to genetics or early stress exposure.[25]

Ultimately, the researchers concluded that the views are not mutually exclusive, and the timing and duration of exposure to stressors may be the most important factors in determining the changes in the brain.

In another study, Reisner showed that aggressive dogs have lower levels of serotonin metabolites, the neurotransmitters associated with mood, in their spinal cords than nonaggressive dogs, making them more likely to act impulsively or aggressively.[26] Dodman concurs, and indicates that increasing serotonin by whatever means necessary can stabilize these dogs' moods and reduce aggression.[27] This is why many dogs with behavioral issues are prescribed selective serotonin reuptake inhibitor medications (SSRIs), such as fluoxetine or paroxetine, among others, and have similar response rates as humans.[28]

In fact, pet medications are a big business in the United States. U.S. retail sales of pet medications, both prescription and over the counter, reached $8.6 billion in 2017.[29] Pet supplement sales reached $800 million in 2021, in part due to demand for CBD products and natural remedies for stress and anxiety.[30]

Environment Matters—or Is It All in the Genes?

Many people say, "It's all in how they are raised." If that were true, abused or shelter dogs would have difficulty being placed into a home, wrote McMillan in an article about her adopted pit bull, Theodore, who was raised by a dog fighter but never showed any negative effects after she adopted him.

"Environment counts, but so do genes," she says. "Ultimately, all dogs are individuals, and that's where we need to meet them."[31]

Many canine anxiety disorders have been observed to be inherited at a relatively high rate, but they also are influenced by several environmental factors, which are still being studied.[32]

Dogs were the first animals to be domesticated by humans, and that process likely played a role in the genetic basis of the fear and aggression behavior traits, researchers suggest. During domestication, dogs developed numerous genetic variations beyond what were already in place prior to the creation of about 400 breeds, including size and fear and aggression toward unknown humans or other dogs. Dogs are the only animal domesticated by humans primarily for their behavioral traits, with some selected for herding, hunting, pointing, protection, and similar useful qualities. Despite the different groupings of breeds, most researchers agree that dog breeds differ in behavior in measurable ways, with many having specific traits.[33] Some of those traits can go to extremes, manifesting in obsessive-compulsive disorder, such as spinning and chasing the tail, repetitive behaviors, or aggression.[34]

A group of researchers at The Ohio State University conducted genetic mapping of fear and aggression in several hundred dogs of various breeds. They found that known *IGF1* and *HMGA2* location variants for small body size were associated with separation anxiety, touch-sensitivity, owner-directed aggression, and dog rivalry. In addition, two locations, between *GNAT3* and *CD36* on chromosome 18, and near *IGSF1* on chromosome X, are associated with touch sensitivity, nonsocial fear, and fear and aggression toward unfamiliar dogs and humans. Mice without *CD36* are known to have significantly increased anxiety and aggression. *GNAT3* and *IGSF1* are expressed in the amygdala and the hypothalamic-pituitary-adrenal (HPA) axis, the brain regions where fear and aggression originate.[35]

As a follow-up study, the researchers and new collaborators evaluated the performance of genetic markers as predictors of canine problematic behavior in the community. Of nearly 400 dogs in the study, 30 percent of them had a behavioral diagnosis and 21 percent of those were on medication for it. From owner-provided cheek swabs from their dogs, the researchers genotyped SNPs (single nucleotide polymorphisms, the most common type of genetic variation) at twenty markers associated with problem behaviors in their studies. They found that female dogs were more likely to have a behavioral diagnosis, and males had increased risk for aggression directed toward familiar dogs and for being more aggressive than females. Female dogs had an increased risk of developing fear of unfamiliar dogs and humans, and intact females had an increased fear of dogs. The researchers did not find a correlation between sex and anxiety traits.[36]

In addition, they tested whether their twenty markers could predict the risk of dogs receiving a behavioral diagnosis. They found a set of five markers on chromosomes 10, 13 and X that could predict a behavioral diagnosis. Multiple DNA variations at the chromosome 10 were associated with various structural and behavioral traits. The chromosome 13 risk variation is associated with increased fear, anxiety, and aggression traits, as well as smaller size. The X chromosome location markers near *IGSF1* are associated with fear, anxiety, aggression, and body size traits, and markers near *HS6ST2* are associated with sociability. While more research is needed, fear, aggression, and anxiety were the most important traits associated with a clinical diagnosis of problem behaviors in dogs.[37]

Interestingly, the researchers also found three markers associated with anxiety disorder: chromosome 1 near *ESR1*; chromosome 20 near *MITF*; and chromosome 24 near *RALY, EIF2S,2* and *ASIP*. While they did not find a marker that predicted a fear diagnosis, they found a marker on chromosome 10 between *MSRB3* and *HMGA2* that was associated with an aggression diagnosis. Ultimately, ten markers at eight locations were associated with having a clinical behavioral diagnosis, and five of those successfully predicted a diagnosis.

Many other researchers have looked at whether behavior traits are heritable, or a measure of how differences in genes account for differences in personality or behavior traits. A heritability score of zero indicates that the trait is due to environmental factors with little genetic influence, while a score of one indicates the variability comes primarily from genetic factors with little environmental influence. A score closer to 0.5 indicates a combination of both influences.[38]

Researchers have found that heritabilities for boldness, or courage, in German Shepherds range from 0.05 to 0.27, reactivity to guns is 0.21, and sociability toward humans is 0.32. In Labrador Retrievers, reactivity to guns was 0.56 and sociability was 0.03. However, Overall and her colleagues indicate that some of this data may be flawed. The test may not measure the trait intended but instead measures the owner's ability to train the dog, or the behavior may not have high heritability. In addition, testing environments may skew the data.[39]

A study published in *Science* in April 2022 revealed that for most behavioral traits, breed is not relevant. The researchers surveyed owners of more than 18,000 dogs, of which almost half were purebred, and sequenced the DNA of more than 2,000 dogs. While they found that most behavioral traits are heritable, behavioral traits do not define breeds in the same way that other traits, such as size, do. While breed explains some variance in a dog's behavior, it is not a reliable predictor of behavior. In their sequencing, they found eleven regions that were associated with behavior, such as sociability with humans, and one hundred and thirty-six regions that were suggestive for behavior. They concluded that the behavioral traits attributed to modern breeds of dogs have been environmentally influenced and are found in all breeds at different levels. They proposed that the breed-specific characteristics developed from dogs' adaptation over thousands of years.[40]

Studies such as these show that there is some genetic basis for behavior problems in dogs, specifically, fear, aggression, and anxiety, but there is still much to be learned. Even researchers studying

4. *Nature vs. Nurture*

the canine genome agree that this is only the beginning, because they still do not know definitively why some breeds are big and others are small, or why some dogs herd and others point.[41] In general, veterinarians recommend providing stable and enriched physical, nutritional, and behavioral environments as possible. However, should pets that experience stress, become reactive, or show behavior problems, it is important to provide treatments, including nutrition, medications, and behavior modification.[42]

The same researchers at Ohio State, along with collaborators from other institutions, looked at MRI scans of sixty-two dogs and compared them with breed-average scores from the C-BARQ test of canine temperament. They found that brain networks involved in social processing and the "flight-or-fight" response were associated with stranger-directed fear and aggression. In addition, a dog's trainability was associated with expansion in regions of the brain's cortex, or the gray matter, while fear, aggression, and other behaviors labeled as problem behaviors were associated with expanded subcortical regions, which are involved in memory, emotion, pleasure, and hormone production. These findings related to volume changes in total brain size, suggesting that a connection between dog body size and behavior is due to a disproportionate enlargement of later-developing regions in dogs with larger brains.[43]

Similarly, researchers have been using functional imaging methods, including single photon emission tomography (SPET) to research the brains of dogs with behavior disorders and how they differ from brains of dogs without behavior disorders. The main regions in the brain associated with impulsive aggressive behavior, also known as dominance aggression, are the limbic system and the prefrontal cortex, which inhibits the amygdala, the region related to aggressive behavior. Other studies found changes in the brains of dogs of other neurophysical and neurochemical biomarkers and function in the regions of the brain areas known to be important in behavior, including anxiety and obsessive-compulsive disorders, similar to what is found in humans with the same disorders.[44]

German Shepherd Dogs are a working breed used often by the military for their self-confidence, temperament, and drive. However, even some German Shepherd Dogs used in the military have been eliminated from service or euthanized for behavior, with studies ranging from 2 percent euthanized for behavior in a three-year period[45] to 20 percent to 88 percent discharged from service for behavior problems. The latter number included German Shepherd Dogs, Belgian Malinois and similar breeds. In the latter study, a dog was discharged for behavior if it was reported to have shown any actions that inhibited its training or had an adverse effect on performing its duties and could not be retrained to eliminate the behavior.[46]

In German Shepherd Dogs kept as pets, behavior problems may be brought on by boredom if the owners fail to provide training and appropriate activity. The breed is known to have more than 50 hereditary disorders, such as hip dysplasia, degenerative myelopathy, von Willebrand disease, and others that can lead to behavior problems.[47]

A study by researchers in Sweden looked at 10,000 behaviorally tested German Shepherd Dogs and Rottweilers in search of inherited behavioral traits. They found a similar pattern of co-inheritance in sixteen chosen behavioral traits. More than half of the additive genetic variation of the behavioral traits could be explained by one principal component, although only aggression appeared to be inherited independently of the other traits. Their results suggest a genetic basis for the shyness/boldness personality trait.[48]

A similar study observed German Shepherd Dogs and Labrador Retrievers for courage, defense drive, prey drive, nerve stability, temperament, cooperation, affability, and gun shyness. They found that males had greater scores than females for sharpness in German Shepherd Dogs, for cooperation and gun shyness in Labrador Retrievers, and for courage, defense drive, prey drive, nerve stability, and hardness in both breeds. They also found that common environment influenced different behavior traits in the two breeds, with German Shepherd Dogs possibly being more sensitive to environmental influences than Labrador Retrievers.[49]

Researchers in Australia analyzed data from nearly 8,000 dogs presented at a veterinary behavior clinic over a thirteen-year period. They identified twenty-two major behaviors among the dogs, with aggression toward people, barking, and anxious behavior the most common. In this group, male dogs were at greater risk of several behavior problems. Other risk factors were the low socioeconomic status of owners and little time spent at home per week. Working dog breeds represented 20 percent of all the dogs, followed closely by terriers (19 percent), toy dogs (15 percent), and gun dogs (11 percent). The breeds most represented were Staffordshire Bull Terrier, Maltese, and Border Collies, with large numbers of unknown or other breeds represented as well.[50]

Researchers at The Ohio State University found that some types of fear and aggression, particularly stranger-oriented fear, and dog- and stranger-directed aggression, are related to each other, but are different from owner-directed aggression, which was associated with *IGF1*. They contend that owner personality does not necessarily contribute to a dog's owner-directed aggression.[51]

I want to believe that my personality—a quiet introvert—did not contribute to Champ's aggression. That leads me to look at his first owners, whom I know nothing about. With us, Champ had a safe and nurturing home in which he lacked for nothing and knew only love. He had everything we could give him. We altered our schedules so that one of us was home with him whenever we weren't working. We passed on social events that took place during times Champ needed medications, or only one of us would go. We traveled infrequently because the kennel was incredibly stressful for him, and we couldn't have anyone come to the house to stay with him. We tried group and individual trainers, agility classes, different leashes, backpacks, medications, and different forms of exercise. Each would help for a while, but nothing worked long-term. He knew he was loved—I loved him so much and told him so multiple times a day—and I believe he loved us. He was rarely aggressive toward us, and when he was, it was redirected because he couldn't get to what was causing his aggression, such as another dog or the e-collar. And I believe he wanted to be a normal dog, but he knew deep down that he couldn't be. His world had become so small—the confines of our small house and backyard. My whole life became managing Champ and his anxiety level. That management was not only financially expensive, but it became taxing on my well-being as I was trying to stay two steps ahead of him. His whole life was managed, and eventually, management almost always fails.

I was getting Champ's prescriptions filled at the same pharmacy I used, but even with a special "savings club" card, it was still too much. I went to a local grocery store pharmacy with a list of his medications and dosages and asked them to give me their best price for a pet. While the pharmacist was kind and professional, I could tell that she was shocked that I was giving my dog so many drugs and at such high doses. However, she was able to save me enough money on each prescription that it was well worth transferring. From then on, I was on a first-name basis with her and the other pharmacist there. They had to special order the quantities of pills that I needed every month, and when I went in to get them, they greeted me by name without me having to tell them who I was.

The Most Painful Choice

I would leave the store with enormous bottles of medications, then come home to sort them out for the week. I had a written schedule of what pills needed to be given at what time every day taped to the backsplash above the pill sorter, which only had four compartments for each day. We needed six, so I had to use other containers. Every night before bed I'd lay out the small bag with the first dose, given at 4:30 a.m. The next dose came with breakfast at 6:30, the next at noon, the next at 5 p.m. when I got home from work, and the last at 9 p.m. He also got two different probiotic powders. I used creamy peanut butter from a big jar, and we went through one and a half jars a week. Occasionally he would refuse the peanut butter, so I had to have braunschweiger, canned dog or cat food, or something else on hand for when this happened. He was usually pretty compliant with taking his medicine, and I was grateful for that.

On one occasion when I returned home from the pharmacy with the big bag of large bottles of medications, and my next-door neighbor asked me about them. I said they were for Champ to help treat some of his issues. He was surprised that I would give Champ so many medications and asked when I would start weaning him off them. I said these were likely lifelong medications to stabilize him, not a short-term treatment. As a person with a young, healthy dog, he had no idea what we were dealing with day to day. I understand that not everyone is in favor of medicating dogs for behavior issues, but nothing else had worked, and we felt like it was our only choice.

Dodman, a veterinary pharmacologist in addition to behavior specialist, writes of being in a veterinary consulting room with owners who had pets like Champ, who were clearly suffering.

> It's very easy to dream about a unicorn world where pets can be healed simply by love and pixie dust. But when a dog or cat is in pain, the stakes turn very serious, very quickly. There are no atheists in foxholes, and there are few starry-eyed herbalists in consulting rooms, holding their suffering pet. In that situation, I challenge anyone to refuse proven scientific measures of relief.[52]

Champ also had terrible skin allergies that would lead to hot spots in the summer. We had him on Apoquel, an antihistamine tablet, for a while, but once he started taking all the other medications, I switched from Apoquel to the Cytopoint injection simply to reduce the number of pills he had to take every day, even if by only one.

Not only did he have skin allergies, but food allergies as well: chicken, chicken egg and possibly beef. He also did not digest dairy products well, such as yogurt or cottage cheese. Often, I made him

70

treats from scratch because it was nearly impossible to find treats in the store that didn't have beef, chicken, or chicken egg.

Behavior issues take their toll on the lifespan of pets. A study out of Pennsylvania State University that looked at 700 dogs posthumously found that stranger-directed fear predicted a shorter lifespan in dogs, while nonsocial fear, body sensitivity, and separation anxiety had no effect. Extreme nonsocial fear and separation anxiety both predicted the severity and incidence of skin problems and shorter lifespans in dogs, and weight and body sensitivity predicted arthritis signs in adult dogs.[53] This leads me to believe that Champ's skin and food allergies and arthritis were likely a byproduct of his anxiety.

We worked with Champ enough that we were finally able to leave for work every day without him getting too upset. He knew that me leaving for work meant he got a food-filled toy. However, if we left again in the evening to go to dinner, a meeting, an errand, or even a special event, he could not handle it. He refused the food-filled toy and would scream and bark and try to get out of the crate—we could hear him from outside as we walked away from the house. He did the same on weekends if Dan and I left together to run an errand or go to lunch. Ultimately, we stopped going out on weekday evenings except in rare circumstances, and Dan and I would stagger our errands on weekends so that one of us was always home with him.

5

Communicating with Champ

"The world would be a nicer place if everyone had the ability to love as unconditionally as a dog."
—M.K. Clinton[1]

In January of 2019, I enrolled in a memoir writing class at the university where I work. We had to write short entries in a daily journal about something in our lives, past or present, then read one aloud to the class each week. One week, I wrote about Champ and read it to the class. It was a difficult decision because it made me very vulnerable to tell others about what I was dealing with every day, but also opened myself to judgment by those who didn't understand.

After class, another student, Caroline, told me that she was trained in Reiki and offered to come over and give Reiki to Champ. Reiki is a Japanese technique intended to reduce stress, encourage relaxation, and promote healing. It is often used with shelter dogs or with dogs with aggression issues, so I thought it was worth a try. Caroline came over one cold Saturday afternoon, and Champ was very excited to see someone. He was always very exuberant and loud when someone came in the house, which frightened most people, so one of us would take him in the backyard until the person got in the house. Once settled, we would let Champ in to greet the visitor. He was rarely aggressive toward visitors after the first six months to a year but was more like a 100-pound tornado barreling toward the person. He did the same with Caroline, but I had her give him a toy to settle him down for a minute, then use the "touch" command with her two fingers. After that, they were friends.

Caroline performed Reiki on him without touching him, but Champ was so anxious by the fact that someone else was in the house that we never saw any relaxation. She was sitting on the couch, and he was on the floor in front of her panting heavily and grabbing his toys. It was hard to tell if he felt anything from it, but it was good to try. She also brought us some rose quartz crystals, said to promote unconditional love and promote healing, to keep near his crate.

Caroline told me she had a friend who was an animal communicator and encouraged me to reach out to her. I wasn't sure what that was, but Caroline told me about her own experience with her cat and the communicator, and it seemed to help her cat. She assured me it wasn't a psychic. Although I did have an open mind, I'll admit I was a bit skeptical about doing this. I had not had any experience with communicators or energy readers or healers before, and I didn't know if it was quite on the up and up. I talked to Dan about it, and we agreed to give it a try. What did we have to lose? We set up a phone meeting with the communicator for a Saturday morning.

I had only given the communicator a little information about Champ in my original email: that he was a rescue, how long we had had him, that he had generalized anxiety disorder and aggression, and that we were running out of ideas on how to help him. The communicator had asked for a photo of Champ via email and that he be in the room when we were on the phone call.

Dan, Champ, and I were in our TV room for the phone call. I wasn't sure how we were going to keep Champ in the room the whole time, but I crossed my fingers that he would not bark or run around. I had a notebook and pen ready to take notes.

The communicator didn't ask us many questions, but relayed what Champ was telling her. She explained that some of the training techniques that we had used were building a wall, and that all that was getting through to him was our anger and frustration. All his emotions were about not being good enough or doing what was wanted of him. In his past, he felt that everyone was out to hurt him, and his only choice was to lash out.

She told me that he needed positive reinforcement, especially in the morning when I would wake him up to go outside. She said that was his most vulnerable time of the day when he was feeling the most emotional, and I needed to pour love and understanding into him. He said he felt like I was rushing him to get up and go outside, and that was triggering his post-traumatic stress disorder and making him anxious. She said the anxiety created aggression, and that created post-traumatic stress and feelings of inferiority.

I described a recent training exercise we had with our trainer during which we took Champ to a parking lot across from an animal shelter to measure his reactivity to the shelter dogs being walked at a significant distance. We had done this one Saturday morning, and Champ shivered during the exercise even though it wasn't cold. We ended it because he couldn't stop shivering.

The communicator said that he saw other dogs having the same emotional struggles that he had and that he was so deep in his own struggles that he couldn't deal with seeing other dogs struggle. He also felt like those dogs were doing better than he was because they could go on walks with shelter volunteers.

Champ said that he wanted to go on walks with us because he liked being outside, but it was too hard for him. It was similar to a war veteran going back to the war zone, and by the time we noticed his stress, it was too late.

Champ said he knew that he was damaged and that he would never be a "normal" dog. "I chose you because you can help me get as close to normal as I can be," he relayed to the communicator for me.

She also said that he had physical pain, but some of it was caused by his emotional pain. He told her that he tenses up when he's anxious, and that causes him pain.

At one point about halfway through the session, the communicator paused, then asked me very tentatively, "Do you read aloud to him?" I said, "Yes, we read every night for about a half an hour." She stopped and started to cry. She said, "Reading is peaceful for him. He likes the storybooks the best where the good outweighs the bad. His favorite is the one with the little girl. It helps him."

I had not told her—or anyone—that I read to him. When she said that, I froze. I looked at Dan, and his jaw was on the floor. And at the time of that call, I was reading *The Bobbsey Twins* books to Champ and doing a different voice for the little girl named Flossie. The Bobbsey Twins were early twentieth-century "do-gooder" children who solved mysteries and always caught "the bad guy." I was stunned.

"That time you spend reading to him is the most special thing that anyone's ever done for him in his life," she said, through her tears. "It shows him pure love."

She told me to read to him when I knew he was having a tough time because he said that was more rewarding to him than any kind of treat.

Before I knew it, our hour was up. I had been taking notes—twelve pages in total—so furiously that I hadn't noticed that Champ was lying quietly on his bed and hadn't moved at all during the call. This was unprecedented behavior for him—he never laid quietly except for when he was sleeping at night, and certainly not when I was in the room or on the phone. He never made a sound through the whole call.

Over the next few days, I reread my notes from the call and processed everything that the communicator had said. I went into it with an open mind, not really knowing what would come out of it, but in the end, I knew that what had taken place was very special. I had been given a gift of being able to know what Champ was thinking and to have someone be able to interpret that. I knew it was real because of Champ's behavior during the call and because she knew about me reading to him.

I tried to implement the suggestions that had come up during the call—not rushing him in the morning when I woke him to go outside, and not rushing him to do anything, just letting him do things on his own time.

We followed up with the communicator about four months later after we'd returned from a six-day vacation, during which Champ was in the kennel. Although it was the same kennel we had always taken him to, where they were fantastic with him, he had a meltdown when I tried to hand him off to the kennel worker. He started screaming and refused to go with her, and it took two kennel workers and me to get him back into the kennel area. He was whining and crying and trying to glue himself to me while the two kennel workers were trying to get him away. We were all sweating and trying to talk sweetly to him to get him to go with them. I finally just had to hand over the leash and leave while he was crying and screaming, then I cried as I walked out to the car. I hated leaving him in that state—I hated leaving him, period—but I had to get a break now and then. I felt horribly guilty, and I prayed that he would settle down once he got in his own kennel space.

We knew from previous experience that it took Champ about as many days as he had been in the kennel to return to his "normal" once at home. But this time was different, and he wasn't eating much, so I reached out to the communicator for a follow up. She told me what I had feared the most—that when he was in the kennel, he had feared that we weren't coming back to get him, and that he was so overwhelmed by that fear that he was out of control when we got home. He tried to be good, but he was too emotionally overwhelmed. He had a strong fear of abandonment and rejection, and while he was in the kennel, he blamed himself for trusting us that we loved him, then we left him there. When we came back to pick him up, he was so overwhelmed because he was proven wrong.

Champ told the communicator that he felt bad that we were paying the price for someone else's mistakes, and that nothing that was happening was our fault.

Again, the communicator surprised us by saying that Champ said it made him feel bad when we had to go in the side door at the vet's office because it made him feel like he was being bad again. I hadn't told her that we had to use the side door at Dr. Koch's office because going in the main doors into the lobby was too stressful for him.

I asked the communicator to ask Champ about potential stomach pain since he wasn't eating. He said that it began as an emotional response and turned into a physical issue, such as an ulcer from stress. He told her that when he eats when he is anxious, the food sits in a ball in his stomach and gives him a feeling of indigestion. He thought it was a good idea to go to the vet and get it checked out, even though going to the vet was stressful for him and that he'd have to be sedated for tests. He said he understood that that needed to happen because it was for his own good. He said he wanted to do it "the usual way." The communicator asked me what that was. I told her that Dr. DeWilde would give him the anesthesia while I was in the room and allow me to stay with him and hold him until he was completely under its effects, so he knew he was safe.

I told her that I'd been hand feeding him to get him to eat. She said that he understood that I was trying to help him and that when someone hand fed him, he knew that the food was safe. In a past life, he was somewhere where the food was often tainted, and it would hurt him. People would bring tainted food, leave it, and walk away. When someone is hand feeding him, they are near him and calmly talking with him. She said that he said that he needed to feel safe about who he gets his food from, and that's why he had food allergies. His body learned that those foods would make him sick.

I asked her to ask him about arthritis pain. He said that when it was humid, his joints would swell and feel tight, mostly in his hips and knees.

The last thing she said was that Champ asked if he could have fresh water put down more often since it was getting warmer. He said he liked cool water and didn't like it when it tasted stale. Then she started to cry and said that request was a big breakthrough for him because we had brought up all the trauma from his kennel stay, and he asked for something so simple as fresh water. After that, I made sure to change his water bowls several times a day.

I had some imaging done on his hips and abdomen in November

2019, which showed moderate arthritis in his elbows and severe arthritis and dysplasia in his hips, as he had predicted, and a shadow in his abdomen on his spleen. The veterinary radiologist indicated that the arthritis could be contributing to his behavior issues, but there was no way to know for sure. Dr. DeWilde and the radiologist weren't sure whether the shadow on the spleen was truly a shadow or if it indicated a mass of some kind. I opted to follow up in three months before proceeding with any further imaging to determine if the mass was truly a mass or a shadow.

In December 2019, a few days before Christmas, Champ and I were out playing fetch with a glow-in-the-dark ball in the backyard one Friday evening after work. He was running back toward me with the ball but didn't stop when he got to me. Instead, he plowed right into me, knocking me off balance. I didn't fall, but my body had to compensate for the impact, and my neck took the worst of it. I had a headache for the rest of the evening. Fortunately, I had a chiropractic appointment the next day, and the chiropractor said I had whiplash from the hit.

In February 2020, as I was researching behavioral euthanasia, I reached out to the communicator again. I had opted not to follow up with more imaging on his spleen, and I wanted to see if I could find out what Champ was thinking. What she told me shocked me.

She said that the very first thing that Champ told her in their first discussion a year prior was that he knew he would have to be euthanized someday. She chose not to tell us that then because it would have been too hard for us to process that as his very first message.

She continued to say that he felt like his brain was degrading, that he was losing his grasp of reality and that he didn't know who he once was. He felt like he had no control of his actions and was going in and out of states where he didn't know what he had done, but he could tell from my emotional reaction that he had done something harmful. He was afraid that he would hurt me or someone else very badly. He knew that I was now fearful of him after he had collided with me and wanted to be let go before something bad happened.

I told her that Champ had been going into the kitchen and stealing food from the counters when he knew he was not supposed to be in there. She started to cry and said it was hard for her to relay his message. He said he was trying to do things to make me not like him to make it easier for me to let him go. He knew that he was getting worse, and he was trying to make things easier for me.

He said that he knew that in my life, I've worked hard at things that were important to me, and when something wasn't working, I would work harder to make it happen. This is very true, so I kept listening. He said he didn't want me to think that I should have or could have tried harder to help him because nothing was going to work. There wasn't anything more that I could have done to make things better. Something was wrong with his brain, and he knew it.

The communicator said that her connection with him during this session was different than the previous two times and that he didn't seem as coherent as he had before.

When I asked her to ask him about his physical pain, she said it was all connected with his brain degeneration. He had constant pain with frequent spikes of severe pain. It was during those times that he was more likely to lash out and cause pain for me.

Champ told her, "I just want her to find a way to not have guilt." He wanted me to remember everything that I had done for him so that I would not feel guilty for having to euthanize him. He also told me to keep myself safe.

This was a lot to process, but it also eventually contributed toward the decision to choose euthanasia. If he was suffering as much as he said he was and was in such pain—both physical and emotional—letting him go was the best thing I could do for him, as difficult as it was. Some may scoff at my choice to take this kind of information into consideration, but there are things that she said that I had not told her in advance and were too specific to be generalities. And I knew from watching Champ during these conversations, calm with his eyes half-closed, that something was happening, because he was never like that otherwise.

I told only a few people close to me that we had worked with the communicator, because this opened me up to judgment. But I was willing to try just about anything—other than more invasive imaging or tests—and was willing to take the risk. I consider those conversations with Champ through the communicator very special gifts. She had told me before our first conversation that some animals don't open up to her for whatever reason, so she couldn't guarantee that Champ would open up to her. I have talked with others who have used a communicator, who said their pet did not or would not communicate, and they were disappointed. I feel so lucky that Champ was able to share his thoughts with the communicator, who relayed them so clearly to me.

Some people in a similar situation have used communicators only after their pets have passed to try to assuage their guilt. I think it provides closure for those of us who had to make the awful decision. I chose not to do that, mostly because I had his reassurance beforehand that he was ready to go and knew it was in his best interest. There have also been some other signs from him that have let me know that he is ok.

6

Making the Decision

"I would give everything I had if it meant that my dog could live as long as me."—Unknown[1]

After talking with the communicator the final time, I knew that euthanasia was the right thing to do, as much as it pained me. I felt like I was giving up and that I had failed him and everyone who had fought so hard to rescue him from his prior life. I felt the guilt that he had said he didn't want me to have, so I knew I needed to work through that before I could let him go.

I follow several blogs about dog behavior and training, and one day in February 2020, I came across a blog post[2] by Deborah Jones, PhD, on her blog, K9 in Focus, from 2019 about a Facebook group called Losing Lulu, which was for pet owners who had to choose behavioral euthanasia (BE) for their pets. Before then, I had not put the words behavior and euthanasia together. I had known of dogs growing up that had to be put to sleep for biting or attacking, but I had never heard anyone refer to that as behavioral euthanasia.

I also came across another post about behavioral euthanasia by Jennifer L. Summerfield, DVM, a veterinarian and dog trainer in West Virginia, who writes Dr. Jen's Dog Blog. As I read the blog post, all the things that Dr. Koch, Dr. DeWilde, and Linda had been saying to me the previous eighteen months started to make sense.

The post highlighted some risk factors that can make an aggressive dog dangerous and difficult to work with. Champ had fear aggression toward dogs and people, but his main issue was the never-ending anxiety that we could not get under control with multiple medications and management. Some of the risk factors Dr. Jen listed included the intensity/severity of aggressive behavior; lack of clear warning signals; size of the dog; and predictability of triggers.[3]

Champ's triggers were predictable, just not manageable, and his size at 100 pounds was a challenge. I could not hold on to him when he pulled, and at times it was even difficult for Dan to do so. We both bear scars from when attempts to restrain Champ caused him to lash out at the restraint and redirect his aggression into biting.

There were links to some other resources, including a web page on behavioral euthanasia from The Ohio State University Veterinary Medical Center. That website had a very helpful document with a checklist to use before considering behavioral euthanasia and one to help make the decision, as well as resources to find emotional support once the decision has been made. While reading it, I realized that I had already done everything the post recommended: checked into medical causes for the behavior and sought professional help. The list also suggested finding a new home for the pet. For Champ and for me, that was not an option. Not only would I never do that, but it would not be fair to him at age nine to hand him off to a new owner, nor would it be fair to a new owner to deal with all his issues. Plus, despite his issues, I could never, ever give him up. I would continue managing his anxiety before I would hand him off to someone else. I couldn't have lived with the guilt.

The checklist for making the decision to euthanize included when re-homing was not an option. In addition, it considered environmental factors, such as young children in the home who may be stressful for the pet; the severity of the problem and progression of signs, referring to the difficulty of managing multiple problems; and the animal's level of suffering.[4]

There was no doubt Champ was suffering. The daily anxiety score I recorded on his spreadsheet was going up, not down. He did enjoy being outside in our backyard, but inside, he was an anxious mess. I suspected he was in pain, and I know from personal experience that chronic pain makes everything harder. Anytime he left the house, he had to wear a basket muzzle, which he didn't mind, but it was a clear indication that we knew he was a risk to others.

Few people talk about behavioral euthanasia because there is so much judgment from others. People with dogs like Champ often hear, "Well, have you tried …?"; "This trainer worked for us,"; "You should use CBD oil," and so many more so-called helpful suggestions, none of which we requested. People accuse us of giving up on or failing our pets. While they mean well, people who have never had dogs, cats, or other animals with these kinds of problems really don't and can't understand that we as owners have already tried literally everything. We have spent a lot of money, tried every trainer, read every book, and tried every drug and supplement. Even seeing a veterinary behavior specialist brought criticism and ridicule. When I first took Lindy to see Dr. Horwitz, some people made fun of me for spending so much money to see a "doggie psychiatrist." It was the same when we took Champ to see Dr. Koch—people shook their heads and asked why we would take time off work, drive forty-five minutes each way, and spend money on a "psychiatrist" for a dog, which showed that people didn't even understand that she wasn't a psychiatrist. We do it all because we love our pets. The last thing we want is to have to resort to euthanasia, so we will go to the ends of the earth to avoid the heartbreak of having to euthanize our beloved family member.

As owners and guardians of these animals, we are their advocates. We are the only people who know them intimately and what their lives are like. As much as we want them to be happy and healthy, sometimes that isn't possible, and letting them go is the best option.

It is a decision that I did not take lightly. In fact, it took me eighteen months to make it, and once I did, I had another month until the scheduled date. I scheduled the appointment for a month out for several reasons: one, that's when Dr. DeWilde was available, and I wanted her to do it; two, I wanted that time to be absolutely sure and to work through the guilt of making the decision; and three, I wanted to spend that time with Champ and savor every moment, knowing that his days were limited.

After I'd made the decision, I let Dr. Koch, Linda, and Dr. DeWilde know, as well as the volunteers we had worked with through Serendipity German Shepherd Dog Rescue. Dan knew, of course, but I asked him not to tell people because I didn't want him to face judgment for it, and it also gave me an out in case I changed my mind.

But I did not change my mind. I was ok until about two days before the scheduled date, then reality set in and I started thinking about all the "lasts" we were experiencing. I knew they were his lasts, but he didn't, and that felt terrible to me. The day before was a nice day, and Champ and I were outside in the backyard watching the world go by. I sat on the grass next to him and hugged him and told him how much I loved him and only wanted to do what was best for him, even if that meant letting him go. As we sat there, I typed his obituary into my phone and cried for the first time since I'd made the decision. I felt like I had to prepare his obituary for my social media account, of which he had been a big part for six years, because I wouldn't be in any condition to do it the day of the euthanasia. I wrote:

6. Making the Decision

Champ
February 2011–March 30, 2020
Adopted May 2014
If love had been enough, you would have
lived forever. Rest in Peace, buddy.
"Love anything, and your heart will be wrung
and possibly be broken."—C.S. Lewis

As I typed that into my phone, I finally really cried. It takes a lot for me to cry, and I rarely do. But at that moment, all the anticipatory grief I had been holding in for the past month since I made the decision for BE came out. Champ didn't seem bothered by my tears, and I kept stroking him and petting him as I cried. I felt like a monster because I knew that he'd be gone within twenty-four hours, and that was completely my decision.

I had scheduled the BE for 8:30 a.m. and had taken a vacation day from work. I went through our normal morning routine and gave Champ his usual medications and breakfast. Due to the Covid-19 pandemic, which was in its first month in the U.S. at that time, our veterinarian's office was not allowing owners inside with their pets for appointments, but since we were doing BE, we were allowed in. They had set up a room for us with blankets on the floor, soft music playing, several boxes of tissues, and bottles of water. As we walked back to the room, the techs were in the hall, already crying, as was the receptionist at the front desk. Dr. DeWilde met us in the room and explained the process, then told us to take all the time we needed with him and let them know when we were ready.

I had brought *The Wind in the Willows*, the last complete book we had read together, and the penguin-shaped cheese crackers that I often fed him while we read. We all sat down on the blankets, and I got out the bag of crackers and started to read. As far as Champ was concerned, we were just having our usual reading time, just somewhere else. I cried as I read and had a tough time getting through it. I kept feeding him crackers, and we were getting crumbs all over the blanket because I was having to feed them through the basket muzzle. Dan was on the other side of Champ, petting him and stroking him softly. After a while—I don't know how long—Dr. DeWilde and a couple of vet techs came in and asked if we were ready for the first shot that would sedate him. They had to shave some of the hair on his back leg, which he didn't like, then the shot was a little painful, so he yipped. I just felt terrible.

I kept reading as he fell asleep with his head in my lap. I wanted my voice to be the last thing he heard on this earth. Once he was asleep, I removed his basket muzzle. Eventually, Dr. DeWilde and the techs returned and asked us if we were ready. He was so peaceful sleeping in my lap, and that's all I wanted for him—to have peace. I don't think I was able to give a verbal answer because I was crying too hard, but I nodded my head. They gave him the final injection, and I kept reading to him until they told me his heart had stopped and he was gone. Then I sobbed.

Since his head was already in my lap, I leaned forward and rested my head on his. I closed his eyes, stroked his soft ears and kissed his long nose like I did every night before bed. Dr. DeWilde and the vet techs were crying, as well, and they told us to take as much time as we needed as they left the room. I'm not sure how long we stayed, but eventually Dan said it was time to go, so I gathered up his leash, Freedom Harness, basket muzzle, the book and what remained of the cheese crackers as well as my pile of sodden tissues. As we left, the longtime receptionist at the front desk cried and said, "I wish I could give you a hug." Thanks to Covid, there could be no hugs that day.

When we got outside of the building, there were other clients waiting in their cars, and I tried not to meet their eyes from under my dark sunglasses. Dan drove us home and dismantled Champ's crate and took it to the basement, along with his other beds. Dan went to work, so I had the rest of the day to myself at home and probably should have taken a few more days off. I gathered up Champ's dishes and washed them, put his toys in a basket, put his remaining medications in a bag, and washed the dog bed covers and towels. I removed the opaque film from the windows and was able to see out of them for the first time in six years. Later, it was warm enough that I could open the front windows, which we hadn't been able to do for that same amount of time.

In the afternoon, I went outside to read. After Lindy died in 2010, I bought a guided journal to use that walked a reader through the grief of losing a beloved pet. I tried to do some of the writing exercises in the journal, but I just couldn't concentrate or focus. It was too soon. Instead, I posted his obituary on my Facebook page with the last photo I had taken of him.

During the six years we had Champ, I frequently posted photos of him in training class, walking on the neighborhood playground equipment, posed in front of different signs or doors or at different parks in the area, or just playing in the backyard. I always referenced him as a rescue and tagged Serendipity German Shepherd Dog Rescue

6. Making the Decision

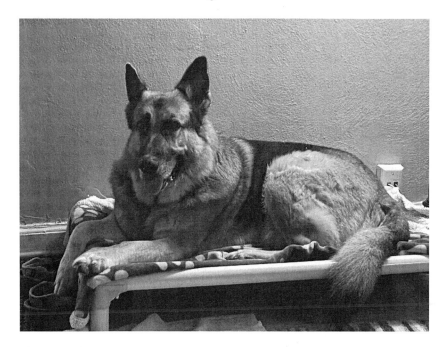

This is the last picture I took of Champ, a couple days before his euthanasia, in 2020.

and Miracle GSD Network. He had a big fan club on Facebook. I never shared any of our difficulties there, though, only the good times. Few people on Facebook knew how much we had struggled to help him, so it came as a shock to many of my "friends," and many private messaged me asking if he had been sick or what had happened. I couldn't tell the truth because I wasn't ready to open myself up for judgment that he was euthanized. Instead, I'd planned to say simply that he passed away in hopes that most people would respect that as a satisfactory answer. Most did, but some probed further. I didn't answer some of the probes by people I didn't know well. For those who were involved in his rescue, I explained that his severe anxiety could no longer be managed, and we suspected he was in physical pain, and I chose to give him some peace.

I felt compelled to reach out individually to the woman who had first found Champ and was instrumental in saving him from his first owner as well as to the man who retrieved him from said owner and took him to the vet, then helped get him to St. Louis and to Serendipity. I explained to both of them that the medications and management techniques were no longer effective for his anxiety or pain, and that

The Most Painful Choice

I chose to give him some peace. I think they understood, but since I hadn't shared the details of the struggle over the years, it likely came as a shock. The volunteers with Serendipity knew what we had been dealing with and were nothing but supportive, and I was grateful for that.

The next day, I returned to work (from home), but this time, I was alone in the house. I didn't have Champ under my feet or next to the table where I worked. I didn't have to give any medications or take him outside. I was able to sit and look out of my front windows while I worked. When I saw the mail carrier coming up the walk, I immediately jumped up to get Champ outside before he saw or heard the carrier coming, and I realized Champ wasn't there. I felt a sense of relief, but also felt conflicted about that relief, like I was betraying Champ's memory by feeling relieved that I could see out of the windows or not having to rush out of the house when the mail carrier came.

The next days and weeks were long. I didn't know what to do with myself after I finished working because I usually spent my evenings taking care of Champ. I couldn't stand to be in the house, so I started taking a walk after dinner, which is when we usually sat down to read. I was finishing a writing class, so I had some things to focus on, but otherwise, with the world shut down, there weren't many distractions from the grief and loss.

About a week after his BE, the veterinarian's office called to let me know his ashes were ready to be picked up. I wasn't sure I could return to the clinic so soon, but because of Covid, I couldn't go in anyway, so they brought them outside for me. I had chosen a cherry wood box similar to what I had chosen for Lindy, Skipper, and Mulligan when I also had them cremated. The gold plate on the front had his name and birth and death years. They also had included two impressions of his paw in clay. On one of them, they had stamped his name. In some ways, having the ashes back was comforting, because Champ was home and was with me. I put the box near my bed where I could see it and set his collar on top with his tags hanging down in front of the box. One of the veterinary technicians had taken a small clump of his hair that they had to shave off to give the injection and put it in a tiny glass bottle with a cork lid.

All those things are exactly where I put them when I brought them home, along with the cards that people sent me after his death. I haven't moved his ashes with the other boxes of ashes, and I'm not sure I will. Most days, it is comforting to see it when I go to bed and when I get up in the morning because I remember the love I had for him that was unlike what I had for any of my other pets. But it also reminds me that

86

6. Making the Decision

I still miss him terribly. His portrait still hangs on the wall in the living room, his toys are still in his toy box, and I still have my collection of antique porcelain German Shepherd figurines on my dresser. His spirit remains alive with me.

Along with his ashes and pawprint impressions, the veterinarian's office had given me a receipt of Champ's treatment history there. On it were their notes for how to best handle him:

"Fear-Free Plan: P(atient) sees Dr. Cook *(sic)* for behavioral issues. O(wner) uses treats and toys throughout appt—P no longer allowed to have tennis balls. Responds to touch command with hand followed by treat. O very good about talking techs/vet about how P best responds to exam, etc. P does well with physical exam with minimal/no restraint as long as O is offering high reward treats. O helped restrain and keep P in check for exam, did not have to handle P at all. Provided some petting for distraction for exam.

Likes: Treats provided by O. P does physical exam with minimal restraint and treats.

Avoid: other dogs, P dog aggressive. P sensitive with genital exam.

Where does Champ prefer to be examined? (i.e., floor, table, owner's lap etc.) Better on floor, would not try to get on table unless necessary

Champ is motivated by? (i.e., treats, toys, petting etc.) Treats provided by O and toys.

Champ was more comfortable with owner present? P looks constantly to O for reassurance, does well with O feeding treats while getting examined."

I can't say enough how fantastic and accommodating our veterinarian's office was throughout Champ's time with us. The notes are a clear indication that they were looking for the best way to handle Champ to minimize stress for him, for me, and to make their job easier. They would even get a room ready for him when it was time for our appointment so we didn't have to sit in the waiting area and risk dealing with the dogs and cats coming into the clinic. I would call them from the car when we arrived, and they would call me back to let me know when it was safe to bring him in.

The few times that Champ had to have anesthesia for imaging, Dr. DeWilde was extremely accommodating. I was allowed to stay in the exam room and hold him while she gave him the anesthetic, then sit on the floor with him until he was completely under. Champ would put his big head on my lap, and I would pet him and talk to him as he was falling asleep. After the imaging, the office would call me when he was about ready to come out of anesthesia so I could be there when he woke up. It made the whole process less stressful for all of us.

About a month after Champ's death, I suggested to Dan that we finally remodel the kitchen now that we didn't have any pets to have to work around, and I was working from home. Again, I had mixed feelings about this because we wouldn't have been able to have the work done with Champ here, but I felt a little guilty that I was looking forward to having it done, like I was almost glad he was gone. I wasn't, but his absence allowed us to do the long-overdue remodel of our outdated kitchen. It was bittersweet to see it torn out because four of our dogs had spent time in there, and it felt like we were erasing part of their memories by tearing out the wood floors damaged by their nails.

During the two-month-long renovation, there was at least one contractor in the house most of the day, and I didn't mind the noise after several months of solitude. The days passed much faster with someone here, even if I didn't have a lot of interaction with them.

Shortly before Champ died, I told Dan that I wanted a Golden Retriever for our next dog, and I wanted a puppy so we could start from scratch. There is a very good Golden Retriever rescue group in St. Louis, but I knew that I could not get another rescue dog for a while and take the chance on getting another dog like Champ. Also, I was too scarred, and frankly, too tired to rehabilitate another rescue dog. I also told Dan that I wanted to get a young cat a few months before we got the puppy so that the cat would feel established in our home before we brought a puppy home.

I had been meeting with my writer's group via Zoom for most of the spring and summer, and all the others were cat people. I told them I had a day off and wanted to go pet cats somewhere, but the local cat café was closed because of Covid. One of the other members told me about another cat café in the city that she thought was open. I looked it up and made a reservation to go pet cats. I wasn't ready for a cat yet, but I wanted to spend some time with them and remember what it was like to play with cats since it had been five years since Mulligan died.

I went to Cheshire Grin Cat Café on historic Cherokee Street in St. Louis one very hot Friday afternoon in June, got an iced green tea, and went into the two-story cat space at the café. A few cats were roaming around playing, and a lot of them were sleeping since it was the middle of the day. I sat on the floor and played with a twelve-year-old cat for a while, then walked around to visit the other cats. A few were friendly, a few were standoffish, and it was nice just to be in the presence of cats again.

About this time, I was on one of my evening walks in the neighborhood when I saw my neighbor in his front yard with a Golden Retriever puppy. He had had two Golden Retrievers previously who were friends with our dogs and had been without a dog for a couple of years. He let me pet the puppy and pick him up and hold him. He had found out through other neighbors that Champ was gone and expressed his sympathy. We had tried to walk with his older Golden Retriever and Champ a few times, but it hadn't gone well. I told him that when we were ready, I wanted to get a Golden Retriever puppy. He told us that they were in short supply and gave us the name of the breeder he had gotten his puppy from as well as another breeder in Michigan. I took the information and shared it with Dan.

We called the local breeder on the first Saturday in July. She talked to us about her dogs and said her next litter would be in spring 2021. We said we were interested, and I was ok with that time frame. Even though I wasn't ready for a dog when we were talking with her, I felt like I would be ready for another dog by that time. She said she already had four deposits, so we would get fifth choice. We said we didn't have a preference of male or female and would be happy with a healthy puppy that came from healthy parents.

While it was going to be nine or ten months until we had a puppy, it gave us both some hope for the future and something to look forward to and plan. With Covid in full swing, our vacation had been canceled, concert tickets were sitting unused, and any other things we had been looking forward to in 2020 were either on hold or rescheduled. I decided to try to adopt a cat in mid–December during my two weeks of vacation for Christmas and the New Year so I could be there to get it acclimated.

I was finally used to the idea of having a puppy in the spring when the breeder called me in mid–August and said her female was in heat earlier than expected. She was reaching out to the people who had put down a deposit to see if they wanted a puppy around the start of 2021 or if they wanted to wait until spring 2021. I said we were ok with either and we would be ready whenever the pups were.

The breeder decided to go ahead breeding her female to the same male as the previous litter, which would mean that our puppy and our neighbor's puppy would have the same parents. She told us we'd be able to bring home our puppy in early January, which is not the greatest time to be outside housebreaking a puppy in the Midwest, but we would make it work.

That meant that I could get a cat much sooner that I had planned. On a hot Sunday afternoon in August, Dan and I went back to Cheshire Grin, and I immediately fell for a tiny black kitten. When I asked about him, they said they only adopted kittens out in pairs, and I knew I could not handle two kittens and a young puppy together. There was another black and white female cat named Mabel that I had petted and played with while we were there. I asked about her, and they said she was about two years old and had been a stray taken to a local shelter, where she was overlooked for months, so she was brought to the café. They said she was very sweet. I had to reach out to the shelter volunteers to get more information. I filled out the application online and waited to hear from someone.

I got a call from the volunteer on Friday, and she had been doing the background checks and calling my references before she called me. After we talked a while, she said Mabel was ours, and we could bring her home that Sunday, which was August 30, five months to the day after Champ died. I took it as a sign that this is what we were supposed to do.

Mabel had been adopted and returned once before, so I tried to give her space once she came to us. She was very scared for the first couple of days and hid in the litter box. Every now and then, I'd sit outside of her box and talk to her. She let me pet her and feed her out of my hand. She cried all night the first two nights. I knew I needed to give her time to decompress and feel comfortable here, so I would check on her every hour or so and give her space the rest of the time. At the cat café, she liked to spend time in a cat tree, so I bought her one and set it in front of a sunny, west-facing window that overlooks the neighborhood. After she was brave enough to leave the safety of her litterbox, she moved to the cat tree.

On the second full Sunday that Mabel was with us, I was sitting on my bed writing. Mabel hopped up on the bed and curled up on the pillow that I had next to me. That was when we started to bond. Since I was home almost all the time, she and I spent a lot of time together, and I quickly became her person. She started sleeping with me shortly after that, and that is a special time of bonding for both of us.

One day when Mabel had been with us a couple of weeks, I could not find her anywhere. I started to panic that she had slipped out the door without us noticing. I went outside twice calling her name and looking for her and searched the whole house, opening every closet and cabinet door, even looking in the washing machine and dryer in case she had jumped in. I was in the basement looking and was getting very upset, then I heard the jingle of the bell on her collar. I got out a flashlight and started looking around. She was sound asleep on the blanket we had kept in Champ's crate that I had put away on a shelf. I was so relieved to find her, and also a little stunned that she had found Champ's blanket and chose to nap on it. I told my friend Caroline about this, and she said that Mabel finding that blanket was Champ telling me that everything was ok. For the next few weeks, Mabel would head down to that shelf and curl up on Champ's blanket every afternoon.

In early November, I got a call from the breeder that the puppies were born October 30—seven months to the day after Champ died. I took that as another sign that this was meant to be. She told us they had five puppies, but both males had died, leaving three females, so we would get the last-choice female. I said we were very excited for a healthy puppy, and Dan and I started preparing for a female Golden Retriever.

A couple weeks later, the breeder called again to tell me that the umbilical cord stumps had fallen off, and our little girl was a little boy! That was ok with us, as we only wanted a healthy dog. And that meant that our boy would have his brother a couple of blocks away.

We were scheduled to bring our puppy home a few days before Christmas. We went back and forth on names, and a few days before we brought him home, I suggested a family name, McKenzie, and shortening it to Mack. After dozens of names that one of us pitched and the other didn't like, this is the one we both liked.

Leading up to this, I started to get very anxious about having a puppy. What if the puppy picked up on my anxiety and PTSD from Champ and I gave it anxiety? What if I couldn't love this puppy because he wasn't Champ? How could I love both the puppy and Mabel and give them both enough attention? I talked with Linda, Champ's trainer, and she assured me that my feelings were normal after the experience I had with Champ. She also said that I needed to give the puppy a chance to show his personality and that I would be very surprised at how normal he would be. She said dogs like Champ are very rare, and the chances that I would get another one, particularly in a puppy from a reputable breeder, were extremely slim.

While the decision to adopt Mabel involved some risk because she was a rescue and not much was known about her background, it was one I was willing to take. Getting a puppy, however, was a whole different level of risk because of so many of my fears. I wasn't sure if I would bond with Mack, or if I did, how long it would take. Bringing a new pet home is basically like bringing a stranger into the house. They don't know you, and you don't really know them—only how to care for them.

The Most Painful Choice

We visited the puppies a couple of weeks before we brought him home. There were two females and Mack. Mack was the biggest and the roughest, but they were all little furry butterballs. I loved sitting there holding them and petting them. When we left, though, I started worrying again on the drive home whether I was ready for another dog. Linda again reassured me that it would all be fine once we brought him home.

The first week with Mack was a real whirlwind. Thankfully, I was on vacation from work for Christmas, so I had the time to focus on him. I needed every second. It felt like we had a newborn, only this newborn didn't wear diapers. The second day he was here, we were in the backyard, and our neighbor with Mack's brother saw us and came in the yard. His dog is seven months older than Mack, so he was much larger, and he wanted to play. Mack was terrified and hid under a chair, so that didn't work well. I was so afraid that I'd ruined their relationship by allowing them to meet too soon before Mack was ready. I worried for a couple of weeks that I'd made Mack afraid of dogs by that one interaction. Thankfully, I didn't, and they became best friends in a short time, but my anxiety was so high about doing something wrong that I was overly focused on it.

As Mack settled in, and we all started to establish a new routine, I started to see signs of PTSD in myself. When I saw the mail carrier or a delivery person approach the house, I would stop what I was doing thinking I had to get Champ outside. But Champ was gone, and Mack was excited to see someone approach the house and stood and wagged his tail. When we were able to start walking him in the neighborhood, I reverted to our management behaviors with Champ by starting to cross the street when another person walking a dog was approaching. I looked down at Mack, and his whole body was wagging in anticipation of being able to meet the dog. I was so conditioned to avoid other dogs and people, but I had to set those old fears and techniques aside so that Mack could become a well-socialized dog. Mack has a good sense for what dogs want to visit and those that don't. When we encounter a reactive dog or one that doesn't want to engage, Mack will shake off, like a dog does after a bath, then keep walking. It's not an issue at all.

I'm still hesitant when we encounter some of Champ's triggers, but I'm trying to remember that Mack is not Champ, and I need to let him decide what he thinks about these things rather than assume he's going to be triggered. So far, he's not bothered by much (other than being afraid of Mabel), and that is better than I could have hoped. Now that I

6. Making the Decision

have some knowledge of dog body language and signs of stress and anxiety, I can monitor him for those signs and evaluate the situation to see what we need to work on with him. My experience with Champ taught me so much, and even though Mack doesn't have the behavior problems that Champ did, that acquired knowledge is so helpful as we work to raise a physically and mentally healthy dog.

7

Grief

"Grief is just love with no place to go."—Jamie Anderson[1]

Since I had a month between the time I made the decision to euthanize Champ and the actual day, I had some time to prepare myself emotionally for both the day itself and the grief. Dr. Koch told me that the University of Missouri College of Veterinary Medicine had a program for clients dealing with the loss of their pets and that I was welcome to take advantage of that. The TIGER (Together in Grief, Easing Recovery) program provides assistance to the humans in making end-of-life choices, anticipatory grief, how to talk to children about losing their pet, and other services. I talked with the grief counselor twice in that month, mostly about the guilt that I felt having to make this choice. She talked with me a lot about anticipatory grief, which occurs before a death. It is common in families and friends of humans who have an extended, terminal illness, but is not often discussed in relation to pets. While it has many of the same symptoms as grief that occurs after a death, it is not the same as grief that follows an unexpected death. Anticipatory grief often allows people to say goodbye to their loved one, and that can be both comforting as well as incredibly difficult, as it was for me.

In some ways, I had been grieving for years for the dog I had wanted but didn't have. I had wanted a friendly, social German Shepherd that I could take places without worry. I wanted another Lindy, but that's not what we had. I had to accept that Champ was who he was and that we were going to have a different kind of life with him. It doesn't mean that I loved him any less. In fact, I probably loved him more because he needed so much more love than any of our previous pets to heal his broken places.

Moira Anderson Allen wrote that anticipatory grief, which she calls pre-loss bereavement, can begin when the pet owner realizes the beginning of the end, either with a devastating diagnosis or visible signs that the pet is in its final days.[2] It is when we begin to grieve the pending loss that we know is coming. In cases of illness or advanced age in the pet, the ending date may not be known and may take years to arrive. But in cases of behavioral euthanasia, sometimes that date is planned ahead of time, while at other times it results after a severe attack or bite.

"Grief is like a swamp; without a map, it's easy to lose any sense of where you are going or where you have been," Allen writes. "Once lost, the more you flail about trying to fight through the morass, the deeper you sink, and the more hopeless things look."[3]

Collin Murray Parkes, MD, a psychiatrist in the UK, indicates the opposite of anticipatory grief is morbid, or complicated, grief in those who express intense distress before and after their loss, then suffer from chronic grief. The person may believe he or she cannot survive without the support of one they lost. In others, their grief is complicated by feelings of anger and guilt that lead them to punish themselves.[4]

Grief is crushing, suffocating, and takes one's breath away. The Old English word for grief, *heartsarnes*, literally means "soreness of the heart." Studies also have found grief to intensify physical pain, increase blood pressure and blood clots, and lead to loss of appetite.[5]

Different Types of Grief

Acute grief, the period immediately following a death, is often characterized by a loss of regulation. This can be observed as increased intensity and frequency of sadness, anger and/or anxiety, and emotional numbness and difficulty concentrating, in addition to disturbed sleep and appetite.[6] Scientists know that grief causes the brain to send stress hormones to the cardiovascular and immune systems that can change how they function and raise the risk of heart attacks, infections, cancer, and chronic diseases.[7]

Grief also has been described as "the cost of commitment" to the lost loved one, or an indirect measure of the strength of attachment.[8] It doesn't have to be the result of a death but is always about someone you cannot bear to have lost, Lars Svendsen writes.[9] He describes grief as "the dark side of love," found in humans and animals because we have the ability to love. But that grief, he says, shows that the relationship with the animal was genuine.[10]

Atlanta psychologist William F. Doverspike, PhD, defines grief as the internal process of regaining equilibrium that requires reorganization on emotional and cognitive levels and re-evaluation of spiritual concerns.[11] He defines bereavement as the state that results from signifi-cant loss and mourning as the public expression of grief. While grief is very personal and private, mourning is more public and subject to cul-tural norms.

After British writer and English literature professor C.S. Lewis' wife, Joy Davidman, passed away from cancer, he kept notebooks in which he wrote about his grief. The notebooks were published in 1961 as *A Grief Observed* and later turned into the movie "Shadowlands." Lewis begins the book:

> No one ever told me that grief felt so like fear. I am not afraid, but the sensa-tion is like being afraid. The same fluttering in the stomach, the same rest-lessness, the yawning. ... At other times it feels like being mildly drunk, or concussed. There is a sort of invisible blanket between the world and me. I find it hard to take in what anyone says. Or perhaps, hard to want to take it in. It is so uninteresting. ... I dread the moments when the house is empty.[12]

Later, he writes:

> And grief still feels like fear. Perhaps, more strictly, like suspense. Or like waiting; just hanging about waiting for something to happen. It gives life a permanently provisional feeling. It doesn't seem worth starting anything. I can't settle down. I yawn, I fidget, I smoke too much. Up till this I always had too little time. Now there is nothing but time. Almost pure time, empty successiveness.[13]

I can relate to many of the words and phrases that Lewis wrote in these passages: empty, restlessness, invisible blanket between the world and me, dread. After Champ died, I felt rather hollow, or like a part of me was missing. I used to donate to Best Friends Animal Sanctu-ary in Utah because they had a beautiful male German Shepherd there whose owner had shot him in the head while in his crate for "barking too much." I really wanted that dog, but he was not adoptable due to the significant physical and emotional trauma he had experienced, and he lived out his life at the sanctuary. In return for my donation, they would send me a few sympathy cards to have on hand when someone lost a pet. One of them is a photograph of a black oval stone on which someone had painted a red heart. Over the heart are lines painted to look like a jigsaw puzzle with one piece missing in the center. I have kept that card, now rather faded and slightly warped, in the corner of a mirror in the bedroom ever since Lindy died, because that's how I felt after she died, after Skipper died, and especially after Champ died—like a piece of my heart was taken, leaving a missing piece. Except with Champ, it felt like most of the pieces of the heart were missing, not just one.

7. Grief

In one study of people who had lost a pet to death in the past year, respondents reported numbness and disbelief; preoccupation with the loss or the lost object; anger, irritability, or self-blame; an urge to search for what was lost; mitigating and avoiding grief; a feeling of loss and self; anxiety and distress; feelings of hopelessness and depression.[14]

Parkes and John Bowlby, MD, both British psychiatrists, describe four stages of grief: shock and numbness; yearning and searching; disorganization and despair; and reorganization and recovery.[15] Parkes describes "pangs of grief," or periods of intense anxiety often marked by uncontrolled crying. These pangs of grief begin shortly after the loss and reach a peak within about fourteen days. They are more frequent at first, then gradually become less frequent and occur only when something happens to remind us of the loss.[16] But grief is a roller coaster—some days we are ok, other days we cry constantly.

Parkes defines grief as "an emotional and behavioral reaction that is set in motion when a love tie is broken." A "love tie" is the relationship between people and their pets: the loss deprives the owner of love.[17]

In a paper on bereavement in adult life, Parkes writes that losses are a common cause of illness, yet they often go unrecognized by physicians. However, he writes, there is evidence that losses can foster maturity and personal growth—they aren't necessarily harmful. He also notes that people may need permission and encouragement to grieve and to stop grieving.[18] I think this is a result of the social and cultural pressures to quickly "get over" a loss, particularly when it involves a pet. Our society doesn't allow us as much time to grieve a pet as it would for a person—we're just expected to move on. To many, a pet is not worth as much as a person, therefore we *should* grieve for a shorter time or with less intensity than we *should* for a person, the culture seems to dictate. So many of us keep our grief to ourselves, not wanting to face the judgment of others.

Panksepp describes the loss of someone close to us as "one of the deepest and most troubling emotional pains of which we, as social creatures, are capable."[19] He writes that we grieve most when we lose those who have helped us to thrive or those with whom we have special bonds.

The grief counselor told me that grieving is a process unique to each person and finding a personal way to acknowledge the bond with our animals is important to process our grief. It is also not linear, so I could expect to feel ok one day yet and in despair the next, and that was perfectly normal.

About a month or two before Champ's BE, I joined the Losing Lulu

97

Facebook group for people who had to choose behavioral euthanasia for their pets. The moderators and administrators of the group are firm about it being a place of support for those who have already lost their pets to BE, not as a place for people to get advice about living pets. Because Champ was still living when I first joined, I could not make any comments or posts. I just absorbed the information and read the stories of people in similar situations who were dealing with the grief of having to choose BE for their dog, cat, horse, or other beloved pet.

This group was a huge place of support and help for me. I can relate so much to the stories and experiences of the others who post there, as they all tried everything they could for their pets like I did, and are grieving like I am. Even as the months have passed since his death, some days I can comment and provide encouragement and support to those who post, and other days, it's just too hard. If the person who posts had a German Shepherd, I can't look at the photo or respond with words but will often just type a heart. It's too close, and I'm not ready to talk about others losing their German Shepherds to BE.

Along with the grief came some relief. I no longer had to stay two steps ahead of Champ, no longer had to be on constant alert for his anxiety or outbursts, no longer had to schedule my life around his medication schedule.

Jessica Pierce, author of *Notes from the Last Walk* about her last year with her dog, Odysseus, summed it up well: "As much as I loved Ody, he was an albatross around my neck and a near constant source of worry. He didn't make life easy for me, and I always told him, 'It's a good thing you're so loveable or you'd be in big trouble.' So mixed with my grief is a certain feeling of release, of relief."[20]

I often told Champ he was lucky he was so handsome because that's what got him through most days. Just looking at his beautiful face and big brown eyes made me forget about all the worry and work it took to keep him going. But after he died, I felt relieved, though very conflicted about that. I really had to sit in my grief, and that was uncomfortable.

I took an online seminar for pet loss, grief, and bereavement in the fall of 2020 taught by three social work students from Virginia Commonwealth University. They said that the grief from pet loss is not acknowledged by society, making it disenfranchised grief. They also said the failure of others to recognize a person's grief over the loss of a pet, called empathic failure, can cause a person's grief to last longer.

There is also what they called "vicarious trauma," or the emotional residue that develops as a result of bearing witness to another's pain, fear, or terror.[21] "The expectation that we can be immersed in suffering and loss daily and not be touched by it is as unrealistic as expecting to be able to walk through water and not get wet," they said in the seminar. While this applies to the owners of the pets, who have to witness their pet's suffering daily, it also applies to the veterinary professionals and trainers who are working with the pet and the family. This could also be considered compassion fatigue.

The seminar leaders shared a variety of ideas for ways to memorialize one's pet, including planting a tree, creating a piece of art, talking to loved ones, joining a pet loss support group, and looking at photos of the pet, among others.

Patty Luckenbach, who wrote *The Kingdom of Heart: A Pet Loss Journal*, encourages grieving pet owners to write a letter to their pet expressing gratitude and telling the pet what he or she gave to you. I also read of a visualization exercise in which one is encouraged to sit comfortably in a quiet room with gentle music and soft lighting and imagine oneself in a peaceful place. Now imagine your dog appearing at that peaceful place and running happily to you. You greet him or her joyfully and spend time together, remembering happy times. When it's time to go, reach down and put your hands against her sides. As you watch, she becomes smaller and smaller, until she is small enough that you can pick her up, cupped in your hands. Now pick her up, hold her in your hands, and place her in your heart, where she will stay with you forever.[22]

Grief is surrounded by well-meaning but unhelpful comments from others, particularly when it is for pet loss. People are told, "It's *only* a pet," when in reality our pets are family members, and the losses are as acute as a human loved one.

The prolific best-selling novelist Dean Koontz wrote a memoir, *A Big Little Life*, about his Golden Retriever named Trixie, whom he and his wife adopted after Trixie was released from the Canine Companions for Independence program in California. Koontz and his wife, Gerda, had never had a dog before, and they fell in love with Trixie at first sight. They referred to her as their daughter.

Koontz wrote about the intense grief he and Gerda suffered after Trixie died a few months short of her ninth birthday.

Some will say, "She was only a dog." Yes, she was a dog, but not only a dog. I am a man, but not only a man. Sentiment is not sentimentality, common sense is not common ignorance, and intuition is not superstition. Living with a recognition of the spiritual dimension of the world not only ensures a happier life but also a more honest intellectual life than if we allow no room for wonder and ruse to acknowledge the mystery of existence.[23]

Others say, "Oh, you can get another dog. There are so many that need homes." While that is true, this invalidates a person's grief for their existing loss. Would someone say to a grieving widow, "Oh, you can get another husband"? Of course not. But for some reason, people think it's acceptable to tell others they can easily replace their pet.

"Those we love can never be replaced," writes Cheri Barton Ross, PhD, a psychology professor and co-author of *Pet Loss and Human Emotion*. "The term replacement is commonly used when referring to the adoption of a new pet. This suggests that animals can be interchanged; it doesn't acknowledge that the unique bond shared with a particular pet can never be duplicated. ... Suggesting replacement trivializes the pet parent's feelings."[24]

Another well-meant but insensitive remark is "Time heals all wounds." This is also a myth, because there is no amount of time that can pass that will heal an emotional wound. "Time can't heal a broken heart any more than time can fix a flat tire," according to Friedman, James, and James in *The Grief Recovery Handbook for Pet Loss*. "Unattended grief tends to get worse with passage of time."[25]

Many children learn early not to show sadness, according to Friedman, James, and James. For many, that carries through to adulthood when we feel that we need to grieve alone and don't want to burden others with our feelings of loss.[26]

Koontz writes that love and loss are inextricably entwined.

We took comfort in the knowledge that God is never cruel, there is a reason for all things. We must know the pain of loss because if we never knew it, we would have no compassion for others, and we would become monsters of self-regard, creatures of unalloyed self interest. The terrible pain of loss teaches humility to our prideful kind, has the power to soften uncaring hearts, to make a better person of a good one.[27]

Koontz describes so vividly the shock that comes when returning home after euthanasia without one's beloved pet.

In the house, Gerda and I were lost. We didn't seem to belong there anymore. Every room was familiar yet as different as a room in someone else's house. We did not know what to do, did not want to do anything, but could not sit idle because, in idleness, the ever-pressing grief became crushing, suffocating.[28]

The late writer Elizabeth Wurtzel, author of *Prozac Nation*, rescued a dog she named Augusta from her local pound in 2003. She had never owned a dog before, and they became inseparable. A year after Augusta passed away, Wurtzel wrote a column for *The Guardian* about the person who changed her, and she chose Augusta as that person. She wrote:

> She is the best thing that ever happened to me.
> She is the love of my life. I am so sorry for the rare times we were apart, because I could never have had enough time with her. I will never love anyone the way I love Augusta. It was about a time and place and situation that only could have happened with Augusta, who I love so much and too much.[29]

What the Research Shows

Several studies have found that attachment to pets can be intense, and the breaking of the bonds with our pets after their deaths can cause a grief reaction comparable to loss of a close relationship with humans.[30] In his paper "Why do people love their pets?" psychologist John Archer, PhD, analyzes various anecdotal and systematic studies of grief in pet owners after their pet's death. He writes that in some circumstances, the characteristics of pets that prompt humans to care for them cause pet owners to get more satisfaction from their pet relationship than those with humans. Pets provide a type of unconditional relationship absent in relationships with other humans. Archer cited a study by psychologist C.S. Stewart, PhD, who reported that 18 percent of pet owners surveyed were so upset by the loss of their pet that they were unable to carry on with their normal routine, and one-third described themselves as very distressed. Another study of nearly 1000 bereaved pet owners in the U.S. found that grief was brief but intense. Sadness was still apparent in over half those surveyed a month after the loss and crying and guilt in about one-fourth.[31]

The *New England Journal of Medicine* published a report in October 2017 about a woman in Texas who went to the emergency room with chest pains that mimicked a heart attack. She reported several recent stressful events in her life, including the death of her dog. She was found to have broken heart syndrome, also known as takotsubo cardiomyopathy, or stress cardiomyopathy, which typically occurs in postmenopausal women and may be preceded by a stressful or emotional event.[32]

While two studies found that that death of a pet was perceived as less stressful than the death of an immediate family member or a close friend and that less depression resulted afterward, two other studies found that the levels of grief following pet loss were comparable to those found after the loss of a human loved one. One study found no significant differences in grief responses of people who had lost a pet with those who had lost a spouse, while another found that the values were comparable with responses for the loss of a parent, child, or spouse.[33]

Another study found that pet owners' adjustment to the loss of their pet may be stalled because of the lack of social support and feeling as though they are unable to confide in others. After surveying pet owners several times up to twenty-six weeks after the pet's death, the researchers found that owners' grief experience associated with the death of their pet is similar to that associated with the loss of a significant person in their life. In addition, the owners who reported deeper relationships with their pets had more difficulty adjusting to the loss and were also less likely to acquire a new pet within six months.[34]

A study of more than 1500 mid-life couples found that losing a pet was among the most frequently occurring stressor, next to children leaving home. M. Geraldine Gage, PhD, and Ralph Holcomb, PhD, found that wives generally experienced higher stress than their husbands for all relationship losses and changes. Forty percent of wives reported the loss of the pet as "quite" or "extremely" disturbing, while 28 percent of husbands responded the same. While both wives and husbands said losing the pet was less stressful than losing a family member or close friend, they said it was more stressful than the death of another relative. The findings indicate that the death of a pet is a stressor to the family system.[35]

Ultimately, what all these studies have shown is that pet owners feel intense grief when their pets die. None of these studies specifically mentioned behavioral euthanasia. The book *Pet Loss and Human Bereavement* does not mention behavioral euthanasia other than to indicate that owners want to avoid it. From my personal experience, and the experiences of those who have also had to euthanize a pet for behavioral reasons, the grief is amplified because we feel like there was more we should have done. In the case of an aging pet or one with a terminal illness, there generally is a time when it's clear no more can be done. But in the case of incurable mental illness or unmanageable behavior issues in a pet, it is much harder to reconcile that everything that could have been done has been done. I hope that with an increased focus on human well-being and mental health following the Covid-19 pandemic that human grief after the loss of one's pet is taken more seriously, particularly in cases of behavioral euthanasia. With little support and the shame associated with having to euthanize, those who have experienced this trauma need support more than ever.

Grief Coaching

Like the grief counselor I spoke with prior to Champ's BE and the bereavement class I took with the social work students, it is becoming more commonly accepted for social workers and grief coaches to help pet owners deal with the pending loss or loss of their pets. Julie Umstead is a grief coach based in Pennsylvania who coaches people experiencing any kind of grief, including the loss of a beloved pet. She said her role is to hold space for people who are grieving and to give them a safe place to say anything they need to say without fear of judgment or condemnation.

"People don't want to talk about grief when they lose people, let alone losing a pet," she said.[36] "To so many people, it was 'just a dog or cat.' There is judgment that comes from other people when we decide we want to be forthcoming about our loss. It's part of the natural grieving process to tell the funny stories about our pet."

Umstead said when others judge pet owners for euthanizing their pet, it reinforces what the owners are telling themselves.

"As humans, we give ourselves far too much power over many things that we don't have control over," she said. "There is an invasive sense of failure when we have tried everything that we can, and we've come to the end of ourselves but there is nothing left but behavioral euthanasia staring us in the face. As a grief counselor, I try to get people past that and to realize that they did the best they could with what they had and what they knew."

Umstead said she sees a difference when people have lost their pet to behavioral euthanasia as opposed to other reasons.

"A high percentage of time in behavioral euthanasia, the pet is not very old, which adds to the grief," she said. "It usually takes some unfortunate event happening, such as the dog attacking a small child causing serious injuries, for owners to realize there is no other recourse, which makes things more complicated because you have a child who is recovering from physical, emotional, and mental injuries as well."

Umstead said veterinarians are now taking the time to take a pawprint, a nose print or a clip of hair from a pet when they perform euthanasia to give to the owner.

"All of that opens up the door for healing so much more than sweeping it under the rug and not talking about it," she said. "We get tired of hearing, 'I'm sorry for your loss.' We want people to use their name and acknowledge that they existed. No matter how long they

103

were here, they were loved, and they loved people to the best of their ability."

Umstead said she would like to see more people in roles like she has to help people through the grief process, similar to how midwives guide mothers through the birth process.

"It would be wonderful to have someone to come alongside the owners and tell them what to expect—not to take their grief away, but to soften the grief," she said. "Holding space for them, listening without judgment, and letting them know they did a really good job and took such good care of their pet, knowing that they did everything they possibly could."

Barton Ross has been hosting pet loss support groups since 1986. Her book, *Pet Loss and Human Emotion: A Guide to Recovery*, is a guide for therapists on how to counsel pet owners after the loss of their beloved pets. She writes that therapists and researchers are only beginning to understand the bonds between people and their pets.

"The significance of a pet's death can have far-reaching ramifications for the guardian," she writes. "Because many pets are considered to be members of the family, the death of a pet can alter the entire structure of a family and reshape the guardian's sense of well-being."[37]

How someone reacts to the death of their pet may be proportional to how much one has personally invested in the pet, the level of attachment and dependence on the animal.[38]

While grief is painful, it is a necessary part of the healing process, said Sandra Barker, PhD, LPC, who studies pet loss at Virginia Commonwealth University Health. "She said there are several factors that can affect the intensity of our grief response, including our previous experiences with death; our physical and mental health and support systems; the circumstances related to the death (was it sudden or was there time to plan, did the pet die naturally or was euthanasia chosen); what the pet symbolized to the owner (companionship, protection, last link to a deceased relative); others' responses to the death (including veterinarians and their staff), and our perception of whether the pet suffered."[39]

Pauline Boss, PhD, a marriage and family therapist and pioneer of the term "ambiguous loss," writes that the more we try to control the pain of loss, the more it controls us. "It is better to flow with the sorry when it comes, have a good cry, and afterward, carry on again as best you can. No pressure. Emotional ups and downs are natural. If we allow them to be felt, the downs become farther and farther apart over time, easing but never totally done."[40]

People in grief often wonder how long is "normal" for them to grieve. I think that question is similar to how much water is in the ocean, or even, how wet is water? I don't think there is a normal or a recommended amount of time for grief—it takes as long as it takes. "But it eases, it lightens, it changes and/or your relationship with it changes, and this is normal too," writes Ann Finkbeiner in the *New York Times*.[41] She writes that prolonged or persistent grief that debilitates a person for up to twelve months is now considered "complicated grief."

It is ok for people to take a break from grieving to prevent complicated or even chronic grief. Parkes describes those who experience severe distress before and after their loss and cannot stop grieving. In such cases, the bereaved may have had a dependent relationship with the one who is deceased and questions his or her survival after the loss. Some may even feel guilty for being able to survive and "move on."[42]

Sometimes, the owners may feel that the euthanasia was an act of selfishness. By looking objectively at the facts, writes Herbert A. Nieburg, PhD, a grief therapist and author of *Pet Loss: A Thoughtful Guide for Adults & Children*, guilt will resolve in time. "Owners are not responsible for their pet's illness," he writes. "And that is the real, if not direct, cause of death."[43]

So how do we get through this grief? Nieburg wrote that "we allow ourselves to mourn—to explore our attachment and admit our sense of loss, to accept our stress and treat it openly. The complication is that we don't want to. We feel embarrassed owning up to grief over the death of an animal. For in our culture, there really is no acceptable way of mourning a pet."[44]

This needs to change. The increase in the number of grief coaches such as Umstead, social workers who are trained to help others deal with pet loss, and pet loss support groups are steps in the right direction. My hope is that with this book, people will learn more about behavioral euthanasia, how difficult it is for those who experience it with their pet, and learn enough to tell those people, "I'm so sorry." Use the pet's name, and tell those grieving, "(Pet's name) knew he was so loved." Those simple words mean the world to those of us who are grieving.

Is There Peace?

When a person loses a loved one—human or animal—people tend to say, "They are now at peace." I said that to myself about Champ. I have even said it to others who have had to have BE on their pets. I told myself Champ was free of his demons and could finally rest because it made me feel better about what I had chosen to do. With his brain no longer functioning, it no longer made him hypervigilant, anxious, and fearful. Does that mean he is now at peace?

Lewis questioned the concept in *A Grief Observed*, writing about his late wife, whom he referred to by her nickname, H.: "They tell me H. is happy now, they tell me she is at peace. What makes them so sure of this? ... But why are they so sure that all anguish ends with death?... How do they know she is 'at rest?'"[45]

No one knows for sure what happens to pets when they die. Either they die, they are reincarnated, they cross the "Rainbow Bridge," or they go into eternal life, depending on one's belief system, or what makes the owner feel best. For me to live with my decision and get through every day, I have to believe that Champ is indeed at peace, and that he is waiting for me in eternity with my loved ones, Lindy, Skipper, Mulligan, Clara, and Luke, and that I will be reunited with him someday. This isn't theological, I admit. For me to see him, whole and unbroken, with a wagging tail and his big German Shepherd smile, would be such a wonderful welcome to eternity for me.

8

Moving Forward

"Don't forget. Somewhere between hello and goodbye, there was love. So much love."—Unknown[1]

Pets have been used to treat loneliness, isolation, and depression as early as the mid-nineteenth century. In 1860, Florence Nightingale said, "a small pet is often an excellent companion for the sick, for long chronic cases especially."[2] But one need not be sick, lonely, isolated, or depressed to enjoy the company of an animal.

We choose to have pets in our life for different reasons. Some want the companionship, some want something to nurture, and others want a partner for their sport, such as hunting. Pets are a major commitment that not everyone is willing to make, but those of us who have pets are willing to do what is necessary so that our pets have good lives.

Nieburg writes that the most meaningful quality that pets provide us with is unqualified love and acceptance. "So often, human affection must be gained with a great deal of effort and sacrifice, but pets give us a readily available, seemingly endless supply of love and ask virtually nothing in return."[3]

We also receive satisfaction and joy from watching a young puppy grow and develop into a well-trained dog, learning its personality quirks, likes and dislikes, and interpreting its sounds and behaviors, and watching it learn the things we teach it. We invest a lot of time and energy into shaping our pets into what they become and are in some sense proud of that. How many of us show off our pet's tricks when people come to visit?

Developing a close relationship with our pet shows loyalty, caring, and strength of character and generally encourages more empathy in owners than in people who do not own pets. This is why we do everything we can to help our pets.[4]

Some researchers have looked at resilience in people after loss and have determined that those who have a more positive outlook on life tend to recover more quickly after losses or physical or mental challenges. Dodman suggests there may be a "resilience gene" that if discovered, may present new opportunities to treat life challenges causing distress.[5]

Arielle Schwartz, PhD, a psychologist in Colorado, defines resilience psychology as a mindset that allows us to adapt and grow in response to loss and painful or traumatic life events. She says that resilience is not a trait that you either have or do not have, but a set of strategies that can be learned and practiced. Part of that resilience includes finding a supportive community, listening to others who are grieving and learning how they are feeling and coping, and understanding that by pacing your grieving process, you can navigate through painful feelings. It also involves staying open, knowing that life will bring loss and painful events.[6]

People who are resilient have been described as "supernormal" by clinical psychologist Meg Jay, PhD, which she defines as exceeding the normal or average. "Their daily struggles are above and beyond what we think of as 'average and expectable,' and their subsequent successes exceed expectations, too. Beating the odds, they live improbable lives, and after decades of academic study no one knows quite why," she wrote.[7]

Resilience is finding a way to cope with loss, which may be with sadness, rage, resentment, grit, or humor.[8]

"In the end, your main benefit at any time of adversity is that you can discover your resiliency; that you are stronger than you thought; that you can withstand long-term hardship and unprecedented loss; that even if sometimes you feel anger or despair, you can take a break, talk with someone, nurture yourself, and when ready, carry on again," Boss writes.[9]

Psychological resilience is defined as an ability to recover from or adjust easily to misfortune or change or the capacity to recover from adversity. It also has a physical definition related to engineering: the capability of a strained body to recover its size and shape after deformation caused especially by compressive stress.[10] An example is a tree that survives a hurricane by bending but not breaking.

Lucy Hone, PhD, a psychologist who studies resilience at the University of Canterbury in New Zealand and author of *Resilient Grieving: Finding Strength and Embracing Life After a Loss That Changes Everything*, encourages those who are grieving a loss to follow several strategies, including accepting the good, or remembering what you have and not only what you have lost; finding positive emotions, either through experiences, music, movies, or spending time with friends or family; and establishing routines to keep the memory of the loved one alive.[11]

Doverspike points to resilience as one of three "Rs": recovery, or the conscious process of moving through the stages of grief; resolution, the gradual acceptance of the reality of the loss; and resilience, one's positive capacity to cope with future crises and catastrophe.[12]

Having to have behavioral euthanasia for a pet can be quite catastrophic. The guilt, the grief, the loss of the beloved pet as well as of one's routine, are overwhelming. Over time, we learn to cope and understand that we did the best we could, or else we stay stuck in our grief and self-blame, continuing to flog ourselves for "failing" our pet.

For me, it was several months before I could dig out of the pit of grief, and it was sweet Mabel who helped me to climb out of it. I was no longer alone in the house all day while working from home during the Covid-19 pandemic shutdown, and I had someone to focus on other than myself. She somehow ended up as a stray in a rural area, and no one knew anything about her prior life, so I wanted to give her a loving home—the same intent I had for Champ when we adopted him. As Mabel and I got to know and trust one another, a process that was much slower for her than it was for me, I realized that even just being able to pet her for the few strokes that she would allow was feeding my soul something I had been missing since Champ died.

It's well known that people who own pets tend to have lower blood pressure than people without pets. I couldn't have agreed with that when Champ was our pet because of the enormous amount of stress that he carried in himself and caused in me as I tried to calm him. But Mabel is such a calming force. She's very quiet, and rarely makes any audible noise. She doesn't ask for a lot other than to be fed twice a day, a few treats in the afternoon, and petting now and then. She seems to know exactly when I need her. Could the same have happened with any other cat available at a shelter? Possibly, but I believe Mabel needs me as much as I need her.

Everyone who has survived some sort of loss or trauma is resilient in some way, or else they would not have survived. This takes tremendous amount of energy, and sometimes we don't have enough energy to live with our memories of our lost loved one and try to function without them. Some days, it's too much. But other days, it is encouraging to see how far we've come since the day of the loss.

After resilience comes resolution of grief, where we accept the loss and decide to go forward with our lives. This does not mean that we are "back to normal" or have forgotten our pet. We are now living in a new phase of life, one without our beloved pet, without our established routine of caring for him or her, and have to find a way to go through our days with these gaping holes of time when we used to go for walks, fill the food and water dishes, play outside, and spend time with our pets.

British illustrator Charlie Mackesy has a lovely book called *The Boy, the Mole, the Fox, and the Horse*, which is full of encouraging messages and illustrations. One of his illustrations, which I saw on social media, stopped me in my tracks about a year after Champ's BE. The boy and the mole are sitting on the back of the white horse, and the fox is standing next to the horse. All are standing in a snow-covered field looking at a winding river. The horse says, "One day you'll look back and realise how hard it was, and just how well you did."[13] That simple yet beautiful illustration was the equivalent of someone saying to me, "Your experience with Champ was so hard, and you did well."

Of course, several people did say something similar to me right after Champ died, but I wasn't in a place where I could really hear and believe it. For several months after Champ's death, I still felt like there was more I could have done. After he died, someone who knew us well said, "Champ tried hard to be everything you wanted and everything he could be." I know it was meant as encouragement, but it made me wonder if I had pushed too hard for him to be something that he wasn't. I wondered if he felt like he couldn't please me because I was always trying to fix his issues. I know this is anthropomorphizing him, but I believe on some level, dogs know when they are pleasing humans and when they aren't. Did I add to his emotional burden by always trying to relieve his anxiety, or did he understand I was doing it all to help him? Should I have stopped trying to change him (for the better), and just let him be himself? Logically, I know the answer to that is no, because the anxiety was literally killing him, mentally and physically, and I was trying to prevent that. I was trying to improve his quality of life, but did he think it was an improvement, or was he just tolerating all the training and activities to please us and make us happy? One of the volunteers from the rescue who had been very involved with his rehabilitation efforts told me multiple times that I was a "warrior" for him. I fought for him every minute of every day, but is that what he wanted? These are questions that may remain forever unanswered, but I will work through these issues as I continue to heal.

I often felt like I had to save Champ from himself, like parents of toddlers who are on constant accident prevention, such as preventing a fall, spilled milk, or a missed-nap meltdown. I've watched parents of toddlers, and they rarely, if ever, take their eyes off their children to be able to intervene when they see something about to happen and redirect the child. That's how I felt with Champ. I rarely stopped watching him so that I could prevent something from causing him fear or anxiety. In that sense, I was a warrior for him. But I also had to know when it was time to wave the white flag of defeat.

A year after Champ's death, Mackesy's words meant something different to me. They meant that it *was* hard, and I *did* do everything I could have. I am so thankful for Mackesy's beautiful book and have given several of them as gifts to those I thought would appreciate his message.

It's important that we allow those who are grieving to feel their feelings without judgment and to reassure them that it is normal to grieve. It's also important for those grieving to understand that moving forward doesn't mean forgetting the one we lost, and it's not a betrayal to their memory. Getting another pet is not a betrayal of loyalty to the pet we lost, and it doesn't mean we've forgotten them. I think our deceased pets would want us to get another pet that needs a loving family and a good home. After our experience with the animal communicator and hearing Champ's "voice," I believe he would have said, "I want you to get another pet because I know you will give him or her the same love, attention, and devotion you gave me, and there are many pets out there who need that as much as I did."

Moving forward doesn't mean the grief is over, either. I went through another wave of grief in January 2021 when President Joe Biden brought his German Shepherd Dogs, Champ and Major, to the White House. At least ten people texted or emailed me links to articles about or videos of them. The Bidens' Champ looked like an older version of my Champ, and Major looked identical to Lindy. I know my friends meant well when sending those videos and photos to me, but I couldn't watch any of the videos and could barely glance at the photos without feeling sick inside. I was so overwhelmed with grief that I shed a few tears after getting several texts in a row.

We can still be grieving when we decide to get a new pet. I certainly was when we brought home Mabel and Mack, and to some extent, I will likely always grieve for Champ due to the intensity of our relationship and the traumatic decision for BE. I grieved for Lindy and Skipper for a very long time. Although I loved each of them deeply, their loss was very different because it was due to age and physical disease. I couldn't do anything to change their aging, and I did all I could for their diseases. I did the same for Champ's disease, though it was a different kind of illness that had nothing to do with his age. In the end, though, the words from the veterinarians were the same: "There is nothing more we can do."

After a loss, people tend to improve as the first year goes by, then when the first anniversary arrives, the feelings resurface, which Doverspike calls anniversary reactions. For me, as the first anniversary of Champ's death approached, I was anticipating that it would cause intense grief. We were starting the second year of the pandemic, I was still working from home while raising a then-five-month-old puppy, I wasn't yet eligible for a vaccine, and life was far from normal. My friend Caroline was the only person who remembered the day. She gave me a card to tell me she was thinking of me in preparation for the day. As it turned out, my aunt died the day before the anniversary, which required my focus to shift away from grieving for Champ to grieving for my aunt and communicating with and caring for family members. I didn't have the opportunity on the actual anniversary to sit with my thoughts about Champ and remember him as I had planned. Maybe that was for the best, as maybe I would have gone down a rabbit hole of grief that would have been detrimental to my well-being. Or maybe I channeled my grief for Champ into the grief over the death of my aunt, which raised many thoughts about the older generation of my family as well as how short our time on earth really is.

Seeing a German Shepherd is still difficult for me most of the time. There is one in the neighborhood I see almost daily, and that is ok. Sometimes when I'm running or riding my bike, I will see a German Shepherd being walked, and I have to look away. It hurts too much: I think about how much I miss Champ, how hard he tried to change, and what a shame it was that his life had to be so restricted. I think about how unfair it was that he didn't get to just relax and enjoy life. On one of my bike routes, I often see a woman walking a German Shepherd who is wearing a pack just like the one we tried on Champ, and it makes me sad. We hoped that the pack would make a difference in Champ, but it really didn't. An external solution was not going to solve his internal problems. Some days, though, seeing that dog wearing the pack makes me smile a little bit, knowing that the pack works for this particular German Shepherd, who seems to enjoy walking with it, and that there are German Shepherds out there for whom life is good.

8. Moving Forward

According to Southwest German Shepherd Rescue, German Shepherd Dogs are the number one breed in rescue. This is for a variety of reasons, including that people get them because they like the way they look, not realizing that they shed constantly, bark a lot, need to have something to do, and are basically "a lot of dog." They don't like to be left alone for long periods of time, and out of instinct, will tend to "herd" children, which many parents don't understand. It absolutely breaks my heart because I love the breed, but I don't know if I can have another one. It hurts too much. And raising another puppy does not appeal right now (they are a lot of work!), and I am not ready to take a risk on another rescued German Shepherd.

Before Champ died, I knew I wanted to have some sort of physical reminder of him. I scanned the clay pawprint that the veterinarian's office gave me and had a pendant made so I would have it close to my heart. It was a temporary solution, however, because I had decided I wanted to get his pawprint as a tattoo, but all the tattoo shops were closed because of the pandemic. I took that time to research what shop I wanted to go to and which artist I wanted to do it. I found the artist I wanted, and when the shop reopened in late July 2020, four months after his death, I made an appointment. I had my friend Beth, a graphic artist, scan the pawprint and size it appropriately since it was bigger than my wrist. I also had her add a tiny heart on one of the paw pads. I had some temporary tattoos made so I could try it in different places, and I decided to put the real one on the inside of my right wrist.

When I gave the artist the printout of the scan of Champ's pawprint, he

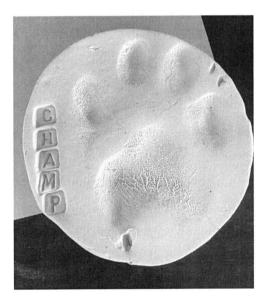

The impression of Champ's paw that the vet techs made for me after his BE. I used this impression for the tattoo that's now on my wrist.

113

asked me what kind of dog it was. I told him it was my German Shepherd who had passed away in March, and I wanted to do this to have a daily reminder of what he meant to me. The artist told me he had grown up with German Shepherds and still had some in his family, so he really understood how I was feeling. During the process, we talked a lot about German Shepherds, and he let me talk about Champ a bit, and that was helpful because it still felt so fresh. I absolutely love my tattoo, and every time I look at it, I think of how much Champ will always be a part of my inside, and now he will always be a part of my outside.

The tattoo also draws a lot of comments from people, both those I know and those I don't. I knew I was starting to move forward when I could smile when I tell people it is the pawprint of my beloved German Shepherd, Champ, who passed away in March 2020, and that this was my way to remember him every day.

I couldn't talk much about Champ for about six months, maybe even longer. But when I could start to talk about him without getting upset, I knew I was starting to move forward. Doverspike says that experiencing the pain of loss involves talking about the one who has passed. I don't talk about Champ a lot, but sometimes something will come up, and talking about him is a natural fit, for instance, when meeting someone at a local park, I said that I used to take Champ there a lot because there weren't many other dogs around. I recently showed someone one of Champ's food puzzles so that they could get one for their dog. I still can't give away his things, but I can show them to someone or describe how we used them.

Rabbi Harold Kushner, who wrote the best-selling book *When Bad Things Happen to Good People*, wrote that recovering from grief involves getting over all the questions we have that start with "why." These are some of my "why" questions:

• Why did this happen to Champ? (In other words, why did he have to go through whatever he experienced in his first home that caused him the lifelong trauma, anxiety and fear and ultimately led to a shorter life?)
• What happened to him that made him anxious and afraid, or was he always that way?
• Why couldn't we help or relieve his anxiety or fear?
• Why did I have to work so hard just to have it end in the pain of loss?

8. Moving Forward

Kushner writes that once we stop asking why, we can ask ourselves what we can do about it now that it has happened.[14] For me, writing our story and educating people about BE is what I can do about it. I want to share with people that there are dogs and other pets out there with severe mental health problems that manifest into physical issues, such as pain, just like in humans.

Kushner writes that pain is the price we pay for being alive.[15] "We may not ever understand why we suffer or be able to control the forces that cause our suffering, but we can have a lot to say about what the suffering does to us, and what sort of people we become because of it," he writes. "Pain makes some people bitter and envious. It makes others sensitive and compassionate. It is the result, not the cause of pain, that makes some experiences of pain meaningful, and others empty and destructive."

My six years with Champ made me more sympathetic to people with dogs who appear to be unruly or out of control. I don't judge them or think to myself that they need to get their dog in line because they may be doing everything they can to help their dog. I don't ever say anything in these situations, but I try to give an empathetic smile. When we were out with Champ and he was having an outburst in view of other people, nothing that they could have said would have helped in that moment—not even something encouraging—because in the heat of that moment, my focus was on getting us all out of the situation as quickly and safely as possible. When he would have an outburst or anxiety attack in group training, some of the other dog owners would look at me like I had a weapon in my hands. There were only a few who understood and knew I was doing the best I could. Sometimes I was embarrassed by his outbursts in these situations, but mostly, it just hurt and frustrated me that he was experiencing something that he didn't know how to deal with, and the tools we were trying to give him to deal with it weren't working.

The hurt I experienced from those times was nothing compared with the hurt from his BE. But even that has helped to make me more compassionate toward "dogs with issues" and their long-suffering owners, fosters, veterinarians, or other caregivers. I'm very compassionate and empathetic with anyone who has had to choose BE for their pet. I'm not ready to talk about it with someone trying to make the decision, but I can talk about it with them afterward. Recently, someone tried to talk to me about whether they should euthanize their dog, and I had to excuse myself from the conversation. I'm not sure if that will ever change.

9

Behavioral Euthanasia
What It Is and What It Is Not

"The only absolute is that the decision is never easy."
—Dr. Jen Summerfield[1]

In North America, behavior problems are the main reason people surrender or euthanize their pets. Behavioral disorders are responsible for the relinquishment and death of more pet animals per year than infectious, cancerous, and metabolic diseases combined, and are the single largest threat to the lifespan of a dog.[2,3] Up to 65 percent of people who surrendered their dogs to a shelter reported behavior issues as the reason.[4] In fact, behavioral issues are among the biggest barriers to adoption, and shelters find themselves with more and more of these animals that are difficult to place.[5]

The word euthanasia comes from the Greek and means a good or easy death: *Eu* means good or well, and *thanatos* means death. Merriam-Webster Dictionary defines it as "the act or practice of killing or permitting the death of hopelessly sick or injured individuals (such as persons or domestic animals) in a relatively painless way for reasons of mercy."[6]

Almost everyone who has ever owned a pet has had to make the decision to euthanize their pet at the end of its life and know what a difficult decision it is to make, even when it is clear the pet is old, very ill, and suffering. It doesn't seem fair that we, as humans, should have the power to make the choice whether another living being lives or dies. After all, euthanasia is a personal—and permanent—decision to make in an impossible situation.

Behavioral euthanasia, then, is euthanasia performed for behavioral reasons, which can include aggression, reactivity, bites and/or attacks of people or other animals, anxiety, obsessive-compulsive disorder and many others. The most commonly cited reason for behavioral euthanasia is aggression.[7] It is for when all treatments and methods to manage the dog have failed.

Behavioral euthanasia is not the same as euthanasia for old age, infirmity, or illness, for irreparable damage caused by an accident or attack, or simply for convenience or because the pet is no longer wanted or is too difficult to care for. It is not punishment for misbehaving, failing to obey, or for being a "bad dog." It is not due to overcrowded shelters, where nearly a million pets were euthanized in 2019 in U.S. facilities.[8]

There is a difference between problem behavior, which is normal dog behavior that causes problems for the owner, such as digging up the backyard, and behavioral disorders, which are pathological or disease-based behaviors that are excessive in some way or used in the wrong context, writes a team of veterinary researchers in The Netherlands.[9] For example, a dog may be afraid of a loud noise, but it becomes problem behavior if its response is so intense that it harms itself or others or escapes.[10] Pathologic behavior may be due to genes, lack of early socialization, or medical conditions. While some of these behaviors can be managed, they may never be cured.

Behavioral euthanasia is a choice one sometimes must make for the greater good, and it hurts the person who doles out the sentence, writes Sarah Stremming of *The Cognitive Canine* blog. "To pretend that it is a callous act is in itself a callous act," she said. "We must take responsibility for these animals, apply effective training, and if it becomes necessary to do so, take a life. It is the deal we have struck."[11]

Alexander said euthanasia is not a welfare question. "The animal is no longer suffering, it is no longer at risk for suffering, and no longer causing anyone else to suffer. It's an alleviation of suffering. We have to accept that some of the time the best welfare outcome for an animal that is suffering is that their welfare will no longer be comprised if they are euthanized," she said.[12]

Jerrold Tannenbaum, professor emeritus of veterinary ethics at University of California, Davis, explains a justified case for euthanasia: (1) the patient is suffering from a condition for which veterinary medicine cannot offer a cure or solution at any cost; (2) the condition is already causing the animal severe pain for which palliative measures are not available; (3) the human client is psychologically able to make a voluntary and rational decision.[13]

But that doesn't make it easy, nor does it justify the situation. Those who have had to choose BE for their pets often feel so many things:

failure, guilt, and shame, as well as great injustice. Many feel that they have failed their pets—that they didn't do enough, that they didn't do the right things, or that they couldn't fix the pet. It's very common to think, "If only I had tried this or that, maybe that would have fixed him." But the reality is, we tried everything, while rearranging our lives and walking on eggshells at home to avoid triggering a reaction.

Being blamed for failing the dog by others who don't understand never helps the grieving family and can lead to increased shame and guilt. Guilt is reported in nearly all people who have lost or are anticipating the loss of a pet, writes Barton Ross, founder of the Redwood Empire Veterinary Medical Association Pet Loss Support Group in Santa Rosa, California. "Guilt is an unproductive, debilitating emotion that often inhibits progress toward resolution," she says. "Guilt also poses the greatest obstacle to the client's attainment of resolution of the loss. It is the enemy of healing and closure."[14]

Guilt is a normal reaction after euthanasia since our moral code states that it is wrong to kill someone or something. While a normal reaction, it's not a truthful one. In those of us who had to choose behavioral euthanasia for our pet, we know deep down that we had exhausted every other option and concluded that euthanasia was the best option, no matter how much it hurt.

Nieburg suggests that to relieve the guilt, we only need to look at the facts. "Are a few extra months of living worth continued pain and suffering? ... If you believe that you have exercised your best judgment in agreeing to euthanasia, then the decision should not be construed as a reason for guilt, but rather as an act of kindness: a loved pet deserves a humane and dignified end to life."[15]

The feeling of failure can be even stronger if the dog is a rescue. Many pet owners adopt rescues with the best of intentions to turn the dog's life around from its previously difficult circumstances. We think that by providing them with a safe, secure, and loving home that they will suddenly get over their past trauma and become normal. McConnell writes that the world is full of dear, damaged dogs who desperately need homes.

> Lots of wonderful people rescue them and those people deserve our heartfelt appreciation. In spite of the importance of early development, patience and hard work can go a long way to rehabilitate dogs damaged in their youth by unsuitable environments. ... Just remember that this might not be the dog who wins you that obedience competition title you've always wanted. Victory with a dog who's been severely damaged by a neglectful upbringing

is more likely to include finally enabling her to tolerate a house sitter when you go on vacation (rather than destroy the house or leap through the second-story window) or teaching him to walk politely down the street without leaping and snarling toward every dog he sees. Don't feel like a failure if you can't make a social butterfly out of the dog you rescued from a nightmarish beginning. Giving him a kind, loving home and helping him to relax enough to nap in your lap are achievements in their own right. If you can manage them, you deserve much more than a blue ribbon and a silver chalice.[16]

Everyone has read stories of rescue dogs who are miraculously transformed after being adopted, have become therapy dogs, or are the constant companions of young children. These stories are true but are by no means the norm. As writer and certified dog trainer Nancy Tanner writes, "There aren't people lining up for dogs with major emotional damage, that have the potential to inflict great damage on other people or animals. That is a fact."[17]

Some rescue dogs cannot be rehabilitated, despite the best efforts of a rescue group, a foster home, or an adoptive owner, leaving BE the only choice. Canadian dog trainer John Wade put it this way:

The irony with regard to euthanasia is that this decision along with all of its horrendous emotional fallout lands on the shoulders of the dog's owner. Whereas anyone with a basic understanding of genetics and behavior would understand that in the vast majority of cases it was not the owner or the dog that was the real problem. Almost without exception, they took in a product that was genetically less than just a roll of the dice.[18]

For many pets who suffer from severe anxiety and fear, BE offers them the peace they could not find while living. BE, then, is not a failure, but a gift that ends our beloved pet's suffering. It also ends the risk of them hurting themselves, a person, or another pet.

Lore I. Haug, DVM, of Texas Veterinary Behavior Services and a certified animal behaviorist, wrote that each animal with a behavior problem is a case study of one, and factors that affect the risk-benefit analysis are unique to each situation.[19] However, researchers have found some similarities.

Overall and her colleagues at the University of Pennsylvania tested the urine of aggressive dogs and compared it with urine from nonaggressive dogs. They found that 88 percent of aggressive dogs had metabolic abnormalities, including high levels of several amino acids known to be excitatory neurotransmitters and are associated with aggression, compared with 23 percent of nonaggressive dogs.[20]

The Most Painful Choice

In a study led by Reisner, a veterinary behaviorist at the University of Pennsylvania School of Veterinary Medicine, she and her collaborators reviewed three hundred and two patient records of dogs who had been taken into their veterinary behavioral service for consultation. They found that dogs who were presented to the service were most commonly diagnosed with generalized anxiety (showing one or more signs of distress including hypervigilance, pacing, jumping, mounting, licking, restlessness, trembling, and vocalizing); fear-related aggression, and resource guarding, sometimes called possession aggression. Many of the patients had more than one diagnosis.[21]

About one-third of owners of these dogs had considered rehoming their dogs before the behavior consultation, while about 20 percent had considered euthanasia. In those owners, the presence of other chronic, non-life-threatening medical problems, such as skin allergies, chronic gastrointestinal problems, or degenerative joint disease, was considered as part of their decision for euthanasia.

A 1987 study by researchers in Georgia observed one hundred and five dogs referred for behavior problem management. They found one hundred and seventy behavior problems in the dogs in three major areas: aggression, or lunging, snarling, growling, or biting postures or signals toward a human or dog; stimulus reactivity, or excessive avoidance or approach in reaction to a particular stimulus; and separation-related, including destruction of items in the home, inappropriate elimination, hyperactivity, escape attempts, excessive barking and behavioral depression in the owner's absence. The dogs were an average of 3.4 years old. In this group, dogs from sporting and mixed breeds had the most diagnoses, followed by working and terrier breeds. Nearly half were intact males. Many owners reported attempting or completing obedience training, which had little effect on resolving the behavior problems, and stated that if nothing could be done about their dog's behavior, it would have to be euthanized.[22]

Most pet owners understand when they need to euthanize a pet in severe physical pain or one who is suffering from incurable disease but euthanizing a pet for mental and/or behavioral reasons is perceived quite differently and can often cause owners to feel tremendous shame. They feel shame because they had a dog with issues that they couldn't solve, because they feel like they did wrong by the dog or let him down by having to choose BE, or because of the judgment from others who don't understand. While most people are sympathetic and well-meaning, others may say they could have done better or that death

120

is never an option. One person I talked to thought that I had eutha-nized Champ for "misbehaving," which is not what behavioral euthana-sia means at all. Comments such as these only exacerbate the guilt and shame felt by the owner.

Many owners, including myself for a long period, would rather tol-erate or try to manage their pet's behavior problems rather than give up or euthanize the animal, even after unsuccessfully trying to correct the problem. A study of one hundred cases brought to the University of Pennsylvania Animal Behavior Clinic for treatment over a four-month period found that 99 percent of the owners said they considered their pet's problem to be serious or very serious. Of the one hundred cases, sixty-one were dogs. The majority of problems seen were aggressive behavior, primarily toward people, including family members. The sec-ond most common problem was separation anxiety, and the third was noise phobia. Study author Victoria L. Voith, DVM, PhD, a professor of animal behavior at Western University College of Veterinary Medicine, wrote that the owners' attachment to their pets was clear in their choice to try to help and keep their pets, but also that the owners faced social ridicule when seeking help from an animal behavior specialist but chose to endure the ridicule in hopes that the treatment would help their pet or save it from euthanasia.[23]

There are several risk factors that lead owners to consider rehom-ing or euthanasia, even after seeking help from a behavior veterinar-ian: heavier weight; mixed breed; aggression to familiar people over resources, resting places, or while being groomed or medicated; aggres-sion to unfamiliar people during interactions; a history of biting; and living in a family with children aged thirteen to seventeen. Related owner risk factors were using punishment-based training and previous consultation with a nonveterinary behaviorist or trainer.[24]

There are several arguments about when euthanasia is justified or performed at the appropriate time. While everyone has the right to his or her own opinion on the subject, ultimately, the decision on whether euthanasia is justified and timely lies with the pet owner, the pet's veter-inarian, any veterinary behavior specialists or other medical specialists, and trainers. These individuals have the most information and perspec-tive on whether euthanasia is the right choice at any time for any pet, for behavior reasons or medical reasons.

Michael Cholbi, PhD, professor of philosophy at the University of Edinburgh and an expert in ethics, writes that knowingly failing to euthanize a companion animal at or near an optimal time fails to respect the animal.[25] He argues that the optimal time to end an animal's life is the point at which additional life would be neither a benefit nor a harm to it. If the animal has nothing more to gain by living longer, yet loses nothing by dying at that time, it would have lived its optimal life span, he writes.[26] If a pet has a condition that detracts from its overall wellbeing, it is up to the owner to make the best judgments he or she can based on the best evidence possible.[27] Not to do so, he writes, is disrespectful to the animal.

> An animal companion that is euthanized at a point in time when its overall quality of life declines with each passing moment has not been adequately respected. For what is "relevant to the issue at hand," what should be "properly attended to" or "taken appropriately into account" in this instance, is precisely the steady decline in overall wellbeing the animal faces by continuing to live. This "reality" should be determinative in deciding to euthanize a companion animal.[28]

Not only is euthanizing too soon disrespectful, but euthanizing too late also is disrespectful, he says.

> Not to euthanize an animal at the point of its optimum life span, based on the best evidence available to us, is therefore wrong because of its cruel effects on the animal—as it amounts to willfully deciding that an animal will live less than the best life available to it—but it also betokens a lack of respect for the animal as a being separate from oneself, with interests and a point of view of its own, worthy of consideration in its own right.[29]

A survey of veterinarians by Clinton R. Sanders, PhD, professor emeritus at the University of Connecticut, found that in behavior cases, veterinarians do take quality of life into account. One veterinarian he interviewed shared her evaluation of the pet's quality of life based on the owner's rationale:

> I can accept putting an animal down for behavioral problems as long as I think you have given it a good shot at trying to rectify the situation. I can sympathize with clients who don't have the facilities to handle a dangerous animal. If the animal is not going to really be an acceptable pet for someone else—the quality of life for an animal like that is not going to be high. I don't have much trouble with euthanasia when I think it is a quality of life question. If the animal's quality of life is not going to be good—this is a hard thing to hear myself say—I think they are better off not being around than being stuck in a cage for the rest of their life.[30]

Animals lack the existential fear of death, Cholbi writes, so euthanizing them depends on whether it would harm the animals, rather than their own fears of death.[31] Pets don't fear death, says Judy Rath, a licensed professional counselor in St. Simons Island, Georgia. "We are fear-based as humans; our pets don't have that fear of the next piece of their existence. We project our emotions on to our dogs."[32]

However, one study showed that animals, particularly dogs, display behavior changes when another animal is euthanized. A survey of veterinarians in South Carolina reported these behavior changes, which included an animal becoming quiet or making unusual sounds. The report explained that companion animals experience grief and empathy in the same way that humans do and read and respond to the emotional cues that humans show. In addition, animals respond to changes in the physical and/or emotional state of the euthanized animal and have the ability to smell death and react to pheromones released at the time of death.[33]

When is the right time for behavioral euthanasia? Does an owner wait until the dog has bitten and severely injured another person or animal? What about if the dog's life is restricted to remaining in its own yard and having to wear a muzzle whenever it is out of its own yard, or having to be crated in the house most of the time? I believe it comes down to quality of life for the dog. While dogs don't have to be social with other dogs and go to dog parks or day care to be healthy, having to be confined to their own fishbowl of a backyard or inside the house for their own safety or the safety of other dogs or people isn't ideal, though sometimes is the only choice for these dogs.

Quality of life of the owner(s) must also be considered. Owners have to determine how much they can handle, how much time and money they are willing to invest, and how much risk they are willing to accept. There should be no judgment for owners who choose not to or are unable to pay for trainers, veterinary behaviorists, and medications. It really is an investment that may not pay off.

Owners must consider the safety of those in the home, especially young children, as well as other pets.[34] If the dog has already bitten a person or another dog, what is the likelihood that it will bite again? What was the damage from prior bites? Is that a risk the owner is willing to take?

The owner must consider if there was a trigger for the bite, such as loud noises, being hit, or being grabbed by a child. If so, can those triggers be avoided in the future? If there wasn't a clear trigger, how can the owner prevent a potential future bite?

Though it sounds unusual, owners must also consider if the dog is a danger to itself. When Champ broke out of his crate, he scraped up his nose and could have easily damaged or broken teeth or a nail. Those injuries are more serious than bending up a crate, which can be replaced at a lesser expense and cause less pain than fixing a broken tooth or nail.

Other things to consider are the dog's comfort. If it is in pain, the owner and veterinarian must determine if there are treatments to relieve the pain. Some dogs don't show signs of pain until they can no longer hide it, so by the time the owner notices the dog in pain, it can be significant. Pets with severe or chronic pain are often thought to be anxious or restless. Pain can hinder normal behaviors and hasten abnormal behaviors and can greatly interfere with the quality of life for both pets and their owners. Research indicates that chronic pain is linked with emotional and cognitive changes and can change the brain on both a structural and functional level, contributing to the development of or increase in emotional and cognitive issues in humans and animals.[35] Various studies with animals have found that molecular and cellular changes in the hippocampus, the region of the brain that plays a large role in both learning and memory, in animals with chronic pain led to behavior changes, including increased anxiety and an inability to stop fear.[36]

In our case, we met Tannenbaum's three criteria to justify euthanasia: Our veterinarians and trainers had told us there was nothing more they could do for Champ; while he was in some physical pain, he also was in a lot of emotional pain from his severe anxiety; and I was able to make a rational decision based on my observations and recommendations from the professionals. Although I could look at the logical reasons that it was time and had the support of those who were closest to him, it did not make the decision any easier. And as Dr. Jen wrote, "There are far worse things in the world than a kind and peaceful euthanasia. ... For some, euthanasia is the least awful option there is. Be kind, and don't judge unless you've been there yourself."[37]

Despite this, there are many groups and owners who say that euthanasia is never warranted; that all dogs can be rehabilitated with the "right" training (whatever that is); more patience, more love, more time, more fill in the blank; or that they personally would never euthanize a dog. I received criticism and questioning for euthanizing Champ from people who knew nothing about our situation, as have others who have had to choose behavioral euthanasia for their pets.

So-called "no-kill" shelters do euthanize pets that are suffering from medical or behavioral issues for which there is no cure or solution, affect their quality of life, and prevent them from finding a permanent home.[38] Best Friends Animal Sanctuary in Utah and many other U.S. shelters advocate for saving at least 90 percent of animals in shelters, though some shelters have varying rates. Another shelter's motto is "No Treatable Animal Is Euthanized."[39] While they have guidelines as to what makes a "treatable" animal, some could be open to interpretation, and that is where the controversy enters.

The Fairfax County Animal Shelter in Virginia conducted a test to assess the risks and outcomes of placing dogs that otherwise would have faced euthanasia in foster homes to find them permanent homes. The shelter sent fifty-two dogs identified as having behavior problems in the shelter and labeled as unadoptable or without many options due to their fear-based aggression, resource guarding, bite history, and other issues to foster homes for a few weeks to several months. Forty-nine of the fifty-two dogs were adopted into permanent homes, including six into their foster homes. Two were returned to the shelter after adoption and were euthanized, and three were euthanized prior to being adopted, giving the shelter a "save rate" of 90.4 percent.[40] This figure is in line the 90 percent target adopted by many shelters as "no-kill."

While this is admirable, it is difficult to say whether this could be replicated nationwide. Rescue groups regularly plea via social media and email for foster families for the dogs and cats they rescue. In this study, just sixteen families fostered the fifty-two dogs in a county with more than one million residents. Finding enough qualified foster homes with families willing to take in a dog with behavior problems may prove difficult for shelters in smaller cities or rural areas.

Where does one draw the line for saving or for euthanizing? Why would one euthanize a dog that has never bitten anyone or has "only" bitten once?

"We should not need a dog to incur a major bite or death on their record or develop a long, dangerous rap sheet before thorough safety and welfare considerations are discussed and euthanasia considered when risk of additional or worse incidents or suffering is high," writes Diane of the Beyond the Walk blog. "It is unkind and unfair to keep a dog alive just so we could say we did."[41]

10

Dogs and Emotions

"After years of having a dog, you know him. You know the meaning of his snuffs and grunts and barks. Every twitch of the ears is a question or statement, every wag of the tail is an exclamation."—Robert McCammon[1]

Because humans spend so much time with their pets, they understand their dog's emotions through its body language. Anyone who has lived with a dog or cat knows that they experience happiness, such as when owners return home from work or when they see their dog friends outside; fear, such as the vacuum cleaner or going to the vet; and sadness, such as when the owner leaves for the day or a toy gets taken away. We learn to recognize that a dog pushing its head forward can be a threat, that a head held high shows confidence, or ears pressed back against their head can mean fear or anger.[2] Dogs that are anxious and afraid will crouch down to make themselves look small or nonthreatening, or make themselves look bigger by raising the hair along their spine; tucking the tail; lunging with an open mouth or biting; and showing dilated pupils.[3]

One study of chronic and acute stress in dogs found that acute stress brought on panting, vocalizing, paw lifting, snout licking, and lowering of posture in the test dogs. More severe stress may induce the dogs to salivate more, pant, and suppress urination. These dogs also showed changes in cortisol and cardiovascular performance. However, the researchers were unable to find any indications of chronic or acute stress on the canine immune system and indicated that adaptations to stress indicate reduced welfare or well-being in the dog.[4] In a follow-up study, they found increased shaking or trembling, crouching, licking, yawning, restlessness, and low posture as indications of acute stress in dogs.[5]

In a survey of pet owners, humans said they could recognize nearly 73 percent of dogs' emotions and that dogs recognize about half of human emotions. The owners said they believed dogs could recognize about two-thirds of primary emotions, including anger, fear, surprise, joy/happiness, sadness, anxiety, disgust, interest, love/affection, and curiosity; while only recognizing about 28 percent of secondary emotions, which included empathy, shame, pride, grief, guilt, jealousy, and embarrassment.[6]

English naturalist Charles Darwin believed that emotions connected us with the rest of our community and with the rest of the earth, so it makes sense that animals would have emotions. While he believed there are six universal emotions—anger, happiness, sadness, disgust, fear, and surprise—he also believed that mammals, which include a wide range of animals including house pets, "have a range of emotions similar to humans, including anxiety, grief, dejection, despair, joy, love, 'tender feelings,' devotion, ill temper, sulkiness, determination, hatred, anger, disdain, contempt, disgust, guilt, pride, helplessness, patience, surprise, astonishment, fear, horror, shame, shyness, and modesty."[7]

We may not recognize all these emotions in our pets, but we can mostly likely recognize suffering, anger, and fear. What we see on the outside tells us a lot about what is going on inside.[8] Anger and fear may show as aggression, while suffering may trigger empathy from others.[9] Pain is typically accompanied by different sounds, such as whining, or shying away from touch; anger is accompanied by growling or barking; and fear is evident by a dog tucking its tail between their legs or crouching.[10] They show excitement by jumping and spinning in circles. Dogs also can mask their emotions and feelings, particularly pain. Often a dog will hide its pain until it becomes too great to bear.

Csányi Volmos, PhD, a Hungarian ethologist who wrote about the canine mind, provided the most important signs that offer insight into a dog's mind: tail wagging, nudging with the nose, pointing with a glance, glancing, eye contact, pointing with the head, requests, questions, complaints, "no," vocalization, immobility, resentment, and miming.[11] Owners must pay close attention to the questions and requests made by their dogs, he writes, or they will stop asking. Highly trained and disciplined dogs are often discouraged from asking questions, instead following the rules as they have been trained.

The various sounds that our pets make all relay a message, and it's our job to learn what that is. A cat's purr usually means it is content, while a meow could mean a variety of things. Dogs bark, whine, growl, and yip in various ways. These sounds can tell us what they are feeling. For instance, a dog who is lonely or bored may howl, bark, jump or nudge humans, or chew or destroy objects. Dogs or cats who are afraid may hide, eliminate in the house, or become suddenly aggressive.

Animals, including dogs, are thought to have a "theory of mind," or the idea of a sense of self—the recognition that others have beliefs, aims, and desires different from our own. This theory of mind then allows animals to experience secondary emotions, such as affection or jealousy.[12] While it can be hard to believe dogs are capable of jealousy, they certainly are. Champ could not tolerate Dan hugging me. Champ would whine, cry, and jump up to get in between us.

Emotions affect a person or animal's relationship with its environment, writes animal behaviorist Daniel S. Mills, PhD, professor of veterinary behavioral medicine at the University of Lincoln in the UK. Emotions affect perception, processing, and voluntary and involuntary processes and provide the basis of the study of individual differences in perception, cognition, and behavior.[13]

How do dogs learn emotions? Many animal behaviorists say they learn from watching humans. One study in Ireland of people who owned "aggressive" dog breeds, including German Shepherd Dogs and Rottweilers, were found to be more aggressive themselves and have more "psychotic tendencies" than owners of "nonaggressive" breeds, such as Golden Retrievers and Labrador Retrievers.[14] In addition, male owners of "aggressive" dogs had lower neuroticism scores (characteristics including anxiety, depression, moodiness, and low self-esteem) than female owners of either "aggressive" or "non-aggressive" dogs.

Larger dogs, such as Labrador Retrievers, German Shepherd Dogs, and other large breeds are more at risk for fearfulness, as well as for anxiety-related conditions such as thunderstorm phobia and lick granuloma, which occurs when a dog obsessively licks a spot on a limb to the point of rawness and infection, Dodman writes.[15]

Dodman asserts that dogs acquire fear from adverse early exposure to a fearful incident, person, or dog.[16] "Fears once learned are never forgotten, although it is possible to ease them by superimposing new learning, with or without the help of medication," Dodman wrote.[17]

Animals and people have the same emotional systems in the brain, researchers have found. In a fifty-page paper that analyzed animal models of human psychiatric disorders, veterinary behaviorist Karen Overall, DVM, found that dogs develop comparable and possibly the same disorders as human psychiatric disorders, including generalized anxiety disorder, attachment disorders, social phobia, obsessive-compulsive disorder, post-traumatic stress disorder (PTSD), panic disorder, Alzheimer's disease, and aggressive impulse control disorders.[18]

Interestingly, some of the physical characteristics of these disorders are the same in humans and dogs, Overall writes. For example, in human generalized anxiety disorder, a person's muscle tension increases, and he or she experiences restlessness, fatigue, sleep disturbances, and irritability, all things also seen in dogs with separation anxiety and hypervigilance. However, she said while veterinary behaviorists have no idea how common the general anxiety disorder diagnosis is in dogs, it may be more common than thought due to the large numbers of dogs given up and euthanized every year.[19]

That makes perfect sense because there are many dogs with similar issues as Champ, and not all of them can be evaluated by a veterinary behaviorist, simply because there aren't enough veterinary behaviorists in the U.S. or the world. In early 2022, there were only 80 board-certified veterinary behaviorists of the American College of Veterinary Behaviorists.[20] In addition, there are few veterinary behavior programs at U.S. veterinary schools. A general veterinarian may attempt to treat the issues, but if those treatments don't work, the owners may give up and either surrender the dog to a shelter or to another owner or choose behavioral euthanasia, though they may not be aware of the term.

Panksepp studied emotions in humans and animals and developed the term affective neuroscience to explain the brain's activities behind emotion. He wrote that what science understands about fear came from research on the brains of animals that showed that the capacity to experience fear comes from a fear circuit that circulates between the central amygdala and a section of the midbrain. These fear behaviors can be artificially produced by activating the circuit, and conditioned fears can be developed by pairing neutral stimuli with unconditional stimuli, such as an electric shock, that can arouse the emotional system.[21]

A study of German Shepherd Dogs that were being trained as guard dogs with electric shock collars found that the dogs exhibited lower body posture; high-pitched yelps and barks; avoidance; redirection aggression; and flicking of the tongue. When allowed to walk freely on the training grounds without the collar on, the dogs that had been trained with the electric collars showed stress signals and lower ear posture than dogs that had received similar training without the use of the electric collars.[22]

I recall how Champ's anxiety skyrocketed during the short period that we used the electronic collar on the advice of the trainers we were using before we started working with Dr. Koch and Linda. The trainer we were working with at the time told us it would pull his attention away from whatever stimulus was triggering him, but instead, it aroused his emotional system and made him even more fearful. In the video that we sent to Dr. Koch before our first visit that showed Champ's reactivity, I can tell when I pressed the button on the electric collar remote because Champ turned around and snapped at my left hand that was holding the leash, a clear behavior of redirection aggression. I was wearing gloves, so no damage was done, but he was letting me know he did not like that shock. It did redirect his attention away from the other dog only for a split second, and he redirected his frustration, aggression, and fear on the source of the shock—my hand. We stopped using the collar shortly after that. While I understand electronic collars have a purpose in the right context, for Champ, it was not the right tool.

Panksepp indicates there are other types of feelings that may contribute to the intensity of fear, including pain, hunger, and thirst. Pain also plays a big role in anxiety. Animals learn to escape from and avoid places where they have been hurt, he writes. However, during fearful episodes, neither animals nor humans focus on their pain.[23]

"There remains little doubt that there exists a highly coherent fear system in the brain that contributes substantially to the overall emotional response that we typically call anxiety, as well as to more intense forms of terror and dread," Panksepp writes.

The Monks of New Skete became well-known for raising and training German Shepherd Dogs at their monastery in New York and have written several books on dog training. They promote the "pack leader" theory, which has become somewhat controversial. In their book *Let Dogs Be Dogs*, they share their ideas on how to treat anxious dogs. At first, they attribute anxiety in dogs to a "lack of structure,"[24] which can be true in some cases, but not in dogs like Champ. They note that some breeds, such as herding breeds, seem to be predisposed to anxiety from places or people that they associate with loud noises, such as a construction site or a garbage truck worker, indicating that the dog learns to be anxious after experiencing trauma that he associates with the noise.[25]

In addition, they indicate that phobia produces anxiety. "It is understandable that a dog that has spent a year chained to a tree might fear storms and lawn mowers. Yet there are dogs that feel anxiety most or all the time even though there is no specific reason for it,"[26] they write. Since Champ was kept on a five-foot chain for at least several

130

months, it's easy to understand how he might become phobic to loud noises or strange people. He never reacted to fireworks or thunderstorms, but would react to other noises, such as car doors closing outside or the neighbor rolling his trashcan down the driveway. He had constant anxiety, and there was a reason for it, though we never determined exactly what it was.

The Monks of New Skete use an analogy to compare some dogs who react strongly to emotional changes in their environment to a box of baking soda used to absorb odors in the refrigerator. At some point, it becomes saturated with odors and must be discarded. Some dogs, they say, will absorb emotions all around them, and when it becomes saturated, it begins to exhibit symptoms such as trembling, constant whining, sudden-onset crate phobia, house soiling, destructive chewing habits, new leash aggression, and vocalizing. Families often punish or rehome the dogs when it gets to this stage because they can't cope with the behaviors.[27] The Monks claim that they can "cleanse the mental state" of these dogs and "restore them to mental health and good behavior."

I appreciate their optimism, but my own experience leaves me skeptical. While I believe that restoring mental health is possible with some dogs, I don't think it's possible with all dogs due to underlying mental or physical issues. Those are the dogs whose lives end with behavioral euthanasia.

A study by Therese Rehn, PhD, a small-animal researcher at the Swedish University of Agricultural Sciences, looked at how adults' attachment style, or how they perceive their relationship with other people, influences how their dog interacts and obtains support from them during challenging events. They exposed owners and their dogs to different situations, including visual surprise, an auditory stressor, and social stressors, such as a person approaching dressed in costume or in a coat, hat, and sunglasses. The dog also was left alone in a new environment for three minutes. They found that the more anxious the owners, the longer the dog oriented toward the owner when the strange person approached and showed less lip licking, a classic sign of stress in dogs, when the dog was separated from the owner. If the owner had a more avoidant attachment style, which tends to avoid dealing with his or her feelings, the longer the dog oriented toward the owner when the visual stressor was presented. But during the auditory stressor, it was less likely to go behind the owner. "These links between owner attachment style and dog behavior imply that dogs may develop different strategies to handle challenging situations, based on the type of support they get from their owner," the study found.[28]

Another study found that while dogs' personalities had little effects on their cortisol levels, or stress hormone, the human personality traits of neuroticism, conscientiousness, and openness significantly affected the cortisol levels in dogs, suggesting that dogs mirror the stress level of their owners.[29]

The American College of Veterinary Behaviorists said it's common for humans to feel stress, fear, and anxiety when feeling challenged or threatened and even to become aggressive. They explain that the part of the brain that is responsible for these emotions, the limbic system, is similar in humans and dogs, therefore it is likely that dogs experience these emotions in the same way we do.[30] Dodman concurs, writing that other mammals have similar brains as humans, so it's understandable that animals respond to incoming sensory information in similar ways. "Under the hood, so to speak, in terms of the nervous system or other organ systems, there is not much difference in how things work," he wrote.[31]

In her book *Animals Make Us Human*, Grandin, who has studied the behavior of dogs, cats, cattle and other farm animals, zoo animals and more, wrote that "the environment that animals live in should activate their positive emotions as much as possible and not activate their negative emotions any more than necessary."[32]

The late Kevin Behan of Natural Dog Training wrote that a dog's behavior and personality are a manifestation and expression of emotion and feelings it is picking up from the ones with whom it has bonded. "I now see a dog as a living, walking, breathing sonogram of the emotional dynamic within its owner," Behan wrote.[33] "I truly believe that one's entire life story can be deduced from understanding one's dog. When we see a problem behavior in a dog, before we set out to fix the messenger, we might first take care to hear the message. No one knows better than what we feel ourselves. But we must always remember, whatever a dog does, it's never about the dog. It's always about us."[34]

Behan implies that emotionally troubled dogs are that way because their owners are also emotionally troubled. By this implication, then, emotionally troubled Champ would have been that way because either his first owner(s) were or I was emotionally troubled. I am not, and I have no way of knowing whether his first owners were. Given the number of emotionally troubled dogs that end up in shelters and in rescue each year, that would indicate a lot of emotionally troubled people in the world.

But we can learn from animals and learn about ourselves through animals. We can learn about our ability to nurture, to care for another besides ourselves, and our patience thresholds. We learn to put another before ourselves and to consider the unique personalities of our pets. And we learn love.

However, as suggests the title of Behan's book, *Your Dog Is Your Mirror*, I do agree with him that dogs can read what is going on within their owner and pick up on the energy. I believe cats can, as well. I also agree that dogs learn from humans through observation, which allows them to follow the rules of the family.[35] Dogs can pick up on whether we are happy, stressed, afraid, or sad. Any pet owner will tell you that when they are having a bad day, their dog or cat will comfort them without being asked—they simply seem to know when their owner needs them. They can do this in most humans, not solely their owners, and they are good judges of character. Dogs who are trained as therapy dogs seem to choose people most in need of their attention.

A study released in early 2022 looked at the influence of dogs on cognitive health in older adults. Of more than 1,300 participants with normal cognitive function, more than half owned pets. They had lower incidence of high blood pressure, but higher rates of depression compared with non-pet owners. Over six years, the non-pet owners had a cognitive score that declined by 0.21 points, compared with 0.08 points in pet owners. The researchers concluded that long-term pet ownership could lessen cognitive decline in older adults.[36]

Interaction between humans and dogs results in a release of oxytocin, a hormone involved in social bonding and can regulate emotional responses such empathy, trust, and relationship-building in both humans and dogs. Human-dog interaction also results in reduced cortisol levels and blood pressure. This goes back as far as when dogs were domesticated. A 2015 study in *Science* showed that when dogs gaze into their owner's eyes, the owner's level of oxytocin goes up. Likewise, when dogs are given oxytocin, it increased their gazing behavior, which also increased oxytocin levels in their owners. The findings indicate a kind of positive loop facilitated by gazing, which supports the idea of human-dog bonding by using common forms of communicating attachment.[37]

A similar study found a correlation between oxytocin and cortisol levels in dogs and owners. Owners with high oxytocin levels may have a more caring and interactive personality and a more positive attitude towards their dogs. Likewise, dogs with high oxytocin levels may be more interactive and more sensitive to their owners' physiological and mental status. The relationship between the dog and its owner may induce long-term, secondary endocrine changes, resulting in increased oxytocin levels.[38] Conversely, owners who had lower levels of cortisol perceived that it would be more traumatic when their dog died.

A study in Portugal of more than 1,000 pet owners suggests that owners' trait anxiety is associated with their dogs' fear and anxiety-related behavior problems, and the level of empathy, or emotional reactivity to owners' emotions, the dogs show their owners may contribute to that. Owners who reported their own anxiety also reported more fear and anxiety-related behaviors in their dogs, such as fear of strangers.[39]

"Fear- and anxiety-related disorders are among the most common behavior disorders in humans and can lead to deleterious effects on health and lifespan in dogs, not to mention negative effects on the owners' emotions," the authors wrote.[40]

Fear is innate in mammals, including in canines. The late novelist Jack London wrote about fear in a wolf in *White Fang*:

> By the time his mother began leaving the cave on hunting expeditions, the cub had learned well the law that forbade his approaching the entrance. Not only had this law been forcibly and many times impressed on him by his mother's nose and paw, but in him the instinct of fear was developing. Never, in his brief cave-life, had he encountered anything of which to be afraid. Yet fear was in him. It had come down to him from a remote ancestry through a thousand thousand lives. It was a heritage he had received directly from One Eye and the she-wolf; but to them, in turn, it had been passed down through all the generations of wolves that had gone before. Fear!—that legacy of the Wild which no animal may escape nor exchange for pottage. So the grey cub knew fear, though he knew not the stuff of which fear was made.[41]

Panksepp called core emotion systems "blue-ribbon emotions" because when the corresponding parts of the brain are stimulated, they always generate the same behaviors from the animal. One of these blue-ribbon emotions is fear, which animals and humans feel when their survival is threatened.[42] The other blue-ribbon emotions are seeing, the basic impulse to make sense of one's environment; rage; panic; lust; care; and play.

A dog's early life experiences, including social exposure in different environments, between the ages of three to twelve weeks play a critical role in their future behavior. A study by British researchers found that the puppy's home environment is critical for its behavioral development in nine of eleven environmental variables, including trainability, distractibility, general anxiety, body sensitivity, stair anxiety, excitability, separation-related behavior, attachment, and attention seeking. Among those nine, the most important were the social variables, such as trainability and excitability.[43]

While many dogs are good at picking up on the emotions and expressions of their owners, there are others whose early life did not give them that experience. Dogs from puppy mills frequently have difficulty making an emotional connection. In a study conducted by the Center for Shelter Dogs at Tufts University Cummings School of Veterinary Medicine of more than 1,000 puppy mill dogs that had been adopted into homes, researchers found that they showed much higher rates of fear to unfamiliar people and dogs and to noises and motions in their environment; house soiling; staring blankly into space; and lower rates of trainability and energy. They also showed about half of the level of aggression that typical pet dogs do toward unfamiliar people and dogs and to their owner due to the high levels of fear. They found that dogs from puppy mills develop extreme and persistent fears and phobias; altered mental functioning; compulsive behaviors; and often have difficulty coping with normal life.[44]

Can dogs and cats suffer from stress? Absolutely, though it is not often the same stress as humans experience. One of the definitions of stress is "a physical, chemical, or emotional factor that causes bodily or mental tension and may be a factor in disease causation."[45] But there is also distress, defined as "pain or suffering affecting the body, a bodily part, or the mind."[46] In distress, the perception of the effort needed to return the body to a normal, healthy state brings about suffering.[47] This is what I believe pets with behavior issues suffer, either temporarily or permanently.

As with humans, pain or physical discomfort can lead to distress in a pet, often changing their behavior in subtle ways, such as staring; compulsive disorders; eating nonfood items; hypersensitivity to heat or cold; increased need for attention from the owner.[48] Reisner wrote that disease is expressed behaviorally through irritability, lethargy, or changes in activity or appetite.[49] Pets can experience distress from difficult relationships at home, for instance, if their owners are frequently fighting, yelling at another pet in the home, or if there are noisy children or teenagers. Loud noises, such as thunder, fireworks, or sirens frequently cause animals distress, so much that more pets go missing during July 4–5 every year in the U.S. due to fireworks than any other days of the year.[50]

Reactivity to noises can have severe, lifelong implications for many dogs, particularly working and service dogs. Surveys have shown up to half of all dogs experience some noise reactivity in their lifetime, whether to fireworks, thunderstorms, or gunshots, and that it often is accompanied by anxiety disorders. A study of noise reactivity by Overall analyzed three breeds of herding dogs commonly used for work and/or service: Australian Shepherds, Border Collies and German Shepherd Dogs. The Border Collies and Australian Shepherds were more severely affected by the sounds of gunshots, storms, and fireworks than the German Shepherd Dogs.[51]

Car rides can cause stress to pets, frequently leading to vomiting or elimination in the car. Some pets get extremely stressed from being confined, whether in a bedroom, bathroom, crate, or carrier. Visits to the veterinarian or groomer also can cause a pet stress. And when humans have stress or distress, they naturally want to feel better, so it follows that animals would want the same thing.

Scientists are beginning to study whether animals can have mental illnesses and are looking at mutations in certain genes in the brain that play a role in disrupting behavior. They have found these genetic changes related to mental illness in both vertebrate and invertebrate animals, attributing mental disorders as the price animals pay for their intelligence.[52]

All these things can lead to behavior issues: fear, anxiety, aggression, reactivity, and compulsive behaviors, such as excessive water drinking, tail chasing, lick granulomas, and sucking on blankets. While these can sometimes be solved with behavior modification and medications, sometimes they cannot, as with Champ and many others like him.

Grandin uses the term "stereotypies" to describe abnormal repetitive behaviors, such as pacing in the same pattern. She writes that abnormal repetitive behavior means one of three things: the animal is suffering; the animal was suffering in the past but isn't now; or the animal is in better shape than the other animals in the same facility that are not stereotyping. In this case, the repetitive behavior may be a way for the animal to soothe itself, while another animal may have given up, reinforcing the fact that all animals are individuals.[53] Two dogs in the same situation may react completely differently.

Dodman ranked tendencies for various behaviors by breed based on dogs he sees in his clinic. German Shepherd Dogs ranked in the top four for biting, lethal attacks, acral lick dermatitis, fly snapping, tail chasing, and chasing things, while herding breeds in general were often seen for fearful behavior.[54] Given these statistics from just one U.S. clinic, it seems likely that there is some genetic link that would cause so many similar behaviors in German Shepherd Dogs.

In the United States, Canada, and Australia, aggression is the most common reason for referrals to veterinary behavior specialty clinics, followed by anxiety and fear-related problems or phobia.[55]

Aggression, defined as "hostile, injurious, or destructive behavior toward an individual, whether human or another animal," can be caused by several factors, including early environment, genetics, learning from past experiences, health (medical and behavioral), fear, reactivity, resource guarding and training.[56,57] It was the top behavior problem reported in dogs ranked by both age and size, according to the medical records of nearly 2.3 million dogs treated at more than 850 Banfield Pet Hospitals in 2013.[58] It is a public safety concern for humans and animals and has a direct impact on the well-being of the dog and the humans in its life.

There are various types of aggression: dominance aggression, the challenge to the dog's control of a social interaction; fear aggression, the defensive reaction that occurs when the dog believes it is in danger; prey aggression, or prey drive, toward cats, squirrels, rabbits, etc.; territorial aggression, the defense of what the dog sees as his property; protective aggression directed toward perceived threats to the dog's family; possessive aggression, when a dog is defending its possessions; and redirected aggression.[59] Other researchers frequently refer to owner-directed aggression, or aggressive behavior toward people who are familiar to the dog. This type of aggression is the most common cause of dog bite injuries reported. They also refer to stranger-directed aggression and dog-directed aggression.[60]

Canine dominance aggression is about control or access to control in situations involving humans, such as postural threats, staring, and biting, often without warning. In these cases, dogs will act aggressively if they are physically disrupted or even when having a leash attached.[61]

One New Jersey dog trainer previously involved in rescue put it this way: "Whether the aggressive behaviors are rooted in 'offensive' aggression or defensive aggression (fear-based, resource guarding, undiagnosed or inoperable pain), dogs that feel they must behave aggressively do not feel good mentally and emotionally (or even physically, as displays of aggression can be taxing and physically uncomfortable)."[62]

Ádám Miklósi, PhD, an ethologist in Hungary and cofounder and leader of the Family Dog Project, wrote that aggressive behavior in social species is a way to communicate and does not necessarily mean physical aggression. Dogs get into a fight if there is no other solution, he wrote.[63]

Most aggressive behaviors are fear-related, he said, and are an attempt to protect food, a toy, or a place to sleep. Females are more likely to initiate aggression within the household, while males are more likely to initiate aggression with dogs outside of the household. Aggression toward humans has declined since dogs were domesticated, however, dogs with aggression toward humans present public health and animal welfare concerns.[64] It can impact the dog's relationship with humans in and out of the house and result in a life with less enrichment.

Aggression is one of the main things that animal shelters test for in temperament tests, because a dog with aggression issues—real or perceived—is likely to be returned. While some of this testing can be useful, it's not a perfect system, because some dogs act differently in a shelter setting than outside of a shelter setting. A 2007 study of temperament testing given to dogs with aggressive tendencies in animal shelters showed that nearly 41 percent of the dogs who had passed a pre-adoption temperament test were lunging, growling, snapping and/or biting a year after adoption. Adding barking to the mix brought the percentage up to 71.2 percent. More than half of the dogs were female, and all but a few were either strays or surrendered by a previous owner. The researchers concluded that the temperament test failed to identify certain types of aggression.[65]

Before we adopted Champ, he was in a boarding kennel for two weeks, where he showed no aggression toward people or dogs, we were told. However, when we brought him home, he immediately showed aggression toward both. Conversely, some dogs show fear aggression in the shelters, but when they are in a home setting, they have none.

A study based on C-BARQ results looking at risk factors associated with stranger-directed aggression in dogs found that adult dogs were more likely to be aggressive compared with younger or senior dogs. In addition, they were less likely to be aggressive if acquired as an adult as compared with as a puppy or younger dog. Dogs were more likely to show stranger-directed aggression if the owner rated them as mildly or severely fearful of strangers, or when mildly fearful in nonsocial situation when compared with dogs without fear. Neutered males were more likely to be aggressive than any other group.[66]

The study also found that dogs acquired from pet stores, friends, or relatives were more likely to be reported as aggressive than those obtained from breeders, and dogs from shelters or other sources or strays were more likely to show severe aggression.[67] This could go back to the maternal and early life stress impacting the HPA axis, which eventually influences behavior in animals.

The researchers also looked at common pure breeds of dogs for risks of aggression. German Shepherd Dogs had increased risks of aggression in all the studies they investigated. "German Shepherds, and other herding breeds, might be more likely to act aggressively due to differences in how they are raised and trained, as well as the types of people who choose to own this breed. German Shepherds are a popular breed for protection and guarding roles, and therefore owners may encourage aggressive behaviors towards strangers."[68]

Again, while this may be true in some cases, it is a statement by the researchers and not a universal truth of German Shepherd Dog owners nor of German Shepherd Dogs.

Male dogs with stranger-directed aggression were more likely to bite or attempt to bite than female dogs. Each year, it is estimated that about 1.5 percent of people in the United States will be bitten by a dog, with 0.3 percent of those requiring medical attention. More than one-third of those bites are toward people with no relationship with the dog. Dogs that bite may have low bite inhibition or impulse control, get pushed beyond their comfort level, or have learned that biting is the only way to protect themselves.[69]

Another study based on C-BARQ data from two sources of data— one a random sample of breed club members and another found online—resulted in significant differences among breeds in aggression toward strangers, owners, and dogs. Eight breeds in both sets of data— Dachshund, English Springer Spaniel, Golden Retriever, Labrador Retriever, Poodle, Rottweiler, Shetland Sheepdog, and Siberian Husky— ranked similarly for aggression directed toward strangers, dogs, and owners, respectively. Dachshunds, Chihuahuas, and Jack Russell Terriers had the greatest percentage of dogs showing serious aggression, such as bites or bite attempts, toward strangers and owners. More than 20 percent of Akitas, Jack Russell Terriers, and Pit Bull Terriers were reported as displaying serious aggression toward unfamiliar dogs.[70]

The researchers also found an interesting balance of fear and aggression behind the aggressive behavior in the different breeds. Some breeds, including Doberman Pinschers, Jack Russell Terriers, West Highland White Terriers, Australian Cattle Dogs, and German Shepherd Dogs, were more aggressive than fearful toward strangers, which they attributed to their heritage as working dogs that require protection, herding, and hunting.[71]

"Differences between lines of distinct breeding stock indicate that the propensity toward aggressive behavior is at least partially rooted in genetics, although substantial within-breed variation suggests that other factors (developmental, environmental) play a major part in determining whether aggressive behavior is expressed in the phenotype," the authors concluded.[72]

A study in Sweden of 503 German Shepherd Dogs evaluated how experiences in the first part of their lives contributed to shaping their long-term behavior, particularly in a stressful situation. When the dogs were between roughly one year and about 1½ years old, they were given temperament tests in four major areas, including confidence, physical engagement, social engagement, and aggression, to assess whether they would be suitable as working dogs. They found that confidence and physical engagement were influenced by the number of litters per mother, growth rate, litter size, and season of birth, while aggression was affected by sex. Social engagement was affected by growth rate and sex. Ultimately, they determined that the first few weeks of life would partly cause life-long adaptations in the way in which these dogs reacted to stressful stimuli.[73]

In Australia, researchers proposed that studying the personality of dogs may help to predict their behavior and help owners manage it. They argue that taking a closer look at the way we interact with and keep animals has the potential to improve animal welfare and improve human-animal interactions. They also claim that every year, "we destroy a significant percentage of the domestic dog population because we find its behavior unacceptable."[74] While genetics play a role in some behavior problems, such as anxiety, the study focused on coping styles, the personality of dogs, and specific behaviors and personality traits. In particular, it focused on boldness, in which researchers included such behaviors as interest in unfamiliar people; playfulness with a variety of dogs or people; fear of noises, unfamiliar dogs or people, or in familiar and unfamiliar situations. In their survey of more than 1,000 dog owners, they found that the age and gender of the owner, the origin of the dog or age when adopted were not factors in the dog's boldness.

Male dogs were bolder than females, and intact dogs were bolder than those that had been spayed or neutered. Boldness decreased with age. The three breeds that were the boldest were, in order, Staffordshire Bull Terrier, Labrador Retriever, and German Shepherd Dog, while the three least bold breeds were Australian Cattle Dog, Jack Russell Terrier, and Greyhound. Ultimately, they found that sociability and playfulness are associated with boldness.[75]

A study by Australian researchers looked at the "big five" personality traits for dogs, including extraversion, neuroticism, self-assuredness/motivation, training focus, and amicability. While they found that extraversion and neuroticism were found in other animals, the other three traits were unique to canines and may reflect their interactions with humans.[76]

Another study found a different top five personality traits, which included energy level; learning, obedience-training ability and problem-solving; sociability; stability vs. excitability; and dominance and territoriality.[77] Coren then classified nearly every breed of dog in each category. German Shepherd Dogs, a member of the herding dog group, rated very high in dominance/territoriality and in intelligence/learning ability; moderately low in emotional reactivity; and moderately high in sociability and energy. Golden Retrievers, a member of the sporting dog group, were rated very low in dominance/territoriality; very high in intelligence/learning ability and sociability; and moderately low in emotional reactivity and energy.[78] Emotional reactivity includes excitability, general activity, snapping at children, excessive barking, demanding affection, and fearfulness or distress.

An interesting study by British researchers compared the facial characteristics of ten breeds of dogs with their behavior. The breeds that shared the most facial characteristics with wolves, such as the Siberian Husky, had more wolf-like behaviors than breeds that did not, such as the Cavalier King Charles Spaniel. The dogs were evaluated for behaviors including growling, showing teeth, and staring, as well as for more submissive behaviors, including licking the muzzle, or looking away. Interestingly, the German Shepherd Dogs, which were deliberately bred to look more like a wolf, showed fewer wolf-type signals than the Siberian Husky, which showed all fifteen of the wolf-like behaviors, or the Golden Retriever, which showed twelve of fifteen behaviors.[79]

Another study evaluated three breeds—Cavalier King Charles Spaniels, Yorkshire Terriers, and German Shepherd Dogs—to identify the onset of fear-related avoidance behavior and to look at the differences in the behavioral development of each breed. Nearly one hundred purebred puppies were evaluated in four tests from age four to five weeks to ten weeks. Their salivary cortisol was measured before and after testing. The onset of fear-related avoidance behavior was later in the Cavalier King Charles Spaniel (fifty-five days) compared with the German Shepherd Dog (thirty-nine days) and Yorkshire Terrier (forty-two days) puppies. The authors suspected that the slower development rate of the Cavalier King Charles Spaniel was the reason. Cavalier King Charles Spaniel puppies that showed fear-related avoidance behavior had a larger percentage change in cortisol before and after testing than those puppies that did not exhibit the behavior.[80]

A study of more than nine hundred dogs identified to have at least one form of aggression examined the effectiveness of various treatments for canine aggression. More than 80 percent of owners who sought help from a veterinarian certified by the American College of Veterinary Behaviorists said it was helpful. About 15 percent of dogs taken to their veterinarian for behavior problems were found to have an underlying health issue. Improved communication between the dog and the owner, relaxation protocols, and short and frequent training sessions were the most consistently beneficial behavior modification techniques, the study found.[81] While more than half of the dogs were of mixed breed, the most common breeds represented in that study were German Shepherd Dogs, Labrador Retrievers, Border Collies, Golden Retrievers, Dachshunds, Chihuahuas, Poodles, Cocker Spaniels, Australian Shepherds, and Pembroke Welsh Corgis. Fifty-six percent were male, and 91 percent of all were neutered. The median age was 9.5 months. Twenty-one percent of dogs received medication as a form of treatment for aggression, but the researchers did not find any significant associations between treatment response and treatment with specific medications.

One rescued mixed breed dog was taken to its veterinarian after two years of worsening aggression and behavior changes. After a slew of bloodwork, the veterinarians found elevated antibodies that suggested gluten sensitivity. The dog was changed to a gluten-free hydrolyzed protein diet, and its aggression stopped within about four days.[82] While this is a rare finding, it does show the importance of ruling out medical causes for behavior changes.

In one study of more than five hundred dog owners, all of them reported at least one behavior problem. More than 60 percent reported some form of anxiety or fear, while more than 33 percent reported aggression toward people or animals. These same owners were asked about using medications for their dog's behavior problem. Twenty-six percent of owners said they would consider giving their dogs medications or supplements for behavior problems, while 56 percent said maybe, and 17 percent said they would not. Ninety percent said that proven effectiveness was important to consider when deciding whether to use psychoactive medications, followed by how easy it was to give the drug to their pet, their veterinarian's recommendation, and cost. Respondents overall were most comfortable giving herbal or nutritional supplements over medications, pheromonal products and CBD products. They reported concern about side effects of medications, including sedation, potential for addiction, and a negative change in the dog's personality. Interestingly, social stigma from giving their dogs these medications was not reported a concern.[83]

Another study of owners of more than four thousand dogs found that owners reported behavior problems in 85 percent of dogs, ranging from everything from anxiety to house soiling to excessive barking to running away. The found that the sex, neuter status, origin, and lineage to have a notable effect on the prevalence of behavior problems and the number of behavior problems per dog. The top five behavior problems reported were fear/anxiety, aggression, jumping, excessive barking, and feces eating. Male dogs were slightly more likely to have behavior problems than females, and neutered males and females were almost twice as likely to exhibit behavior problems as intact dogs. The study indicated that with this information, veterinarians may incorporate some behavior problem management into their work, which would have major implications on the welfare of dogs and could reduce the number of dogs surrendered to shelters for behavior reasons as well as euthanasia.[84]

Fear aggression is often found in fearful and insecure dogs that feel like they must fend off threats. Their philosophy, according to Dodman, is that a good offense is the best defense.[85]

Dodman said it is often possible to identify a point in these dogs' lives when they were exposed to an unpleasant experience involving another dog or a human. "In post-traumatic stress syndrome, a single catastrophic incident has effects that are usually lifelong," he writes. "Burns of epinephrine released during the traumatic incident are instrumental in making the memory indelible."

Champ was aggressive and reactive outside of our home and yard because he was afraid. He was afraid of everything—people, other dogs, leaves crunching under someone's feet, riding in the car, and so many other things. He got aggressive when he was afraid so that people and dogs would stay away from him. And it worked all too well. He was so big and out of control that no one but us wanted to be around him.

Over the past few years, I've been studying the effects of trauma on the body and the brain. The things that happen in our lives are indelibly stamped in our mind, even though we might not be able to recall them immediately. For example, one of my earliest memories is a car accident my family was in when I was four or five years old. I was sitting in the back seat of our Chevrolet Chevelle drinking a red Mr. Misty from Dairy Queen. My dad was driving, and my mom was holding my brother on her lap in the passenger seat (this was before car seats). A wrong-way driver hit us, and my brother hit his head on the windshield or dashboard. I remember crying because my Mr. Misty spilled all over me in the back seat. I didn't realize I remembered this until I saw a similar Chevy Chevelle at a car show recently and told Dan the story. Just the sight of the same type of car triggered that memory in my mind. That was just one incident in my life, so imagine the other memories that are stored in my mind of other things that happened to me—the time in kindergarten or first grade when I stood too close to someone batting on a baseball field and got hit in the eye with the swinging bat and got a black eye; or the time in first grade when my school bus broke down and I walked home along a highway with the older kids from the neighborhood. While those don't qualify as Trauma (capital T), they left an imprint in my mind and unpleasant memories, which could be classified as trauma (lowercase t).

One of the best descriptions of trauma that I have ever heard was an analogy to the patterns that running water makes in dirt. For example, when water runs downhill, it often flows the same way, and over time, it makes a deep indent in the ground so that the water will always take the same pathway. The brain is the same. When we have an experience or a trauma in our life, especially early in life, the brain reacts by making a pathway. Over time, the same indent that develops in the ground from water develops in the brain, so when a trauma is experienced again, the brain takes that same pathway, so we react the same way. It is possible to reroute those pathways with a lot of therapy.

For Champ, whenever he saw another dog, his brain took that pathway that made him fearful and reactive, so he barked aggressively to keep the dog away from him. The same thing happened in his brain when someone walked by the house or when he was noisy and agitated in the car.

10. Dogs and Emotions

Some emotional symptoms of trauma include shock, denial, disbelief, anger, irritability, mood swings, guilt, shame, self-blame, feeling sad or hopeless, confusion, difficulty concentrating, anxiety and fear, withdrawing from others, and feeling disconnected or numb.[86]

There have been studies that suggest there are differences in the effects of trauma on human neurobiology, depending on the stage of development at which the trauma occurs. The normal human brain changes across the lifespan, but researchers can determine the differences between normal changes and those that vary from normal. Three areas of the brain, the amygdala, hippocampus, and prefrontal cortex, show stress response and play a role in memory. Children who were abused and develop PTSD have shown decreased volume in the hippocampus, and studies in rats show that stress affects these brain areas, so it is likely it applies to dogs and other mammals, as well.[87,88]

Newer research into trauma shows chemical changes in the blood, brain, sperm, and ova of mice led to behavior issues, such as anxiety and depression, in later generations. The stress of mice pups being separated from their mother caused changes in their gene expression that could be traced for three generations.[89] This phenomenon, known as intergenerational trauma or transgenerational epigenetic inheritance, has been seen in rats and humans as well, so it is likely that it could also be present in dogs.

11

Behavior Problems and the Owners' Well-Being

"When I look into the eyes of an animal, I do not see an animal. I see a living being. I see a friend. I feel a soul."
—Anthony Douglas Williams[1]

Champ's issues, as well as his care and constant management of his life, took a toll on my well-being and Dan's. Champ's constant anxiety burdened me as the caregiver.

A study of owners of pets with behavioral issues found that many felt the same way. Respondents noted caretaking, emotions, coping strategies, and lack of understanding and support as their primary issues. They noted the extra time it took for management and training, the need to plan to keep the pet and others safe, and limited time away from the home as caretaking issues. Regarding emotions, owners had both positive and negative emotions about the situation, including anger, frustration, stress, worry, fear, and sadness, while at the same time love for their pets and their relationship with their pets. Many reported feeling bad for their pet, while at the same time being embarrassed by its behavior. Respondents also said they found support from friends, family, support groups, veterinarians, and therapists who took the time to learn about their pet's behaviors and how to help. However, many more cited a lack of understanding and support from friends and family, the community, and some who were hired to help the situation but were not understanding or helpful.[2]

Not surprisingly, owners of pets with chronic or terminal illnesses were found to experience more caregiver burden, which is linked to stress, depression, anxiety, and reduced quality of life, than owners of healthy pets. While not specifically included among the chronic illnesses of pets in this study, behavior illnesses in pets should qualify as chronic illnesses because they take the same toll on the owners and caregivers and require as much management as physical illnesses.

This study also found that having a pet with chronic illness could lead to more visits to the veterinarian, which in turn could exacerbate compassion fatigue and distress in already overburdened veterinarians.[3] The authors indicate that they were unable to determine if higher caregiver burden leads to poorer psychological and social functioning, or if these owners already had greater levels of stress, depression, or anxiety symptoms before the animal's diagnosis and therefore found the caregiving more of a burden. Most of the owners in the study had animals that were older, therefore they had owned the pets for longer and their attachment was greater, and it may be more likely that they would choose to provide long-term care for the pets over euthanasia.[4] Owners who participated in this study were primarily white, female, well-educated, had relatively high socioeconomic status, and were an average age of forty-eight years old. Study authors noted that these demographics showed that these participants opted to keep the pet despite of the potentially high financial and personal costs. Many of them also were part of a social media group for owners of chronically ill pets where they sought support.[5]

In a follow-up study, the researchers found greater symptoms of depression, anxiety, and stress, and reduced quality of life in owners of chronically ill pets. The owners reported poor psychological and emotional function than owners of healthy pets. In addition, these owners used more veterinary care, particularly through phone calls and emails that were not billed, than owners of healthy pets. The researchers concluded that more studies are needed to appreciate the characteristics of caregivers of chronically ill pets, which may help to improve patient care and the experience of the owner and caregiver.[6]

The same group of researchers set out to predict caregiver burden in veterinary clients, which may help communication between veterinarians and their clients. They found the most caregiver burden when their pets showed weakness; appeared depressed, anxious, or in pain or showed a change in personality; lethargy; and frequent urination.[7] The authors conclude that reducing the burden on the owner may ultimately benefit the veterinarian, and that future work needs to address how euthanasia impacts the burden of owners.[8]

Another study of owners of chronically ill dogs found that owners reported having to provide extra care, make changes in the use of their home, and implement restrictions relating to work, social life, and finances. It brought changes in their relationship with their dogs, which led to sadness, frustration, guilt, and feelings of loss, as well as concerns about its well-being and potential euthanasia.[9]

The Most Painful Choice

A survey of people in the UK who had dogs diagnosed with osteo-arthritis found similar results, including increasing worry about their pet's condition; the need for and cost of medications and other treatments; the inability to take vacations because of having no one else to care for the dog or being unable to take the dog with them; guilt over the dog's reduced activity level; and physical and emotional burden of the caregiver. However, nearly all the owners surveyed said they were not resentful about the changes their dog's diagnosis brought to their lives.[10]

In addition, all these owners expressed concern over knowing when their dog would need to be euthanized. One owner said, "You can be blind because of loving them so much, so I think you need a bit of help when things get really hard."

This describes my situation exactly. I loved Champ so much, and even when the three professionals caring for him each provided that bit of help when they told me it was time to consider letting him go, I couldn't see their point for another 18 months.

It is truly a helpless feeling when a dog is so ill and there is little one can do. When caring for chronically ill humans, there is often an option for temporary or permanent in-home nursing care or hospitalization. With a chronically ill pet, owners must manage at home with instructions from the veterinarian. This feeling of helplessness is overwhelming at times, and there are only two real choices to deal with it: keep caring for the pet or euthanize. In most studies I found, respondents chose to keep caring for their pets, feeling that the dog deserved everything possible, as considering euthanasia brought on significant distress.[11]

I consider myself extremely lucky that I had a veterinarian, Dr. DeWilde, who was always willing to work with us on Champ's behavior issues and made sure we got into see Dr. Koch. I realize that not everyone has a veterinarian who is willing to work with them. A study in the UK found that very little time at a veterinary visit is spent discussing behavioral issues. At a health problem visit, 90 percent of the conversation was gathering biomedical information. At wellness appointments, such as for annual vaccines and checkups, 50 percent of the conversation was related to information gathering, and 27 percent was on client education. In this particular study, all owners reported a concerning behavior of their pet, such as aggression to people or animals, training, and destruction of property. However, only ten of the fifty-eight problems presented were discussed by the veterinarian, and none of them were further explored or managed after the initial visit.[12]

148

A similar study in the U.S. showed that veterinarians in small animal practices were not addressing behavior problems in dogs and cats as effectively as they could, leading to underdiagnosed and inadequately treated behavior problems and likely more relinquishment of those pets to shelters or euthanasia. Fewer than 75 percent of veterinarians said they routinely discussed a pet's behavior and lacked clinical confidence to treat behavior problems.[13]

This needs to change. There are thousands of animals out there like Champ who need treatment for their behavior disorders and options other than rehoming or surrendering to a shelter, both of which pass the problem on to someone else, or euthanasia. While I realize that veterinarians are overworked, especially now that so many people adopted pets during the Covid-19 pandemic, the mental health and behavior of pets should be a part of every wellness exam. Not every pet will have any behavior issues to be discussed, but questions about behavior should be a routine part of exams. This would help owners to feel validated for their concerns and open the discussion for treatment options. Not every case will be as complex as Champ's. While behavior problems are preferably prevented, some may have a solution that is simple and straightforward and may prevent relinquishment to shelters or eventual euthanasia.

Some researchers in California surveyed dog owners who were surrendering their dog to a shelter about why they chose to do so. Sixty-five percent of the owners said there was a behavior reason that led them to surrender their dog, and nearly half said there was at least one problem behavior that strongly influenced their decision to give up their dog. The researchers also found that the dog owners' level of attachment to, or the interaction with, their pet was much lower than for owners who chose to keep their dogs, most likely because of the dog's behavior problems.[14] The owners who surrendered their dogs were more likely to have always kept the dogs outside and had more children living in the home.

The National Council on Pet Population Study and Policy Regional Shelter Relinquishment Study found that behavior problems, including aggression toward people or animals, were the most frequently given reason for relinquishing a dog and the second most frequently given reason for relinquishing a cat. At least one behavioral reason was given for 40 percent of the dogs and 28 percent of the cats relinquished. In addition, owners surrendering these dogs had them for less than three months before relinquishing them,[15] which is not nearly enough time for a pet to acclimate to its new environment.

The Most Painful Choice

As considerable research has shown that at least some level of positive, reward-based training is related with a decrease in unwanted behaviors, this is an opportunity for more education for owners to address some of these behavior issues and prevent so many dogs from being turned over to shelters, where their problems will likely be passed on to an unsuspecting new owner, or the dog will be euthanized.

In the study that surveyed dog owners about medication use for behavior problems, nearly 97 percent of the owners surveyed said dogs' behavior problems can be based on anxiety or other emotional problems, and 57 percent said their dog had two or more behavior problems. However, only 6 percent of the respondents' veterinarians had referred them to a veterinary behaviorist or nonveterinary animal behaviorist, and only half were aware that psychoactive medications and supplements were available for use in dogs.[16] Delaying treatment for behavior problems prolongs the negative effects on dog's and the owner's well-being. Discussing behavior problems with owners during veterinary visits opens an opportunity for veterinarians to discuss possible treatments for behavior issues and address the owners' concerns about them.

Another study out of the UK found that with certain behavior problems, there is evidence of an association between dominance aggression in the dog and the involvement of the owner, such as considering the dog a family member, talking with the dog, and celebrating its birthday. In addition, there is an association with over-excitement and displacement activities in the dog and anxiety in the owner. Owner anxiety is not associated with a higher incidence of phobias in the dog, but the dog's phobia did cause greater distress to a more anxious owner.[17]

Another study from the early 1990s sought to determine if there was a relationship between behavior problems in dogs and its owners "spoiling" it, treating it like a person, or not providing obedience training. Some of the variables included sharing food with the dog, allowing it to sleep in the bed with owners, and taking the dog on trips. They found no more behavior problems in dogs that met these criteria than dogs that were not "spoiled," treated like a person, or had obedience training.[18]

"Obedience training is certainly of help to many owners in the general management and control of their dog," the authors wrote. "What is apparent, however, is that obedience training does not necessarily result in a behavior-problem-free dog, any more than the lack of obedience training automatically results in a problem-laden dog."[19]

In our case, this was true. Champ had more than three years of weekly training, which included obedience, socialization, agility, tricks, and other exercises that worked his brain. If obedience training had been the cure for his fears, anxiety, or aggression, we would have taken care of his problems fairly quickly.

Some researchers and trainers have associated with fears and phobias in the dog with the owner's "fear transmitted down the leash." For instance, when the owner tightens the leash when he or she sees another dog approaching, the dog feels that tightness and learns to associate it with negativity. A 2021 study in the *Journal of Veterinary Behavior* affirmed this notion, finding that dogs may respond to their owners' anxiety in a sort of empathy. In a survey of more than 1,000 dog owners, they found a significant correlation between the owners' trait anxiety, or when fear and worry are part of a person's personality, and the degree of their dogs' fear and anxiety-related behavior. In addition, they found that owners scoring higher for trait anxiety reported higher fear and anxiety-related behavior problems in their dogs as assessed by the C-BARQ test. They also affirmed other studies that indicated that anxiety aggregates in families, which includes their pets. However, the researchers found that there was no relation between an owner's overprotective behavior or using "coercive" training methods on a pet's anxiety.[20]

Dodman and colleagues also studied whether the owner's personality and psychological well-being influenced their dog's behavior. In surveys of more than 1,500 dog owners, they found associations between owners' use of aversive or confrontational training methods and the severity of various behavior problems, including aggression, separation anxiety, persistent barking, chasing, and house soiling. They also found some association between owners' low scores on four of the "Big Five" personality traits—openness, conscientiousness, extroversion, agreeableness, and neuroticism—and their dogs' more frequent display of aggression, stranger-directed fear, or urination when left alone. They found little evidence that these relationships were enabled by using harsh training methods but did find a significant number of men with moderate depression using confrontational training with their dogs.[21]

Hal Herzog, PhD, a psychologist who studies animals and their behavior, writes that animals are anxious because their owners are anxious. He points to the Dodman study and others conducted worldwide that show that owners who are high in the neuroticism trait had dogs that were more anxious, fearful, or less responsive to training than owners who were lower in this area. While he acknowledges that the anxiety could be traveling from a fearful and anxious dog to the owner, what is more likely, he says, is that neurotic owners partly create anxious dogs.[22]

McConnell writes that while some anxious people may be more attracted to anxious animals, the best hypothesis is what she calls "emotional contagion," or that human emotions are "catching," which activates our dogs' empathy.[23] There are several breeds that are known particularly for their empathy, which makes them excellent candidates for service and therapy dogs.

I believe that in some cases the owner's influence on a dog's behavior is valid. I have seen neighbors who are first-time dog owners get puppies and make numerous mistakes in raising and training them. However, I don't think this is universally true. In our case, Champ was anxious when he came to us. I have no way of knowing if his first owners were anxious, had other psychological problems, or used aversive or abusive training methods—if they did any training with him at all. It's easy for me to blame them, but he also could have been anxious when they got him due to his breeding and weaning situation. He could have come from a puppy mill, a backyard breeder, or some other source where he didn't have a healthy, nurturing environment in his earliest weeks of life. Therefore, I don't think it's entirely fair to blame all owners for dogs' behavior problems.

Conclusion

*"Some people will never understand how much someone
can love a dog, but that's ok—the dog knows."*—Unknown[1]

In 1969, Elisabeth Kübler-Ross's book *On Death & Dying* introduced the concept of the five stages of grief: denial, anger, bargaining,
depression, and acceptance.[2] People experience these stages very differently and not always in that order. While these are now considered
outdated and not necessarily accurate, I still believe people who are
grieving go through stages in the grieving process. Her co-author, David
Kessler, has since introduced a sixth stage: meaning.[3]

Finding meaning in a loss is a process of trying to make sense of the
loss, writes Pauline Boss. Some losses will never make sense, which may
lead to feelings of helplessness. The key question, she writes, is asking
what the loss means to us.[4]

This book is my effort to find meaning in Champ's life and the way
his life ended through behavioral euthanasia. I have scoured scientific
research to try to find answers why Champ was the way he was. Mostly,
I wanted to find out if it was something that I did that made him how
he was. Most of the research I found confirms that it wasn't something
I did, however, not all of it does. Some of the research I found insisted
that a dog's anxiety was caused by its owner's anxiety. I don't consider
myself an anxious person and have no diagnosis of anxiety. However,
I was anxious when handling Champ because I always had to be two
steps ahead of him, watching for his triggers; trying to redirect his fear,
anxiety, or aggression; and being concerned about the toll his mental
health was taking on his physical health, as well as the toll his medications were taking on his physical health and overall well-being over the
long term. I was anxious when I had to leave him at the kennel because
I knew it would be extremely stressful for him. I was anxious when he
could no longer be walked because I was afraid he wasn't getting enough
exercise. And I was on edge every time I had to drive him somewhere

Conclusion

because of his screaming in my ear, pacing, inability to be restrained, and repeated attempts to get in the front seat on my lap.

But did my attempts to prevent his outbursts cause his anxiety? I don't think so. He came to us with tremendous anxiety that everyone thought would go away once he got settled with us, and it never did. It only got worse, and I've always wondered in the back of my mind if it was my fault. Many owners of pets who had to have BE wonder if it was our fault or something we did or didn't do that caused them to be how they were. And through this research and the hundreds of papers and books that I have read in my research, the answer is probably not. Champ was wired differently from the beginning, and his early traumatic experiences before he went into rescue were too much for him to overcome. We did everything we possibly could to help him recover. The only things I ever said no to were another abdominal scan to look at his spleen and a brain and spinal MRI, because if they showed a brain tumor or other physical issue, it wouldn't have changed my actions at all, so I opted not to put either of us through that.

If I knew then what I know now, would I still have adopted Champ? Of course, I would have because I still believe that he was meant to be ours. I knew it from the moment I first saw his picture—he was *my* dog. And that means all of him, behavior problems and everything else that came with it. We had a lot of good times together. We walked in so many parks and trails and had a lot of fun playing games and learning new things. Every night before I went to bed, I kissed his long nose and told him I loved him. I believe he was about as happy as he could be, given the circumstances. He taught me so much about dogs, mental health, trauma, PTSD, life, and love. He also taught me that no matter how hard I try, I will never be able to change some things. While I couldn't change his brain, I could give him the best life possible, and I hope that I succeeded in that.

To those struggling with the decision for BE: I'm sorry that you are in such a position. It is something no pet owner ever expects to or a situation anyone wants to be in. I hope that this book has helped in some way, whether it's to know that you're not alone or helped provide some context for your decision. Please reach out to your behavioral veterinarian or regular veterinarian and ask about any resources they might have. Also, check into local or online pet loss support groups. I've found that talking about it helps. Keeping it inside just allowed it to fester, while talking about Champ acknowledged that he was real, he had a life, he was so loved, and he won't ever be forgotten.

Conclusion

To those struggling with guilt after BE: Please give yourself some grace. You did the very best you could. You did not take the easy way out—you took the hardest route there is and are likely questioning and second-guessing yourself. Second-guessing will only bring on more guilt and shame under the circumstances. Do not listen to the naysayers. No one else outside of your home and veterinary clinic really knows what you have been dealing with and has no right to judge. No one else has seen the tears you have cried or the bruises or scars you've hidden. Please tell yourself that you made the best decision possible for your pet, and that he/she is now at peace.

And to those who have gone through BE and are wondering if they should or could get another pet, the answer is yes. There are so many pets out there who need homes. The chances of getting another pet with behavioral issues severe enough to require BE are very slim. Take the opportunity to open your heart again to another pet. You have so much love to give, and the pet you lost would want another pet to have the same care and love you gave it.

Chapter Notes

Introduction

1. Goodreads.com.

Chapter 2

1. Blythe Baird, *If My Body Could Speak* (Minneapolis: Button Poetry, 2019).

Chapter 3

1. Temple Grandin, *Animals Make Us Human* (Orlando: Houghton Mifflin Harcourt, 2009), 53.
2. Frauke Ohl, Saskia S. Arndt, and F. Josef van der Staay, "Pathological Anxiety in Animals," *The Veterinary Journal* 175, no. 1 (2008): 18–26. doi: 10.1016/j.tvjl.2006.12.013.
3. *Ibid.*, 2.
4. Centers for Disease Control and Prevention. https://www.cdc.gov/genomics/disease/epigenetics.htm.
5. Debra Horwitz and John Ciribassi, eds., with Steve Dale, *Decoding Your Dog* (New York: Haughton Mifflin Harcourt, 2014), 237.
6. Franklin D. McMillan, *Unlocking the Animal Mind* (Emmaus, PA: Rodale Press, 2004), 146.
7. Stefanie Schwartz, "Separation Anxiety Syndrome in Dogs and Cats," *Journal of the American Veterinary Medical Association* 222, no. 11 (2003): 1526–1532. doi:10.2460/JAVMA.2003.222.1526.
8. Karen Overall, "Natural Animal Models of Human Psychiatric Condition: Assessment of Mechanism and Validity," *Progress in Neuro-Psychopharmacology & Biological Psychiatry* 24, no. 5 (2000): 741. https://doi.org/10.1016/S0278-5846(00)00104-4.
9. Barbara L. Sherman, "Separation Anxiety in Dogs," *Compendium on Continuing Education for the Practising Veterinarian—North American Edition* 30, no. 1 (2008): 27–32.
10. Schwartz, 1529.
11. Horwitz and Ciribassi, 237.
12. Brian J. Burton, "Literature Review: Behavior Modification for Canine Separation Anxiety," *IAABC Journal.* https://iaabcjournal.org/literature-review-behavior-modification-canine-separation-anxiety/.
13. Niwako Ogata, "Exploring Future Possibilities for Studies in Canine Anxiety Disorders," *Journal of Veterinary Behavior* 10 (2015): 438–448.
14. Marta Arnat, Susana Le Brech, Tomas Camps, and Xavier Manteca, "Separation-Related Problems in Dogs," *Advances in Small Animal Care* 1, no. 1 (2020): 1–8. doi: 10.1016/j.yasa.2020.07.001.
15. Niwako Ogata, "Separation Anxiety in Dogs: What Progress Has Been Made in Our Understanding of the Most Common Behavioral Problems in Dogs," *Journal of Veterinary Behavior* 16 (2016): 28–35. doi: 10.1016/j.jveb/2016.02.005.
16. Sherman, 28.
17. Arnat, Le Brech, Camps, and Manteca, 3.
18. *Ibid.*, 5.
19. Ádám Miklósi, "The Science of a Friendship," *Scientific American Mind* 26, no. 3 (2015): 41.
20. Overall, "Natural Animal Models of Human Psychiatric Condition," 742.

21. Nicholas Dodman, *Dogs Behaving Badly: An A-to-Z Guide to Understanding & Curing Behavioral Problems in Dogs* (New York: Bantam, 1999), 20.

22. Natural Dog Company, "6 Natural Ways to Treat Dog Anxiety." https://naturaldogcompany.com/know-treating-dog-anxiety.

23. Chiara Mariti, Angelo Gazzano, Jane Lansdown Moore, Paolo Baragli, L. Chelli and Claudio Sighieri, "Perception of Dogs' Stress by Their Owners," *Journal of Veterinary Behavior—Clinical Applications and Research* 7 (2012): 213–219. doi:10.1016/j.jveb.2011.09.004.

24. Nancy A. Dreschel, "The Effects of Fear and Anxiety on Health and Lifespan in Pet Dogs," *Applied Animal Behavior Science* 125 (2010): 157–162. doi:10.1016/j.applanim.2010.04.003.

25. Nicole Wilde, *Don't Leave Me!* (Santa Clarita: Phantom Publishing, 2010), 15–18.

26. Shreya Dasgupta, "Many Animals Can Become Mentally Ill." *BBC Earth*, Sept. 9, 2015. http://www.bbc.co.uk/earth/story/20150909-many-animals-can-become-mentally-ill.

27. Lisa Dietz, Anne-Marie K. Arnold, Vivian C. Goerlich-Jansson, and Claudia M. Vinke, "The Importance of Early Life Experiences for the Development of Behavioral Disorders in Domestic Dogs," *Behavior* 155 (2018): 88–89. doi:10.1163/1568539X-00003486.

28. Ogata, "Separation Anxiety in Dogs," 32.

29. Schwartz, 1529.

30. Burton.

31. Rita Lenkei, Sara Alvarez Gomez, and Peter Pongracz, "Fear vs. Frustration—Possible Factors Behind Canine Separation Related Behaviour," *Behavioral Processes* 157 (2018): 115–124. doi:10.1016/j.beproc.2018.08.002.

32. Milla Salonin, Sini Sulkama, Salla Mikkoa, Jenni Puurunen, Emma Hakanen, Katriina Tiira, Cesar Araujo, and Hannes Lohi, "Prevalence, Comorbidity, and Breed Differences in Canine Anxiety in 13,700 Finnish Pet Dogs," *Scientific Reports* 10, no. 2962 (2020). doi:10.1038/s41598-020-59837-z.

33. Texas A&M University Veterinary Medicine & Biomedical Sciences, CVMBS News online, "PTSD in Dogs," Oct. 7, 2010. https://vetmed.tamu.edu/news/pet-talk/ptsd-in-dogs/.

34. Jaak Panksepp, *Affective Neuroscience: The Foundations of Human and Animal Emotions* (New York: Oxford University Press, 1998), 206–207.

35. Robert Sapolsky, *Behave: The Biology of Humans at Our Best and Worst* (New York: Penguin, 2017), 34.

36. James Dao, "After Duty, Dogs Suffer Like Soldiers," *The New York Times*, Dec. 1, 2011. https://www.nytimes.com/2011/12/02/us/more-military-dogs-show-signs-of-combat-stress.html.

37. Dodman, *Dogs Behaving Badly*, 33–34.

38. *Ibid.*, 35–36.

39. Best Friends Animal Sanctuary. https://bestfriends.org/sanctuary/about-sanctuary/vicktory-dogs.

40. Patricia B. McConnell, *The Education of Will* (New York: Atria Books, 2017), 156.

41. *Ibid.*, 250–251.

42. Dao.

43. Karen L. Overall, "How Asking 'What Don't We Know' Improves Behavior and Welfare," *Journal of Veterinary Behavior* 36 (2020): 70–71. doi:10.1016/j.jveb.2020.04.001.

44. Sarah Jane Reaney, Helen Zulch, Daniel Mills, Sarah Gardner, and Lisa Collins, "Emotional Affect and the Occurrence of Owner-Reported Health Problems in the Domestic Dog," *Applied Animal Behavior Science* 196 (2017): 76–83. doi:10.1016.j.applanim.2017.06.011.

Chapter 4

1. John Grogan, *Marley & Me: Life and Love with the World's Worst Dog* (New York: Harper, 2005).

2. Deb Jones, "Losing Lulu: Introduction to Behavioral Euthanasia," Zoom seminar, Fall 2020.

3. Nicholas Dodman, *Pets on the Couch* (New York: Atria Books, 2016), 53.

4. Dodman, *Dogs Behaving Badly*, 94.

Notes—Chapter 4

5. *Ibid.*, 60.

6. Nancy Tanner, "Building a Dangerous Dog—the Indicators," Feb. 21, 2015. https://nancytanner.com/2015/02/21/building-a-dangerous-dog-the-indicators/.

7. Stanley Coren, *Why Does My Dog Act This Way?* (New York: Free Press, 2006), 184–185.

8. Karen L. Overall, Katriina Tiira, Desiree Broach, and Deborah Bryant, "Genetics and Behavior: A Guide for Practitioners," *Veterinary Clinics of North America: Small Animal Practice* 44, no. 3 (2014): 483–505. doi:10.1016/j.cvsm.2014.01.006.

9. *Ibid.*, 484.

10. *Ibid.*

11. Alexander and McMillan.

12. Ádám Miklósi, *The Dog: A Natural History* (Princeton: Princeton University Press, 2018), 164.

13. American Kennel Club. https://www.akc.org/dog-breeds/labrador-retriever/.

14. Benjamin L. Hart and Michael F. Miller, "Behavioral Profiles of Dog Breeds," *Journal of the American Veterinary Medical Association* 186, no. 11 (1985): 1175–1180.

15. Lindsay R. Mehrkam and Clive D.L. Wynne, "Behavioral Differences Among Breeds of Domestic Dogs (*Canis lupus familiaris*): Current Status of the Science," *Applied Animal Behaviour Science* 155 (2014): 12–27. doi.org/10.1016/j.applanim.2014.03.005.

16. John Paul Scott and John L. Fuller, *Dog Behavior: The Genetic Basis* (Chicago: University of Chicago Press, 1965), 358, 378.

17. Horwitz and Ciribassi, 211.

18. Sonia J. Lupien, Bruce S. McEwen, Megan R. Gunnar, and Christine Heim, "Effects of Stress Throughout the Lifespan on the Brain, Behaviour and Cognition," *Nature Reviews Neuroscience* 10 (2009): 434–445. https://doi.org/10.1038/nrn2639.

19. Kayla Fratt and Jackie Maffucci, "Glucocorticoids, Stress and Behavior Consulting," *IAABC Journal* 9 (2018). https://iaabcjournal.org/glucocorticoids/.

20. Lupien, McEwen, Gunnar, and Heim, 435.

21. Fratt and Maffucci.

22. Dietz, Arnold, Goerlich-Jansson, and Vinke, 87.

23. Miho Nagasawa, Yoh Shibata, Akiko Yoneawa, Tomoko Morita, Masanori Kanai, Kazutaka Mogi, and Takefumi Kikusui, "The Behavioral and Endocrinological Development of Stress Response in Dogs," *Developmental Psychobiology* 56 (2014): 726–733. doi.org/10.1002/dev.21141.

24. Dietz, Arnold, Goerlich-Jansson, and Vinke, 87–88.

25. Lupien, McEwen, Gunnar, and Heim, 439.

26. Horwitz and Ciribassi, 210.

27. Dodman, *Dogs Behaving Badly*, 124.

28. Kathleen Morrill, Jessica Hekman, Xue Li, Jesse McClure, Brittney Logan, Linda Goodman, Mingshi Gao, Yinan Dong, Marjie Alonso, Elena Carmichael, Noah Snyder-Mackler, Jacob Alonso, Hyun Ji Noh, Jeremy Johnson, Michele Koltookian, Charlie Lieu, Kate Megquier, Ross Swofford, Jason Turner-Maier, Michelle E. White, Zhiping Weng, Andrés Colubri, Diane P. Genereux, Kathryn A. Lord, and Elinor K. Karlsson, "Ancestry-Inclusive Dog Genomics Challenges Popular Breed Stereotypes," *Science*, April 29, 2022. DOI: 10.1126/science.abk0639.

29. Packaged Facts, "Pet Medications in the U.S.," 5th Edition, Aug. 25, 2017. https://www.packagedfacts.com/Pet-Medications-Edition-11058305/.

30. Packaged Facts, "Pet Supplements in the U.S.," 8th Edition, Jan. 20, 2021. https://www.packagedfacts.com/Pet-Supplements-Edition-14015218/.

31. Trish McMillan, "No, It's Not All How They're Raised," *The Huffington Post*, Aug. 24, 2015, updated Dec. 6, 2017. www.huffpost.com/entry/how-theyre-raised-pit-bulls_b_8029078.

32. Katriina Tiira, "Canine Anxiety Genetics: Challenges of Phenotyping Complex Traits," *Journal of Veterinary Behavior* 10 (2015): 438–448.

33. Mehrkam and Wynne, 14.

34. Karen L. Overall and Arthur E. Dunham, "Clinical Features and

Notes—Chapters 5 and 6

Outcome in Dogs and Cats with Obsessive-Compulsive Disorder: 126 cases (1989–2000)," *Journal of the American Veterinary Medical Association* 221, no. 10 (2002): 1445–52. doi: 10.2460/javma.2002.221.1445.

35. Isain Zapata, James A. Serpell, and Carlos E. Alvarez, "Genetic Mapping of Canine Fear and aggression," *BMC Genomics* 17 (2002): 572. doi: 10.1186/s12864-016-2936-3.

36. Isain Zapata, M. Leanne Lilly, Meghan E. Herron, James A. Serpell, and Carlos E. Alvarez, "Genetic Testing of Dogs Predicts Problem Behaviors in Clinical and Nonclinical Samples," *bioRxiv* preprint, 4 (2020). doi: 10.1101/2020.08.13.249805.

37. *Ibid.*, 6.

38. National Library of Medicine, MedLine Plus, "What Is Heritability?" https://medlineplus.gov/genetics/understanding/inheritance/heritability/.

39. Overall, Tiira, Broach, and Bryant, 487.

40. Morrill, et al.

41. Heidi G. Parker and Elaine A. Ostrander, "Canine Genomics and Genetics: Running with the Pack," *PLoS Genetics* 1, no. 5 (2005): 0512. DOI: 10.1371/journal.pgen.0010058.

42. Overall, Tiira, Broach, and Bryant, 496.

43. E.E. Hecht, I. Zapata, C.E. Alvarez, D.A. Gutman, T.M. Preuss, M. Kent, and J.A. Serpell, "Neurodevelopmental Scaling Is a Major Driver of Brain-Behavior Differences in Temperament Across Dog Breeds," *Brain Structure and Function* 226 (2021): 2725–2739. doi: 10.1007/s00429-021-02368-8.

44. Olivia Taylor, Kurt Audenaert, Chris Baeken, Jimmy Saunders, and Kathelijne Peremans, "Nuclear Medicine for the Investigation of Canine Behavioral Disorders," *Journal of Veterinary Behavior* 16 (2016): 94–103. doi:10/1016/j.jveb.2016.08.005.

45. George E. Moore, Kay D. Burkman, Margaret N. Carter, and Michael R. Peterson, "Causes of Death or Reasons for Euthanasia in Military Working Dogs: 927 Cases (1993–1996)," *Journal of*

the American Veterinary Medical Association 219, no. 2 (1991): 209–214. doi: 10.2460/javma.2001.219.209.

46. Rebecca I. Evans, John R. Herbold, Benjamin S. Bradshaw, and George E. Moore, "Causes for Discharge of Military Working Dogs from Service: 268 Cases (2000–2004)," *Journal of the American Veterinary Medical Association* 231, no. 8 (2007). doi: 10.2460/javma.231.8.1215.

47. Jacquelyn M. Wahl, Stephanie M. Herbst, Leigh Anne Clark, Kate L. Tsai, and Keith E. Murphy, "A Review of Hereditary Diseases of the German Shepherd Dog," *Journal of Veterinary Behavior* 3 (2008): 255–265. doi:10.1016/j.jveb.2008.05.004.

48. P. Saitre, E. Stranberg, P-E Sundgren, U. Pettersson, E. Jazin, and T.F. Bergstrom, "The Genetic Contribution to Canine Personality," *Genes, Brain and Behavior* 5 (2006): 240–248. doi: 10.1111/j.1601-183X.2005.00155.x.

49. E.H. van der Waaij, E. Wilsson, and E. Strandberg, "Genetic Analysis of Results of a Swedish Behavior Test on German Shepherd Dogs and Labrador Retrievers," *Journal of Animal Science* 86 (2008): 2853–2861. doi: 10.2527/jas.2007-0616.

50. Ramazan Col, Cam Day, and Clive J.C. Phillips, "An Epidemiological Analysis of Dog Behavior Problems Presented to an Australian Behavior Clinic, with Associated Risk Factors," *Journal of Veterinary Behavior* 15 (2016): 1–11. doi: 10.1016/j.jveb.2016.07.001.

51. Zapata, Serpell and Alvarez, 14.

52. Dodman, *Pets on the Couch*, 253.

53. Dreschel, 157.

Chapter 5

1. Goodreads.com.

Chapter 6

1. Chapter 6

2. Deb Jones, "Losing Lulu," Aug. 17, 2019. https://k9infocus.com/losing-lulu/.

3. Jennifer L. Summerfield, "Harsh Truths and Difficult Choices: The Reality

160

of Behavioral Euthanasia," Dr. Jen's Dog Blog, Feb. 6, 2017. http://www.drjensdogblog.com/harsh-truths-and-difficult-choices-the-reality-of-behavioral-euthanasia/.

4. The Ohio State University Veterinary Medical Center, "Euthanasia for Behavioral Issues: A Complicated and Difficult Decision." http://vet.osu.edu/honoringthebond.

Chapter 7

1. Goodreads.com.

2. Moira Anderson Allen, *Coping with Sorrow on the Loss of Your Pet*, Third Edition (Kearney, NE: Morris Publishing, 2009), 98–100.

3. *Ibid.*, 11.

4. Colin Murray Parkes, "Coping with Loss: Bereavement in Adult Life," *British Medical Journal* 316 (1998): 856–859.

5. Cari Romm, "Understanding How Grief Weakens the Body," *The Atlantic*, Sept. 11, 2014. https://www.theatlantic.com/health/archive/2014/09/understanding-how-grief-weakens-the-body/380006/.

6. Mary-Frances O'Connor, "Grief: A Brief History of Research on How Body, Mind, and Brain Adapt," *Psychosomatic Medicine* 81, no. 8 (2019): 731–738. https://www.ncbi.nlm.nih.gov/pmc/articles/PMC6844541/.

7. Ann Finkbeiner, "The Biology of Grief," *The New York Times*, April 22, 2021. https://www.nytimes.com/2021/04/22/well/what-happens-in-the-body-during-grief.html.

8. John Archer, "Why Do People Love Their Pets?" *Evolution and Human Behavior* 18 (1997): 237–259.

9. Lars Svendsen, *Understanding Animals: Philosophy for Dog and Cat Lovers* (London: Reaktion Books, 2019), 152.

10. *Ibid.*, 154.

11. W.F. Doverspike, "Grief: The Journey from Suffering to Resilience," Dec. 2008. http://drwilliamdoverspike.com.

12. C.S. Lewis, *A Grief Observed* (New York: HarperCollins, 1989), 15.

13. *Ibid.*, 46.

14. John Archer and Gillian Winchester, "Bereavement Following Death of a Pet," *British Journal of Psychology* 85 (1994): 261.

15. University of Colorado Boulder, "Four Phases of Grief: Grieving the Loss of a Loved One." https://www.colorado.edu/ova/four-phases-grief-grieving-loss-loved-one.

16. Herbert A. Nieburg and Arlene Fischer, *Pet Loss: A Thoughtful Guide for Adults & Children* (New York: Harper & Row, 1982), 19.

17. *Ibid.*, 14.

18. Parkes, 856–859.

19. Panksepp, 261.

20. Jessica Pierce, *Notes from the Last Walk* (Chicago: University of Chicago Press, 2012), 219–220.

21. Liz Becker, Lindsay Goodrich-Komline, and Angelique Gordon, Pet Loss Grief and Bereavement seminar, Richmond SPCA in conjunction with VCU School of Social Work, Nov. 16, 2020.

22. Pat Miller, "How to Cope with Losing a Dog," *Whole Dog Journal*, March 4, 2018, updated March 21, 2019. https://www.whole-dog-journal.com/care/saying-goodbye/how-to-cope-with-losing-a-dog/.

23. Dean Koontz, *A Big Little Life: A Memoir of a Joyful Dog Named Trixie* (New York: Bantam, 2011), 263.

24. Cheri Barton Ross and Jane Baron-Sorenson, *Pet Loss and Human Emotion: A Guide to Recovery* (New York: Taylor & Francis, 2007), 122.

25. Russell Friedman, Cole James, and John W. James, *The Grief Recovery Handbook for Pet Loss* (Lanham, MD: Taylor Trade, 2014), 21–30.

26. *Ibid.*

27. Koontz, 261.

28. *Ibid.*, 260.

29. Elizabeth Wurtzel, "You Changed Me: I Rescued My Dog Augusta, but Really She Rescued Me," *The Guardian*, May 8, 2016. https://www.theguardian.com/lifeandstyle/2016/may/08/you-changed-me-rescue-dog-augusta-elizabeth-wurtzel.

30. Archer, "Why Do People Love Their Pets?" 4.

31. *Ibid.*, 3.

32. Abhishek Maiti and Abhijeet Dhoble, "Takotsubo Cardiomyopathy," *New England Journal of Medicine* 377, no. e24 (2017). doi: 10.1056/NEJMicm1615835.

33. Archer, "Why Do People Love Their Pets?" 4.

34. Marilyn K. Gerwolls and Susan M. Labott, "Adjustment to the Death of a Companion Animal," *Anthrozoös*, 7, no. 3 (1994): 172–187.

35. M. Geraldine Gage and Ralph Holcomb, "Couples' Perception of Stressfulness of Death of the Family Pet," *Family Relations* 40 (1991): 103–105. https://www.jstor.org/stable/585666.

36. Personal interview with Julie Umstead, May 19, 2021.

37. Barton Ross and Baron-Sorenson, 4.

38. M.W. Fox, "Pet Animals and Human Well-Being," in *Pet Loss and Human Bereavement*, eds. William J. Kay, Herbert A. Nieburg, Austin H. Kutscher, Ross M. Grey, and Carole E. Fudin (Ames: Iowa State University Press, 1984), 17–18.

39. Lisa Rodier, "How to Prepare for a Dog's Death," *Whole Dog Journal*, April 16, 2010, updated March 21, 2019. https://www.whole-dog-journal.com/care/saying-goodbye/how-to-prepare-for-a-dogs-death/.

40. Pauline Boss, *The Myth of Closure: Ambiguous Loss in a Time of Pandemic and Change* (New York: W.W. Norton, 2022), 76.

41. Finkbeiner.

42. Parkes, 858.

43. Nieburg and Fischer, 56.

44. *Ibid.*, xiii.

45. Lewis, 39.

Chapter 8

1. Goodreads.com.

2. Margo A Halm, "The Healing Power of the Human-Animal Connection," *American Journal of Critical Care* 17, no. 4 (2008): 373–376. doi:10.4037/ajcc2008.17.4.37.3

3. Nieburg and Fishcer, 3–4.

4. Dodman, *Dogs Behaving Badly*, 247, 249.

5. Dodman, *Pets on the Couch*, 35–36.

6. Arielle Schwartz, "Resilience Psychology and Coping with Grief," https://drarielleschwartz.com/resilience-psychology-and-coping-with-grief/#.YN9a1RNKgdU.

7. Meg Jay, *Supernormal: The Secret World of the Family Hero* (New York: Twelve, 2017), 15–16.

8. Boss, 116.

9. *Ibid.*, 116.

10. Merriam-Webster Dictionary. https://www.merriam-webster.com/.

11. Lucy Hone, "What I Learned About Resilience in the Midst of Grief," *Greater Good Magazine.* https://greatergood.berkeley.edu/article/item/what_i_learned_about_resilience_in_the_midst_of_grief.

12. Doverspike, 4.

13. Charlie Mackesy, *The Boy, the Mole, the Fox, and the Horse* (New York: Harper One, 2019).

14. Harold S. Kushner, *When Bad Things Happen to Good People* (New York: Schocken Books, 1989), 71.

15. *Ibid.*, 64.

Chapter 9

1. Summerfield.

2. Overall, "Natural Animal Models of Human Psychiatric Condition," 727–776.

3. Karen Overall, "Evidence-Based Paradigm Shifts in Veterinary Behavioral Medicine," *Journal of the American Veterinary Medical Association* 254, no. 7 (2019): 799. doi: 10.2460/javma.254.7.798.

4. Jennifer Y. Kwan and Melissa J. Bain, "Owner Attachment and Problem Behaviors Related to Relinquishment and Training Techniques of Dogs," *Journal of Applied Animal Welfare Science* 16, no. 2 (2013): 168–183. https://doi.org/10.1080/10888705.2013.768923.

5. The Association for Animal Welfare Advancement, National Council on Pet Population. https://theaawa.org/page/nationalcouncil.

6. Merriam-Webster Dictionary. https://www.merriam-webster.com/dictionary/euthanasia.

7. Carlo Siracusa, Lena Provoost, Ilana R. Reisner, "Dog- and Owner-Related Risk Factors for Consideration of Euthanasia or Rehoming Before a Referral Behavioral Consultation and for Euthanizing or Rehoming the Dog After the Consultation," *Journal of Veterinary Behavior* 22 (2017): 46. https://doi.org/10.1016/j.jveb.2017.09.007.

8. American Society for the Prevention of Cruelty to Animals. https://www.aspca.org/helping-people-pets/shelter-intake-and-surrender/pet-statistics.

9. Dietz, Arnold, Goerlich-Jansson, and Vinke, 84.

10. Daniel S. Mills, "Perspectives on Assessing the Emotional Behavior of Animals with Behavior Problems," *Current Opinion in Behavioral Sciences* 16 (2017): 66–72. http://dx.doi.org/10.1016/j.cobeha.2017.04.002.

11. Sarah Stremming, "We Need to Talk About Behavioral Euthanasia," *The Cognitive Canine*, Sept. 6, 2017. https://thecognitivecanine.com/blog/we-need-to-talk-about-behavioral-euthanasia/.

12. Jones, "Losing Lulu."

13. Pierce, 167–168.

14. Barton Ross and Baron-Sorenson, 21, 141.

15. Nieburg and Fischer, 55–56.

16. Patricia B. McConnell, *For the Love of a Dog: Understanding Emotion in you and your friend* (New York: Ballantine, 2005), 87–88.

17. Nancy Tanner, "When Is Euthanasia the Right Answer for Behavioral Issues?" NancyTanner.com, April 9, 2015. https://nancytanner.com/2015/04/09/when-is-euthanasia-the-right-answer-for-behavioral-issues/.

18. John Wade, "Seven Options Available to Dog Owners with Dogs with Very Serious Behavior Problems (Aggression)." https://www.askthedogguy.com/six-options-available-to-dog-owners-with-dogs-with-very-serious-behavior-problems-aggression/.

19. Lore I. Haug, "Treat or Euthanize? Helping Owners Make Critical Decisions Regarding Pets with Behavior Problems," Dvm360.com, Oct. 31, 2011. https://www.dvm360.com/view/treat-or-euthanize-helping-owners-make-critical-decisions-regarding-pets-with-behavior-problems.

20. Karen Overall, *Clinical Behavioral Medicine for Small Animals* (St. Louis: Elsevier, 1997), 120.

21. Siracusa, Provoost, and Reisner, 49.

22. John C. Wright and Marc S. Nesselrot, "Classification of Behavior Problems in Dogs: Distributions of Age, Breed, Sex and Reproductive Status," *Applied Animal Behavior Science* 19 (1987): 169–178.

23. Victoria L. Voith. "Owner/Pet Attachment Despite Behavior Problems," in *Pet Loss and Human Bereavement*, edited by William J. Kay, Herbert A. Nieburg, Austin H. Kutscher, Ross M. Grey, and Carole E. Fudin (Ames: Iowa State University Press, 1984), 140.

24. Siracusa, Provoost, and Reisner, 46.

25. Michael Cholbi, "The Euthanasia of Companion Animals," in *Pets and People: The Ethics of Companion Animals*, edited by Christine Overall, Oxford Scholarship Online, Feb. 2017, 2. Doi: 10.1093/acprof:oso/97801 90456085.001.0001.

26. *Ibid.*, 6.

27. *Ibid.*, 7.

28. *Ibid.*, 8.

29. *Ibid.*, 9.

30. Clinton R. Sanders, "Killing with Kindness. Veterinary Euthanasia and the Social Construction of Personhood," *Sociological Forum* 10, no. 2 (2005): 195–214.

31. Cholbi, 4.

32. Rodier.

33. George E. Dickinson and Heath C. Hoffman, "The Difference Between Dead and Away: An Exploratory Study of Behavior Change During Companion Animal Euthanasia," *Journal of Veterinary Behavior* 15 (2016): 61–65. http://dx.doi.org/10.1016/j.jveb.2016.08.073.

34. K9 Turbo Training, "Euthanasia for Behavior, Part Two: How Do You Decide?" https://www.k9turbotraining.com/post/euthanasia-for-behavior-part-two-how-do-you-decide.

35. Nicole Ribeiro, "Chronic Pain, the Brain, and Behavior," *IAABC Journal*. https://iaabcjournal.org/chronic-pain-the-brain-and-behavior/.
36. *Ibid.*
37. Summerfield.
38. Best Friends Animal Sanctuary, "What Does No Kill Mean?" https://bestfriends.org/no-kill-2025/what-does-no-kill-mean.
39. Family Dogs New Life, "What Is No Kill?" https://www.familydogsnewlife.org/what-is-no-kill.
40. Association for Animal Welfare Advancement, 2015 SAWA Research Symposium, "Placing Medium and Large Breed Shelter Dogs with Behavioral Challenges in Foster Homes: Results and Outcomes." https://www.maddiesfund.org/assets/documents/Institute/2015%20SAWA%20Article%20-%20Foster%20Study.pdf.
41. "Behavioral Euthanasia Before the Bite," Beyond the Walk blog, Dec. 27, 2020. www.beyondthewalkdogs.com/f/-behavioral-euthanasia-before-the-bite.

Chapter 10

1. Goodreads.com.
2. Nicholas E. Dodman, *If Only They Could Speak* (New York: W.W. Norton, 2002), 244.
3. Dodman, *Dogs Behaving Badly*, 59–60.
4. Bonne Beerda, Matthijs B.H. Schilder, Jan A.R.A.M. van Hoof, and Hans W. de Vries, "Manifestations of Chronic and Acute Stress in Dogs," *Applied Animal Behavior Science* 52 (1997): 207–219.
5. Bonne Beerda, Matthijs B.H. Schilder, Jan A.R.A.M. van Hoof, Hans W. de Vries, and Jan A. Mol, "Behavioural, Saliva Cortisol and Heart Rate Responses to Different Types of Stimuli in Dogs," *Applied Animal Behaviour Science* 58 (1998): 365–381.
6. Veronika Konok, Krisztina Nagy, and Ádám Miklósi, "How Do Humans Represent the Emotions of Dogs? The Resemblance Between the Human Representation of the Canine and Human Affective Space," *Applied Animal Behavior Science* 162 (2015): 37–46. http://dx.doi.org/10.1016/j.applanim.2014.11.003.
7. Marc Bekoff, *The Emotional Lives of Animals* (Novato, CA: New World Library, 2007), 21, 31.
8. McConnell, *For the Love of a Dog*.
9. Vilmos Csányi, *If Dogs Could Talk: Exploring the Canine Mind* (New York: North Point Press, 2000), 58.
10. *Ibid.*, 68.
11. *Ibid.*, 135.
12. Dodman, *Pets on the Couch*, 51.
13. Mills, 66.
14. Deborah L. Wells, and Peter G. Hepper, "The Personality of 'Aggressive' and 'Nonaggressive' Dog Owners," *Personality and Individual Differences* 53 (2012): 770–773.
15. Dodman, *Dogs Behaving Badly*, 66–68.
16. *Ibid.*, 61.
17. *Ibid.*, 30.
18. Overall, "Natural Animal Models of Human Psychiatric Condition," 742.
19. *Ibid.*
20. American College of Veterinary Behaviorists. https://www.dacvb.org/search/custom.asp?id=5985.
21. Panksepp, 206.
22. Matthijs B.J. Schilder and Joanne A.M. van der Borg, "Training Dogs with the Help of the Shock Collar: Short and Long Term Behavioural Effects," *Applied Animal Behavior Science* 85 (2004): 319–334. doi:10.1016/j.applanim.2003.10.004.
23. Panksepp, 215.
24. The Monks of New Skete and Marc Goldberg, *Let Dogs Be Dogs* (New York: Little, Brown, 2017), 215.
25. *Ibid.*, 216.
26. *Ibid.*, 218.
27. *Ibid.*, 221–222.
28. Therese Rehn, Andrea Beetz, and Linda J. Keeling, "Links Between and Owner's Adult Attachment Style and the Support-Seeking Behavior of Their Dog," *Personality and Social Psychology*, Nov. 30, 2017. doi: 10.3389/fpsyg.2017.02059.
29. Ann-Sofie Sundman, Enya Van Poucke, Ann-Charlotte Svensson Holm,

Ashild Faresjo, Elvar Theodorsson, Per Jensen, and Lina S.V. Roth, "Long-Term Stress Levels Are Synchronized in Dogs and Their Owners," *Scientific Reports* 9, 7391 (2019): 1–7. https://doi.org/10.1038/s41598-019-43851-x.

30. The American College of Veterinary Behaviorists, "Dogs and Humans Have Similar Social and Emotional Brains," *Psychology Today*, June 18, 2018. https://www.psychologytoday.com/us/blog/decoding-your-pet/201806/dogs-and-humans-have-similar-social-and-emotional-brains.

31. Dodman, *Pets on the Couch*, 51.

32. Grandin, 3.

33. Kevin Behan, *Your Dog Is Your Mirror* (Novato, CA: New World Library, 2011), xv–xvii.

34. Behan, xxii.

35. Ádám Miklósi, "The Science of a Friendship," *Scientific American Mind* 26, no. 3 (2015), 39.

36. Monica Shieu, Jennifer Applebaum, Galit Dunietz, and Tiffany Braley, "Companion Animals and Cognitive Health: A Population-Based Study," American Association of Neurology AAN 74th Annual Meeting Abstract, published Feb. 23, 2022.

37. Miho Nagasawa, Shouhei Mitsui, Shiori En, Nobuyo Ohtani, Mitsuaki Ohta, Yasuo Sakuma, Tatsushi Onaka, Kazutaka Mogi, and Takefumi Kikusui, "Oxytocin-Gaze Positive Loop and the Coevolution of Human-Dog Bonds," *Science* 348, no. 6232 (2015): doi: 10.1126/science.1261022.

38. Linda Handlin, Anne Nilsson, Mikael Ejdebäck, Eva Hydbring-Sandberg, and Kerstin Uvnäs-Moberg, "Associations Between the Psychological Characteristics of the Human-Dog Relationship and Oxytocin and Cortisol Levels," *Anthrozoös* 25, no. 2 (2015): 215–228. doi: 10.2752/175303712X13316289505468.

39. Maria Pereira, Antonio Lourenco, Mariely Lima, James Serpell, and Karine Silva, "Evaluation of Mediating and Moderating Effects on the Relationship Between Owners' and Dogs' Anxiety: A Tool to Understand a Complex Problem," *Journal of Veterinary Behavior* 44 (2021): 55–61. Doi: 10.1016/j.jveb.2021.03.004.

40. *Ibid.*, 55.

41. Jack London, *White Fang* (Salt Lake City: Project Gutenberg Literary Archive Foundation, 1997). Electronic resource.

42. Grandin, 8.

43. Naomi D. Harvey, Peter J. Craigon, Simon A. Blythe, Gary C.W. England, and Lucy Asher "Social Rearing Environment Influences Dog Behavioral Development," *Journal of Veterinary Behavior* 16 (2016): 13–21.

44. Tufts University Cummings School of Veterinary Medicine, "Puppy Mills: The Scientific Evidence of Harm They Cause to Dogs." https://centerforshelterdogs.tufts.edu/blog/puppy-mills-the-scientific-evidence-of-harm-they-cause-to-dogs/.

45. Merriam-Webster Dictionary. https://www.merriam-webster.com/dictionary/stress.

46. *Ibid.*, https://www.merriam-webster.com/dictionary/distress.

47. Mariti Chiara, Angelo Gazzano, Jane Lansdown Moore, Paolo Baragli, Laura Chelli, and Claudio Sighieri, "Perception of Dogs' Stress by Their Owners," *Journal of Veterinary Behavior* 7 (2012): 213–219.

48. Jessica Hekman, "Pain's Effect on Behavior," *Whole Dog Journal*, March 23, 2020, updated June 30, 2020. https://www.whole-dog-journal.com/health/pains-effect-on-behavior/.

49. Ilana Reisner, "Behavioral Medicine: Top 10 Tools for Success," *Today's Veterinary Practice*. https://todaysveterinarypractice.com/top-ten-behavioral-medicine-top-10-tools-for-success/.

50. American Kennel Club, "Be Prepared! More Pets Go Missing July 4 & 5 Than Any Other Day." https://www.akc.org/expert-advice/health/prepared-pets-go-missing-july-4-5-day/

51. Karen L. Overall, Arthur E. Dunham, and Soraya V. Juarbe-Diaz, "Phenotypic Determination of Noise Reactivity in 3 Breeds of Working Dogs:

Notes—Chapter 10

A Cautionary Tale of Age, Breed, Behavioral Assessment, and Genetics," *Journal of Veterinary Behavior* 16 (2016): 113–125.

52. Dasgupta.

53. Grandin, 19–20.

54. Dodman, *If Only They Could Speak*, 260–261.

55. Ogata, "Separation Anxiety in Dogs," 28–35.

56. Debra Horwitz, "How to Help Dogs That Are Aggressive During Leash Walking," *Today's Veterinary Practice.* https://todaysveterinarypractice.com/how-to-help-dogs-that-are-aggressive-during-leash-walking/.

57. Erin Rakosky, "What Is Aggression? Dog Reactivity vs. Dog Aggression," American Kennel Club, Aug. 19, 2020. https://www.akc.org/expert-advice/training/reactivity-vs-aggression/#:~:text=Aggression%20in%20dogs%20can%20be,guarding%20behaviors%20to%20being%20aggressive.

58. Ilana Reisner, "Focus on Canine Behavior," *Today's Veterinary Practice.* https://todaysveterinarypractice.com/pet-health-by-the-numbers-focus-on-canine-behavior/.

59. Sherry Woodard, "Dog Aggression," Best Friends Animal Sanctuary. https://resources.bestfriends.org/article/dog-aggression.

60. Mehrkam and Wynne, 15.

61. Overall, "Natural Animal Models of Human Psychiatric Condition," 750.

62. "Behavioral Euthanasia Before the Bite," Dec. 27, 2020. https://beyondthewalkdogs.com/blog/f/behavioral-euthanasia-before-the-bite.

63. Miklósi, 76.

64. *Ibid.*, 77.

65. E'Lise Christensen, Janet Scarlett, Michael Campagna, and Katherine Albro Houpt, "Aggressive Behavior in Adopted Dogs That Passed a Temperament Test," *Applied Animal Behavior Science* 106 (2007): 85–95. doi:10.1016/j.applanim.2006.07.002.

66. Hanna E. Flint, Jason B. Coe, James A. Serpell, David L. Pearl, and Lee Niel, "Risk factors Associated with Stranger-Directed Aggression in Domestic Dogs," *Applied Animal Behavior Science* (2017): 45–54. Doi:10.1016/j.applanim.2017.08.007.

67. *Ibid.*, 49.

68. *Ibid.*, 52.

69. *Ibid.*, 45.

70. Deborah L. Duffy, Yuying Hsu, and James A. Serpell, "Breed Differences in Canine Aggression," *Applied Animal Behaviour Science* 114 (2008): 441–460. doi: 10.1016/j.applanim.2008.04.006.

71. *Ibid.*, 456.

72. *Ibid.*, 457.

73. Pernilla Foyer, Erik Wilsson, Dominic Wright, and Per Jensen, "Early Experiences Modulate Stress Coping in a Population of German Shepherd Dogs," *Applied Animal Behaviour Science* 146 (2013): 79–87. Doi: 10.1016/j.applanim.2013.03.013.

74. Paul D. McGreevy and Pauleen C. Bennett, "Challenges and Paradoxes in the Companion-Animal Niche," *Animal Welfare* 19, Suppl. 1 (2010), 11–16.

75. Melissa J. Starling, Nicholas Branson, Peter C. Thompson, and Paul D. McGreevy, "'Boldness' in the Domestic Dog Differs Among Breeds and Breed Groups," *Behavioural Processes* 97 (2013): 53–62. DOI: 10.1016/j.beproc.2013.04.008.

76. Jacqueline Ley, Pauleen Bennett, and Grahame Coleman, "Personality Dimensions That Emerge in Companion Canines," *Journal of Applied Animal Behavior Science* 110 (2008): 305–317. Doi: 10.1016/j.applanim.2007.04.016.

77. Stanley Coren, *Why Does My Dog Act That Way?* (New York: Free Press, 2006), 68–69.

78. *Ibid.*, 256–262.

79. Deborah Goodwin, John W.S. Bradshaw, and Stephen M. Wickens, "Paedomorphosis Affects Agonistic Visual Signals of Domestic Dogs," *Animal Behaviour* 53 (1997): 297–304. Doi: 10.1006/anbe.1996.0370.

80. Mary Morrow, Joseph Ottobre, Ann Ottobre, Peter Neville, Normand St. Pierre, Nancy Dreschel, Joy L. Pate, and "Breed-Dependent Differences in the Onset of Fear-Related Avoidance Behavior in Puppies," *Journal of*

Veterinary Behavior 10 (2015): 286-294. doi: 10.1016/j.jveb.2015.03.002.

81. Ian R Dinwoodie, Vivian Zottola, and Nicholas H. Dodman, "An Investigation Into the Effectiveness of Various Professionals and Behavior Modification Programs, with or Without Medication, for the Treatment of Canine Aggression," *Journal of Veterinary Behavior* 43 (2021): 46–53. https://doi.org/10.1016/j.jveb.2021.02.002.

82. Anna Sunol, Jorge Perez-Accino, Molly Kelley, Giacomo Rossi, and Silke Salavati Schmitz, "Successful Dietary Treatment of Aggression and Behavioral Changes in a Dog," *Journal of Veterinary Behavior* 37 (2020): 56–60. https://doi.org/10.1016/j.jveb.2020.04.009.

83. Karen A. Van Haaften, Emma K. Grigg, Cheryl Kolus, Lynette Hart, and Lori R. Kogan, "A Survey of Dog Owners' Perceptions on the Use of Psychoactive Medications and Alternatives for the Treatment of Canine Behavior Problems," *Journal of Veterinary Behavior* 35 (2020): 27–33. Doi: 10.1016/j.jveb.2019.10.002.

84. Ian R., Dinwoodie, Barbara Dwyer, Vivian Zottola, Donna Gleason, and Nicholas H. Dodman, "Demographics and Comorbidity of Behavior Problems in Dogs," *Journal of Veterinary Behavior* 32 (2019): 62–71. https://doi.org/10.1016/j.jveb.2019.04.007.

85. Dodman, *Dogs Behaving Badly*, 9.

86. Children's of Alabama, "How Emotional/ Psychological Trauma Affects the Body." https://www.childrensal.org/workfiles/Clinical_Services/CBH/How_Trauma_Affects_the_Body.pdf.

87. J. Douglas Bremner, "Traumatic Stress: Effects on the Brain," *Dialogues in Clinical Neuroscience* 8, no. 4 (2006): 445–461. doi: 10.31887/DCNS.2006.8.4/jbremner.

88. Sapolsky, 195.

89. Mark Wolynn, *It Didn't Start with You* (New York: Viking, 2016), 35.

Chapter 11

1. Goodreads.com.

2. Kristin Buller and Kelly C. Ballentyne, "Living with and Loving a Pet with Behavioral Problems: Pet Owners' Experiences," *Journal of Veterinary Behavior* 37 (2020) doi: 10.1016/j.jveb.2020.04.003.

3. Mary Beth Spitznagel, Dana M. Jacobson, Melanie D. Cox, and Mark D. Carlson, "Caregiver Burden in Owners of a Sick Companion Animal: A Cross-Sectional Observational Study," *Veterinary Record* 181, no. 12 (2017). doi: 10.1136/vr.104295.

4. *Ibid.*, 5.

5. *Ibid.*

6. Mary Beth Spitznagel, Melanie D. Cox, Dana M. Jacobson, Angela L. Albers, and Mark D. Carlson, "Assessment of Caregiver Burden and Associations with Psychosocial Function, Veterinary Service Use, and Factors Related to Treatment Plan Adherence Among Owners of Dogs and Cats," *Journal of the American Veterinary Medical Association* 254, no. 1 (2019): 124–132. DOI: https://doi.org/10.2460/javma.254.1.124.

7. Mary Beth Spitznagel, Dana M. Jacobson, Melanie D. Cox, Mark D. Carlson, "Predicting Caregiver Burden in General Veterinary Clients: Contribution of Companion Animal Clinical Signs and Problem Behaviors," *The Veterinary Journal* 236 (2018): 23–30. DOI: 10.1016/j.tvjl.2018.04.007.

8. *Ibid.*, 29.

9. Stine B. Christiansen, Annemarie T. Kristensen, Peter Sandøe and Jesper Lanssen, "Looking After Chronically Ill Dogs: Impacts on the Caregiver's Life," *Anthrozoös* 26, no. 4 (2015): 519–533. DOI: 10.2752/175303713X13795775536174.

10. Zoe Belshaw, Rachel Dean, and Lucy Asher, "'You can be blind because of loving them so much': The Impact on Owners in the United Kingdom of Living with a Dog with Osteoarthritis," *BMC Veterinary Research* 16 (2020): 190. DOI: 10.1186/s12917-020-02404-5.

11. Christiansen, Kristensen, Sandøe, and Lanssen, 530.

12. A.L. Roshier and E.A. McBride, "Canine Behavior Problems: Discussions Between Veterinarians and Dog Owners

During Annual Booster Consultations," *Veterinary Record* 172, no. 9 (2012). doi: 10.1136/vr.101125.

13. Gary J. Patronek and Nicholas H. Dodman, "Attitudes, Procedures, and Delivery of Behavior Services by Veterinarians in Small Animal Practice," *Journal of the American Veterinary Medical Association* 215, no. 11 (1999): 1606–1611.

14. Jennifer Y. Kwan and Melissa J. Bain, "Owner Attachment and Problem Behaviors Related to Relinquishment and Training Techniques of Dogs," *Journal of Applied Animal Welfare Science* 16 (2013): 168–183. Doi:10.1080/10888705.2 013.768923.

15. Mo D. Salman, Jennifer Hutchinson, Rebecca Ruch-Gallie, Lori Kogan, John C. New, Jr., Phillip H. Kass, and Janet M. Scarlett, "Behavioral Reasons for Relinquishment of Dogs and Cats to 12 Shelters," *Journal of Applied Animal Welfare Science* 3, no. 2 (2000): 93–106. Doi: 10.1207/S15327604JAWS0302_2.

16. Karen A. Van Haaften, Emma K. Grigg, Cheryl Kolus, Lynnette Hart, and Lori R. Kogan, "A Survey of Dog Owners' Perceptions on the Use of Psychoactive Medications and Alternatives for the Treatment of Canine Behavior Problems," *Journal of Veterinary Behavior* 35 (2020): 27–33. Doi: 10.1016/j.jveb.2019.10.002.

17. Valerie O'Farrell, "Owner Attitudes and Dog Behavior Problems," *Applied Animal Behavior Science* 52 (1997): 205–213. Doi: 10.1016/S0168-1591(96)01123-9.

18. Victoria L. Voith, John C. Wright, and Peggy J. Danneman, "Is There a Relationship Between Canine Behavior Problems and Spoiling Activities, Anthropomorphism and Obedience Training?" *Applied Animal Behavior Science* 34 (1992): 263–272. Doi: 10.1016/S0168-1591(05)80121-2.

19. *Ibid.*, 271.

20. Pereira, Lourenco, Lima, Serpell, and Silva, 55–61.

21. Nicholas H. Dodman, Dorothy C. Brown, and James A. Serpell, "Associations Between Owner Personality and Psychological Status and the Prevalence of Canine Behavior Problems," *PLoS One* 13, no. 2 (2018). Doi: 10.1371/journal.pone.0192846.

22. Hal Herzog, "Do Anxious Owners Raise More Anxious Dogs?" *Psychology Today*, Sept. 21, 2021. https://www.psychologytoday.com/us/blog/animals-and-us/202109/do-anxious-owners-raise-more-anxious-dogs.

23. Patricia B. McConnell, "Anxious Owners, Anxious Dogs?" The Other End of the Leash blog, Sept. 27, 2021. https://www.patriciamcconnell.com/theotherendoftheleash/anxious-owners-anxious-dogs.

Conclusion

1. Goodreads.com.

2. Grief.com, https://grief.com/the-five-stages-of-grief/.

3. David Kessler, "Finding Meaning: The Sixth Stage of Grief." https://grief.com/sixth-stage-of-grief/.

4. Boss, 71–72.

Bibliography

Allen, Moira Anderson. *Coping with Sorrow on the Loss of Your Pet.* Third Edition. Kearney, NE: Morris Publishing, 2009.

American Association of Neurology. AAN 74th Annual Meeting Abstract, published Feb. 23, 2022. https://aan files.blob.core.windows.net/aanfiles/ d8da7df0-1248-4b85-a858-8aad7 d6b6b83/EMBARGOED%202022 %20AAN%20AM%20Abstract%20 671%20-%20Companion%20Animals %20and%20Cognitive%20Health%20 A%20Population-Based%20Study%20 -%20Braley%20titled%20(2).pdf.

American College of Veterinary Behaviorists. "Dogs and Humans Have Similar Social and Emotional Brains." *Psychology Today,* June 18, 2018.

American College of Veterinary Behaviorists. https://www.dacvb.org/search/ custom.asp?id=5985.

American Kennel Club. https://www.akc. org/dog-breeds/labrador-retriever/.

Archer, John. "Why Do People Love Their Pets?" *Evolution and Human Behavior* 18 (1997).

_____, and Gillian Winchester. "Bereavement Following Death of a Pet." *British Journal of Psychology* 85 (1994).

Arnat, Marta, Susana Le Brech, Tomas Camps, and Xavier Manteca. "Separation-Related Problems in Dogs." *Advances in Small Animal Care* 1 (2020).

Association for Animal Welfare Advancement. 2015 SAWA Research Symposium, "Placing Medium and Large Breed Shelter Dogs with Behavioral Challenges in Foster Homes:

Results and Outcomes." https://www. maddiesfund.org/assets/documents/ Institute/2015%20SAWA%20 Article%20-%20Foster%20Study.pdf.

Barton Ross, Cheri, and Jane Baron-Sorenson. *Pet Loss and Human Emotion: A Guide to Recovery.* New York: Taylor & Francis, 2007.

Becker, Liz, Lindsay Goodrich-Komline, and Angelique Gordon. Pet Loss Grief and Bereavement seminar, Richmond SPCA in conjunction with VCU School of Social Work, Nov. 16, 2020.

Beerda, Bonne, Matthijs B.H. Schilder, Jan A.R.A.M. van Hoof, and Hans W. de Vries. "Manifestations of Chronic and Acute Stress in Dogs." *Applied Animal Behavior Science* 52 (1997).

_____, Matthijs B.H. Schilder, Jan A.R.A.M. van Hoof, Hans W. de Vries, and Jan A. Mol. "Behavioural, Saliva Cortisol and Heart Rate Responses to Different Types of Stimuli in Dogs." *Applied Animal Behaviour Science* 58 (1998).

Behan, Kevin. *Your Dog Is Your Mirror.* Novato, CA: New World Library, 2011.

"Behavioral Euthanasia Before the Bite." Beyond the Walk blog, Dec. 27, 2020. www.beyondthewalkdogs.com/f/- behavioral-euthanasia-before-the-bite.

Bekoff, Marc. *The Emotional Lives of Animals.* Novato, CA: New World Library, 2007.

Belshaw, Zoe, Rachel Dean, and Lucy Asher. "'You Can Be Blind Because of Loving Them So Much': The Impact on Owners in the United Kingdom of Living with a Dog with Osteoarthritis." *BMC Veterinary Research* 16 (2020).

Bibliography

Best Friends Animal Society. https://
bestfriends.org.

Boss, Pauline. *The Myth of Closure: Ambiguous Loss in a Time of Pandemic and Change.* New York: W.W. Norton, 2022.

Bremner, J. Douglas. "Traumatic Stress: Effects on the Brain." *Dialogues in Clinical Neuroscience* 8, no. 4 (2006).

Buller, Kristin, and Kelly C. Ballentyne. "Living with and Loving a Pet with Behavioral Problems: Pet Owners' Experiences." *Journal of Veterinary Behavior* 37 (2020).

Burton, B.J. "Literature Review: Behavior Modification for Canine Separation Anxiety." *IAABC Journal.* https://iaabcjournal.org/literature-review-behavior-modification-canine-separation-anxiety/.

Centers for Disease Control and Prevention. https://www.cdc.gov/ .

Children's of Alabama. "How Emotional/Psychological Trauma Affects the Body." https://www.childrensal.org/.

Cholbi, Michael. "The Euthanasia of Companion Animals." *Pets and People: The Ethics of Companion Animals,* Christine Overall, ed. Oxford Scholarship Online, 2017.

Christensen, E'Lise, Janet Scarlett, Michael Campagna, and Katherine Albro Houpt. "Aggressive Behavior in Adopted Dogs That Passed a Temperament Test." *Applied Animal Behavior Science* 106 (2007).

Christiansen, Stine B., Annemarie T. Kristensen, Peter Sandøe, and Jesper Lanssen. "Looking After Chronically Ill Dogs: Impacts on the Caregiver's Life." *Anthrozoös* 26, no. 4 (2015).

Col, Ramazan, Cam Day, and Clive J.C. Phillips. "An Epidemiological Analysis of Dog Behavior Problems Presented to an Australian Behavior Clinic, with Associated Risk Factors." *Journal of Veterinary Behavior* 15 (2016).

Coren, Stanley. *Why Does My Dog Act That Way?* New York: Free Press, 2006.

Csányi, Vilmos. *If Dogs Could Talk: Exploring the Canine Mind.* New York: North Point Press, 2000.

Dao, James. "After Duty, Dogs Suffer Like Soldiers." *The New York Times,* Dec. 1, 2011. https://www.nytimes.com/2011/12/02/us/more-military-dogs-show-signs-of-combat-stress.html.

Dasgupta, Shreya. "Many Animals Can Become Mentally Ill." *BBC Earth,* Sept. 9, 2015. http://www.bbc.co.uk/earth/story/20150909-many-animals-can-become-mentally-ill.

Dickinson, George E., and Heath C. Hoffman. "The Difference Between Dead and Away: An Exploratory Study of Behavior Change During Companion Animal Euthanasia." *Journal of Veterinary Behavior* 15 (2016).

Dietz, Lisa, Anne-Marie K. Arnold, Vivian C. Goerlich-Jansson, and Claudia M. Vinke. "The Importance of Early Life Experiences for the Development of Behavioral Disorders in Domestic Dogs." *Behavior* 155 (2018).

Dinwoodie, Ian R., Barbara Dwyer, Vivian Zottola, Donna Gleason, and Nicholas H. Dodman. "Demographics and Comorbidity of Behavior Problems in Dogs." *Journal of Veterinary Behavior* 32 (2019).

Dinwoodie, Ian R., Vivian Zottola, Nicholas H. Dodman. "An Investigation Into the Effectiveness of Various Professionals and Behavior Modification Programs, with or Without Medication, for the Treatment of Canine Aggression." *Journal of Veterinary Behavior* 43 (2021).

Dodman, Nicholas H. *Dogs Behaving Badly: An A-to-Z Guide to Understanding & Curing Behavioral Problems in Dogs.* New York: Bantam Books, 1999.

———. *If Only They Could Speak.* New York: W.W. Norton, 2002.

———. *Pets on the Couch.* New York: Atria Books, 2016.

Dodman, Nicholas H., Dorothy C. Brown, and James A. Serpell. "Associations Between Owner Personality and Psychological Status and the Prevalence of Canine Behavior Problems." *PLoS One* 13, no. 2 (2018).

Doverspike, W.F. "Grief: The Journey from Suffering to Resilience." December 2008. http://drwilliamdoverspike.com.

Dreschel, Nancy A. "The Effects of Fear

and Anxiety on Health and Lifespan in Pet Dogs." *Applied Animal Behavior Science* 125 (2010).

Duffy, Deborah L., Yuying Hsu, and James A. Serpell. "Breed Differences in Canine Aggression." *Applied Animal Behaviour Science* 114 (2008).

Evans, Rebecca I., John R. Herbold, Benjamin S. Bradshaw, and George E. Moore. "Causes for Discharge of Military Working Dogs from Service: 268 Cases (2000–2004)." *Journal of the American Veterinary Medical Association* 231, no. 8 (2007).

Family Dogs New Life. "What Is No Kill?" https://www.familydogsnewlife.org/what-is-no-kill.

Finkbeiner, Ann. "The Biology of Grief." *The New York Times*, April 22, 2021. https://www.nytimes.com/2021/04/22/well/what-happens-in-the-body-during-grief.html.

Flint, Hanna E., Jason B. Coe, James A. Serpell, David L. Pearl, and Lee Niel. "Risk Factors Associated with Stranger-directed Aggression in Domestic Dogs." *Applied Animal Behavior Science* (2017).

Fox, M.W. "Pet Animals and Human Well-Being." *Pet Loss and Human Bereavement*. Eds. William J. Kay, Herbert A Nieburg, Austin H. Kutscher, Ross M. Grey, Carole E. Fudin. Ames: Iowa State University Press, 1984.

Foyer, Pernilla, Erik Wilsson, Dominic Wright, and Per Jensen. "Early Experiences Modulate Stress Coping in a Population of German Shepherd Dogs." *Applied Animal Behaviour Science* 146 (2013).

Fratt, Kayla, and Jackie Maffucci. "Glucocorticoids, Stress and Behavior Consulting." *IAABC Journal* 9 (2018).

Friedman, Russell, Cole James, and John W. James. *The Grief Recovery Handbook for Pet Loss*. Lanham, MD: Taylor Trade, 2014.

Gage, M. Geraldine, and Ralph Holcomb. "Couples' Perception of Stressfulness of Death of the Family Pet." *Family Relations* 40 (1991).

Gerwolls, Marilyn K., and Susan M. Labott. "Adjustment to the Death of a Companion Animal." *Anthrozoös* 7, no. 3 (1994).

Goodwin, Deborah, John W.S. Bradshaw, and Stephen M. Wickens. "Paedomorphosis Affects Agonistic Visual Signals of Domestic Dogs." *Animal Behaviour* 53 (1997).

Grandin, Temple. *Animals Make Us Human*. Orlando: Houghton Mifflin Harcourt, 2009.

Grief.com. https://grief.com/the-five-stages-of-grief/.

Halm, Margo A. "The Healing Power of the Human-Animal Connection." *American Journal of Critical Care* 17, no. 4 (2008).

Handlin, Linda Anne Nilsson, Mikael Ejdebäck, Eva Hydbring-Sandberg, and Kerstin Uvnäs-Moberg. "Associations Between the Psychological Characteristics of the Human-Dog Relationship and Oxytocin and Cortisol Levels." *Anthrozoös* 25, no. 2 (2015).

Hart, Benjamin L., and Michael F. Miller. "Behavioral Profiles of Dog Breeds." *Journal of the American Veterinary Medical Association*. 186, no. 11 (1985).

Harvey, Naomi D., Peter J. Craigon, Simon A. Blythe, Gary C.W. England, and Lucy Asher. "Social Rearing Environment Influences Dog Behavioral Development." *Journal of Veterinary Behavior* 16 (2016).

Haug, Lore I. "Treat or Euthanize? Helping Owners Make Critical Decisions Regarding Pets with Behavior Problems." Dvm360.com, Oct. 31, 2011. https://www.dvm360.com/view/treat-or-euthanize-helping-owners-make-critical-decisions-regarding-pets-with-behavior-problems.

Hecht E.E., I. Zapata, C.E. Alvarez, D.A. Gutman, T.M. Preuss, M. Kent, and J.A. Serpell. "Neurodevelopmental Scaling Is a Major Driver of Brain-behavior Differences in Temperament Across Dog Breeds." *Brain Structure and Function* 226 (2021).

Hekman, Jessica. "Pain's Effect on Behavior." *Whole Dog Journal*, March 23, 2020, updated June 30, 2020. https://www.whole-dog-journal.com/health/pains-effect-on-behavior/.

Herzog, Hal. "Do Anxious Owners

Bibliography

Raise More Anxious Dogs?" *Psychology Today*, Sept. 21, 2021. https://www.psychologytoday.com/us/blog/animals-and-us/202109/do-anxious-owners-raise-more-anxious-dogs.

Hone, Lucy. "What I Learned About Resilience in the Midst of Grief." *Greater Good Magazine*. https://greatergood.berkeley.edu/article/item/what_i_learned_about_resilience_in_the_midst_of_grief.

Horwitz, Debra. "How to Help Dogs That Are Aggressive During Leash Walking." *Today's Veterinary Practice*. https://todaysveterinarypractice.com/how-to-help-dogs-that-are-aggressive-during-leash-walking/.

Horwitz, Debra, and John Ciribassi, eds., with Steve Dale. *Decoding Your Dog*. New York: Houghton Mifflin Harcourt, 2014.

Jay, Meg. *Supernormal: The Secret World of the Family Hero*. New York: Twelve, 2017.

Jones, Deb. "Losing Lulu." K9 in Focus blog, Aug. 17, 2019. https://k9infocus.com/losing-lulu/.

Kessler, David. "Finding Meaning: The Sixth Stage of Grief." https://grief.com/sixth-stage-of-grief/.

K9 Turbo Training. "Euthanasia for Behavior, Part Two: How Do You Decide?" https://www.k9turbotraining.com/post/euthanasia-for-behavior-part-two-how-do-you-decide.

Konok, Veronika, Krisztina Nagy, and Àdàìm Mikloìsi. "How Do Humans Represent the Emotions of Dogs? the Resemblance Between the Human Representation of the Canine and Human Affective Space." *Applied Animal Behavior Science* 162 (2015).

Koontz, Dean. *A Big Little Life: A Memoir of a Joyful Dog Named Trixie*." New York: Bantam, 2011.

Kushner, Harold S. *When Bad Things Happen to Good People*. New York: Schocken Books, 1989.

Kwan, Jennifer Y., and Melissa J. Bain. "Owner Attachment and Problem Behaviors Related to Relinquishment and Training Techniques of Dogs." *Journal of Applied Animal Welfare Science* 16, no. 2 (2013).

Lenkei, Rita, Sara Alvarez Gomez, and Peter Pongracz. "Fear Vs. Frustration—Possible Factors Behind Canine Separation Related Behaviour." *Behavioral Processes* 157 (2018).

Lewis, C.S. *A Grief Observed*. New York: HarperCollins, 1989.

Ley, Jacqueline, Pauleen Bennett, and Grahame Coleman. "Personality Dimensions That Emerge in Companion Canines." *Journal of Applied Animal Behavior Science* 110 (2008).

London, Jack. *White Fang*. Salt Lake City: Project Gutenberg Literary Archive Foundation, 1997. Electronic resource.

Lupien, Sonia J., Bruce S. McEwen, Megan R. Gunnar, and Christine Heim. "Effects of Stress Throughout the Lifespan on the Brain, Behaviour and Cognition." *Nature Reviews Neuroscience* 10 (2009).

Mackesy, Charlie. *The Boy, the Mole, the Fox, and the Horse*. New York: Harper One, 2019.

Maiti, Abhishek, and Abhijeet Dhoble. "Takotsubo Cardiomyopathy." *New England Journal of Medicine* 377, no. e24 (2017).

Mariti, Chiara, Angela Gazzano, Jane Lansdown Moore, Paolo Baragli, Laura Chelli, and Claudio Sighieri. "Perception of Dogs' Stress by Their Owners." *Journal of Veterinary Behavior* 7 (2012).

McConnell, Patricia B. "Anxious Owners, Anxious Dogs?" The Other End of the Leash blog, Sept. 27, 2021. https://www.patriciamcconnell.com/theotherendoftheleash/anxious-owners-anxious-dogs.

_____. *The Education of Will*. New York: Atria Books, 2017.

_____. *For the Love of a Dog: Understanding Emotion in You and Your Friend*. New York: Ballantine, 2005.

McGreevy, Paul D., and Pauleen C. Bennett. "Challenges and Paradoxes in the Companion-animal Niche." *Animal Welfare* 19, Suppl. 1 (2010).

McMillan, Franklin D. *Unlocking the Animal Mind*. Emmaus, PA: Rodale Press, 2004.

McMillan, Trish. "No, It's Not All How They're Raised," *The Huffington*

Bibliography

Post, Aug. 24, 2015. www.huffpost.com/entry/how-theyre-raised-pit-bulls_b_8029078.

Mehrkam, Lindsay R., and Clive D.L. Wynne. "Behavioral Differences Among Breeds of Domestic Dogs (*Canis lupus familiaris*): Current Status of the Science." *Applied Animal Behaviour Science* 155 (2014).

Miklósi, Ádám. *The Dog: A Natural History.* Princeton: Princeton University Press, 2018.

——. "The Science of a Friendship." *Scientific American Mind* 26, no. 3 (2015).

Miller, Pat. "How to Cope with Losing a Dog." *Whole Dog Journal,* March 4, 2018, updated March 21, 2019. https://www.whole-dog-journal.com/care/saying-goodbye/how-to-cope-with-losing-a-dog/.

Mills, Daniel S. "Perspectives on Assessing the Emotional Behavior of Animals with Behavior Problems." *Current Opinion in Behavioral Sciences* 16 (2017).

The Monks of New Skete and Marc Goldberg. *Let Dogs Be Dogs.* New York: Little, Brown, 2017.

Moore, George E., Kay D. Burkman, Margaret N. Carter, and Michael R. Peterson. "Causes of Death or Reasons for Euthanasia in Military Working Dogs: 927 Cases (1993–1996)." *Journal of the American Veterinary Medical Association* 219, no. 2 (1991).

Morrill, Kathleen, Jessica Hekman, Xue Li, Jesse McClure, Brittney Logan, Linda Goodman, Mingshi Gao, Yinan Dong, Marjie Alonso, Elena Carmichael, Noah Snyder-Mackler, Jacob Alonso, Hyun Ji Noh, Jeremy Johnson, Michele Koltookian, Charlie Lieu, Kate Megquier, Ross Swofford, Jason Turner-Maier, Michelle E. White, Zhiping Weng, Andrès Colubri, Diane P. Genereux, Kathryn A. Lord, and Elinor K. Karlsson. "Ancestry-Inclusive Dog Genomics Challenges Popular Breed Stereotypes." *Science* 376, eabk0639 (2022).

Morrow, Mary, Joseph Ottobre, Ann Ottobre, Peter Neville, Normand St. Pierre, Nancy Dreschel, and Joy L. Pate. "Breed-Dependent Differences in the Onset of Fear-Related Avoidance Behavior in Puppies." *Journal of Veterinary Behavior* 10 (2015).

Nagasawa, Miho, Shouhei Mitsui, Shiori En, Nobuyo Ohtani, Mitsuaki Ohta, Yasuo Sakuma, Tatsushi Onaka, Kazutaka Mogi, and Takefumi Kikusui. "Oxytocin-Gaze Positive Loop and the Coevolution of Human-Dog Bonds." *Science* 348, no. 6232 (2015).

——, Yoh Shibata, Akiko Yoneawa, Tomoko Morita, Masanori Kanai, Kazutaka Mogi, and Takefumi Kikusui. "The Behavioral and Endocrinological Development of Stress Response in Dogs." *Developmental Psychobiology* 56 (2014).

National Library of Medicine MedLine Plus. "What Is Heritability?" https://medlineplus.gov/genetics/understanding/inheritance/heritability/.

Natural Dog Company. "6 Natural Ways to Treat Dog Anxiety." https://naturaldogcompany.com/know-treating-dog-anxiety.

Nieburg, Herbert A., and Arlene Fischer. *Pet Loss: A Thoughtful Guide for Adults & Children.* New York: Harper & Row, 1982.

O'Connor, Mary-Frances. "Grief: A Brief History of Research on How Body, Mind, and Brain Adapt." *Psychosomatic Medicine* 81, no. 8 (2019).

O'Farrell, Valerie. "Owner Attitudes and Dog Behavior Problems." *Applied Animal Behavior Science* 52 (1997).

Ogata, Niwako. "Exploring Future Possibilities for Studies in Canine Anxiety Disorders." *Journal of Veterinary Behavior* 10 (2015).

——. "Separation Anxiety in Dogs: What Progress Has Been Made in Our Understanding of the Most Common Behavioral Problems in Dogs?" *Journal of Veterinary Behavior* 16 (2016).

The Ohio State University Veterinary Medical Center. "Euthanasia for Behavioral Issues: A Complicated and Difficult Decision." http://vet.osu.edu/honoringthebond.

Ohl, Frauke, Saskia S. Arndt, AND F. Josef van der Staay. "Pathological Anxiety in

Bibliography

Animals." *The Veterinary Journal* 175, no. 1 (2008).

Overall, Karen L. "Evidence-Based Paradigm Shifts in Veterinary Behavioral Medicine." *Journal of the American Veterinary Medical Association* 254, no. 7 (2019).

———. "How Asking 'What Don't We Know' Improves Behavior and Welfare." *Journal of Veterinary Behavior* 36 (2020).

———. "Natural Animal Models of Human Psychiatric Condition: Assessment of Mechanism and Validity." *Progress in Neuro-Psychopharmacology & Biological Psychiatry* 24 (2000).

Overall, Karen L., and Arthur E. Dunham. *Clinical Behavioral Medicine for Small Animals.* St. Louis: Elsevier, 1997.

Overall, Karen L., and Arthur E. Dunham. "Clinical Features and Outcome in Dogs and Cats with Obsessive-Compulsive Disorder: 126 Cases (1989–2000)." *Journal of the American Veterinary Medical Association* 221, no. 10 (2002).

Overall, Karen L., Arthur E. Dunham, AND Soraya V. Juarbe-Diaz. "Phenotypic Determination of Noise Reactivity in 3 Breeds of Working Dogs: A Cautionary Tale of Age, Breed, Behavioral Assessment, and Genetics." *Journal of Veterinary Behavior* 16 (2016).

Overall, Karen L., Katriina Tiira, Desiree Roach, and Deborah Bryant. "Genetics and Behavior: A Guide for Practitioners." *Veterinary Clinics: Small Animal Practices* 44 (2014).

Packaged Facts. Pet Medications in the U.S., 5th Edition, Aug. 25, 2017. https://www.packagedfacts.com/Pet-Medications-Edition-11058305/.

———. Pet Supplements in the U.S., 8th Edition, Jan. 20, 2021. https://www.packagedfacts.com/Pet-Supplements-Edition-14015218/.

Panksepp, Jaak. *Affective Neuroscience: The Foundations of Human and Animal Emotions.* New York: Oxford University Press, 1998.

Parker, Heidi G., and Elaine A. Ostrander. "Canine Genomics and Genetics: Running with the Pack." *PLoS Genetics* 1, no. 5 (2005).

Parkes, Colin Murray. "Coping with Loss: Bereavement in Adult Life." *British Medical Journal* 316 (1998).

Patronek, Gary J., and Nicholas H. Dodman. "Attitudes, Procedures, and Delivery of Behavior Services by Veterinarians in Small Animal Practice." *Journal of the American Veterinary Medical Association* 215, no. 11 (1999).

Pereira, Maria, Antonio Lourenco, Mariely Lima, James Serpell, and Karine Silva. "Evaluation of Mediating and Moderating Effects on the Relationship Between Owners' and Dogs' Anxiety: A Tool to Understand a Complex Problem." *Journal of Veterinary Behavior* 44 (2021).

Pierce, Jessica. *Notes from the Last Walk.* Chicago: University of Chicago Press, 2012.

Rakosky, Erin. "What Is Aggression? Dog Reactivity vs. Dog Aggression." American Kennel Club, Aug. 19, 2020. https://www.akc.org/expert-advice/training/reactivity-vs-aggression/#:~:text=Aggression%20in%20dogs%20can%20be,guarding%20behaviors%20to%20being%20aggressive.

Reaney, Sarah Jane, Helen Zulch, Daniel Mills, Sarah Gardner, and Lisa Collins. "Emotional Affect and the Occurrence of Owner-reported Health Problems in the Domestic Dog." *Applied Animal Behavior Science* 196 (2017).

Rehn, Therese, Andrea Beetz, and Linda J. Keeling. "Links Between and Owner's Adult Attachment Style and the Support-Seeking Behavior of Their Dog." *Personality and Social Psychology,* Nov. 30, 2017.

Reisner, Ilana. "Behavioral Medicine: Top 10 Tools for Success." *Today's Veterinary Practice.* https://todaysveterinarypractice.com/top-ten-behavioral-medicine-top-10-tools-for-success/.

———. "Focus on Canine Behavior." *Today's Veterinary Practice.* https://todaysveterinarypractice.com/pet-health-by-the-numbers-focus-on-canine-behavior/.

Ribeiro, Nicole. "Chronic Pain, the Brain,

Bibliography

and Behavior." *IAABC Journal.* https://
iaabcjournal.org/chronic-pain-the-
brain-and-behavior/.

Rodier, Lisa. "How to Prepare for a Dog's
Death." *Whole Dog Journal,* April 16,
2010, updated March 21, 2019.

Romm, Cari. "Understanding How Grief
Weakens the Body." *The Atlantic,* Sept.
11, 2014. https://www.theatlantic.
com/health/archive/2014/09/under
standing-how-grief-weakens-the-
body/380006/.

Roshier, A.L., and E.A. McBride. "Canine
Behavior Problems: Discussions
Between Veterinarians and Dog Owners
During Annual Booster Consultations."
Veterinary Record 172, no. 9 (2012).

Saitre P., E. Stranberg, P-E Sundgren,
U. Pettersson, E. Jazin, and T.F. Berg-
strom. "The Genetic Contribution to
Canine Personality." *Genes, Brain and
Behavior* 5 (2006).

Salman, Mo D., Jennifer Hutchinson,
Rebecca Ruch-Gallie, Lori Kogan, John
C. New, Jr., Phillip H. Kass, and Janet
M. Scarlett. "Behavioral Reasons for
Relinquishment of Dogs and Cats to 12
Shelters." *Journal of Applied Animal
Welfare Science* 3 (2000).

Salonin, Milla, Sini Sulkama, Salla Mik-
koa, Jenni Puurunen, Emma Hakanen,
Katriina Tiira, Cesar Araujo, and
Hannes Lohi. "Prevalence, Comorbid-
ity, and Breed Differences in Canine
Anxiety in 13,700 Finnish Pet Dogs."
Scientific Reports (2020).

Sanders, Clinton R. "Killing with Kind-
ness: Veterinary Euthanasia and the
Social Construction of Personhood."
Sociological Forum 10, no. 2 (2005).

Sapolsky, Robert. *Behave: The Biology of
Humans at Our Best and Worst.* New
York: Penguin, 2017.

Schilder, Matthijs B.J., and Joanne A.M.
van der Borg. "Training Dogs with
the Help of the Shock Collar: Short
and Long Term Behavioural Effects."
Applied Animal Behavior Science 85
(2004).

Schwartz, Arielle. "Resilience Psychology and Coping with Grief." https://
drarielleschwartz.com/resilience-
psychology-and-coping-with-grief/#.
YN9a1RNKgdU.

Schwartz, Stefanie. "Separation Anxiety
Syndrome in Dogs and Cats." *Journal
of the American Veterinary Medical
Association* 222, no. 11 (2003).

Scott, John Paul, and John L. Fuller. *Dog
Behavior: The Genetic Basis.* Chicago:
University of Chicago Press, 1965.

Sherman, Barbara L. "Separation Anxiety in Dogs." *Compendium on Continuing Education for the Practising
Veterinarian—North American Edition* (2008).

Siracusa, Carlo, Lena Provoost, and Ilana
R. Reisner. "Dog- and Owner-related
Risk Factors for Consideration of
Euthanasia or Rehoming Before a
Referral Behavioral Consultation and
for Euthanizing or Rehoming the Dog
After the Consultation." *Journal of
Veterinary Behavior* 22 (2017).

Spitznagel, Mary Beth, Dana M. Jacobson, Melanie D. Cox, and Mark D.
Carlson. "Caregiver Burden in Owners of a Sick Companion Animal:
A Cross-sectional Observational
Study." *Veterinary Record* 181, no. 12
(2017).

Spitznagel, Mary Beth, Dana M. Jacobson, Melanie D. Cox, Mark D. Carlson.
"Predicting Caregiver Burden in General Veterinary Clients: Contribution
of Companion Animal Clinical Signs
and Problem Behaviors." *The Veterinary Journal* 236 (2018).

Spitznagel, Mary Beth, Melanie D. Cox,
Dana M. Jacobson, Angela L. Albers,
and Mark D. Carlson. "Assessment of
Caregiver Burden and Associations
with Psychosocial Function, Veterinary Service Use, and Factors Related
to Treatment Plan Adherence Among
Owners of Dogs and Cats." *Journal
of the American Veterinary Medical
Association* 254, no. 1 (2019).

Starling, Melissa J., Nicholas Branson, Peter C. Thompson, and Paul D.
McGreevy. "'Boldness' in the Domestic Dog Differs Among Breeds and
Breed Groups." *Behavioural Processes*
97 (2013).

Stremming, Sarah. "We Need to Talk
About Behavioral Euthanasia." The
Cognitive Canine, Sept. 6, 2017.
https://thecognitivecanine.com/blog/

Bibliography

we-need-to-talk-about-behavioral-euthanasia/.

Summerfield, Jennifer L. "Harsh Truths and Difficult Choices: The Reality of Behavioral Euthanasia," Dr. Jen's Dog Blog, Feb. 6, 2017. http://www.drjensdogblog.com/harsh-truths-and-difficult-choices-the-reality-of-behavioral-euthanasia/.

Sundman, Ann-Sofie, Enya Van Poucke, Ann-Charlotte Svensson Holm, Ashild Faresjo, Elvar Theodorsson, Per Jensen, and Lina S.V. Roth. "Long-Term Stress Levels Are Synchronized in Dogs and Their Owners." *Scientific Reports* 9, no. 7391 (2019).

Sunol, Anna, Jorge Perez-Accino, Molly Kelley, Giacomo Rossi, and Silke Salavati Schmitz. "Successful Dietary Treatment of Aggression and Behavioral Changes in a Dog." *Journal of Veterinary Behavior* 37 (2020).

Svendsen, Lars. *Understanding Animals: Philosophy for Dog and Cat Lovers.* London: Reaktion Books, 2019.

Tanner, Nancy. "Building a Dangerous Dog—The Indicators." NancyTanner.com, Feb. 21, 2015. https://nancytanner.com/2015/02/21/building-a-dangerous-dog-the-indicators/.

———. "When Is Euthanasia the Right Answer for Behavioral Issues?," NancyTanner.com, April 9, 2015. https://nancytanner.com/2015/04/09/when-is-euthanasia-the-right-answer-for-behavioral-issues/.

Taylor, Olivia, Kurt Audenaert, Chris Baeken, Jimmy Saunders, and Kathelijne Peremans. "Nuclear Medicine for the Investigation of Canine Behavioral Disorders." *Journal of Veterinary Behavior* 16 (2016).

Texas A&M University Veterinary Medicine & Biomedical Sciences. "PTSD in Dogs." CVMBS News, Oct. 7, 2010. https://vetmed.tamu.edu/news/pet-talk/ptsd-in-dogs/.

Tiira, Katriina. "Canine Anxiety Genetics: Challenges of Phenotyping Complex Traits." *Journal of Veterinary Behavior* 10 (2015).

Tufts University Cummings School of Veterinary Medicine. "Puppy Mills: The Scientific Evidence of

Harm They Cause to Dogs." https://centerforshelterdogs.tufts.edu/blog/puppy-mills-the-scientific-evidence-of-harm-they-cause-to-dogs/.

Umstead, Julie. Personal interview, May 19, 2021.

University of Colorado Boulder. "Four Phases of Grief: Grieving the Loss of a Loved One." https://www.colorado.edu/ova/four-phases-grief-grieving-loss-loved-one.

Van der Waaij, E.H., E. Wilsson, and E. Strandberg. "Genetic Analysis of Results of a Swedish Behavior Test on German Shepherd Dogs and Labrador Retrievers." *Journal of Animal Science* 86 (2008): 2853–2861.

Van Haaften, Karen A., Emma K. Grigg, Cheryl Kolus, Lynette Hart, and Lori R. Kogan. "A Survey of Dog Owners' Perceptions on the Use of Psychoactive Medications and Alternatives for the Treatment of Canine Behavior Problems." *Journal of Veterinary Behavior* 35 (2020).

Voith, Victoria L. "Owner/Pet Attachment Despite Behavior Problems." *Pet Loss and Human Bereavement.* William J. Kay, Herbert A. Nieburg, Austin H. Kutscher, Ross M. Grey and Carole E. Fudin, eds. Ames: Iowa State University Press, 1984.

Voith, Victoria L., John C. Wright, and Peggy J. Danneman, "Is There a Relationship Between Canine Behavior Problems and Spoiling Activities, Anthropomorphism and Obedience Training?" *Applied Animal Behavior Science* 34 (1992).

Wade, John. "Seven Options Available to Dog Owners with Dogs with Very Serious Behavior Problems (Aggression)." https://www.askthedogguy.com/six-options-available-to-dog-owners-with-dogs-with-very-serious-behavior-problems-aggression/.

Wahl, Jacquelyn M., Stephanie M. Herbst, Leigh Anne Clark, Kate L. Tsai, and Keith E. Murphy. "A Review of Hereditary Diseases of the German Shepherd Dog." *Journal of Veterinary Behavior* 3 (2008).

Wells, Deborah L., and Peter G. Hepper. "The Personality of 'Aggressive' and

Bibliography

"nonaggressive" dog owners. *Personality and Individual Differences* 53 (2012).

Wilde, Nicole. *Don't Leave Me!* Santa Clarita: Phantom Publishing, 2010.

Wolynn, Mark. *It Didn't Start with You.* New York: Viking, 2016.

Woodard, Sherry. "Dog Aggression." https://resources.bestfriends.org/article/dog-aggression.

Wright, John C., and Marc S. Nesselrote. "Classification of Behavior Problems in Dogs: Distributions of Age, Breed, Sex and Reproductive Status." *Applied Animal Behavior Science* 19 (1987).

Wurtzel, Elizabeth. "You Changed Me: I Rescued My Dog Augusta, but Really She Rescued Me." *The Guardian*, May 8, 2016. https://www.theguardian.com/lifeandstyle/2016/may/08/you-changed-me-rescue-dog-augusta-elizabeth-wurtzel.

Zapata, Isain, James A. Serpell, and Carlos E. Alvarez. "Genetic Mapping of Canine Fear and Aggression." *BMC Genomics* 17 (2002).

Zapata, Isain, M. Leanne Lilly, Meghan E. Herron, James A. Serpell, and Carlos E. Alvarez. "Genetic Testing of Dogs Predicts Problem Behaviors in Clinical and Nonclinical Samples." *bioRxiv* preprint, 4 (2020).

Index

Index

Index

Index